Benoit Prieur

ULYSSES
TRAVEL PUBLICATIONS
Travel better... enjoy more

Series Director
Claude Morneau

Project Coordinator
Pascale Couture

Research and Composition
Benoit Prieur

Collaboration
Daniel Desjardins

English Translation
Tracy Kendrick
Jennifer McMorran
Andrea Szakos

English Editor
Jennifer McMorran

Page Layout
Pierre Daveluy
Jennifer McMorran

Cartography
André Duchesne

Graphic Design
Jean-François Bienvenue

Photography
Pierre Philippe Brunet
Peggy's Cove Lighthouse

Special thanks to: New Brunswick Ministry of Economic Development and Tourism, Diane Roux and Perry Mallet; Nova Scotia Marketing Agency, Randy Brooks; P.E.I. Enterprises, Carol Horne.

Distributors

CANADA:
Ulysses Books & Maps
4176 Saint-Denis
Montréal, Québec
H2W 2M5
☎ (514) 843-9882, ext.
Fax: 514-843-9448

GERMANY:
Brettschneider Fernreisebedarf
GmbH
D-8011 Poing bei München
Hauptstr. 5
☎ 08121-71436
Fax: 08121-71419

ITALY:
Edizioni del Riccio
50143 Firenze-
Via di Soffiano
☎ (055) 71 63 50
Fax: (055) 71 33 33

NETHERLANDS and FLANDERS:
Nilsson & Lamm
Pampuslaan 212-214
Postbus 195
1380 AD Weesp (NL)
☎ 02940-65044
Fax: 02940-15054

U.S.A.:
Seven Hills Book Distributors
49 Central Avenue
Cincinnati, Ohio, 45202
☎ 1-800-545-2005
Fax: (513) 381-0753

AUSTRALIA:
Little Hills Press Pty Ltd
11/37-43 Alexander Street
Crows Nest NSW 2065
☎ (612) 437-6995
Fax: (612) 438-5762

Other countries, contact Ulysses Books & Maps (Montréal), Fax : (514) 843-9448

Canadian Cataloguing in Publication Data

Prieur, Benoit, 1965-

    Canada's Maritime Provinces

    (Ulysses Travel Guides)
    Includes index
    Translation of: Provinces maritimes

ISBN 2-921444-18-6

1. Maritime Provinces - Guidebooks. I. Titile. II. Series.

FC2024.P7413 1995   917.1504'4   C95-940770-7   F1035.8.P7413 1995

"*There was a freshness in the air as of a wind that had blown over the honey-sweet fields of clover... Beyond lay the sea, misty and purple with its haunting, unceasing murmur.*"

Lucy Maud Montgomery, *Anne of Green Gables*

TABLE OF CONTENTS

A PORTRAIT OF
    CANADA'S
MARITIME PROVINCES 9
    Geography 10
    History 10
    Politics and the Economy . 16
    Arts and Culture 17

PRACTICAL INFORMATION . 19
    Entrance Formalities 19
    Embassies and Consulates 20
    Tourist Information 22
    Customs 23
    Finding Your Way Around 23
    Transportation 25
    Time Difference 28
    Currency 28
    Business Hours and Public
        Holidays 28
    Currency Exchange and
        Banks 29
    Climate and Clothing 29
    Health 30
    Shopping 30
    Accommodation 31
    Taxes and Tipping 32
    Restaurants and Bars 33
    Wine, Beer and Alcohol . . 33
    Advice for Smokers 33
    Safety 34
    Children 34
    Weights and Measures . . . 34
    General Information 34

OUTDOOR ACTIVITIES 37
    Parks 37
    Summer Activities 38
    Winter Activities 41

NEW BRUNSWICK 43
    Finding Your Way Around 44
    Practical Information 47
    Exploring 47
    Parks 78
    Beaches 80
    Outdoor Activities 81
    Accommodation 83
    Restaurants 93
    Entertainment 98
    Shopping 99

NOVA SCOTIA 103
    Finding Your Way Around 104
    Practical Information 107
    Exploring 108
    Parks and Beaches 136
    Outdoor Activities 137
    Accommodation 141
    Restaurants 150
    Entertainment 156
    Shopping 156

PRINCE EDWARD ISLAND . . 159
    Finding Your Way Around 160
    Practical Information 160
    Exploring 162
    Parks and Beaches 174
    Accommodation 178
    Restaurants 182
    Entertainment 186
    Shopping 187

INDEX . . . .

Help make Ulysses Travel Guides even better!

The information contained in this guide was correct at press time. However, mistakes can slip in, omissions are always possible, places can disappear, etc. The author and publisher hereby disclaim any liability for loss or damage resulting from omissions or errors.

We value your comments, corrections and suggestions, as they allow us to keep each guide up to date. The best contributions will be rewarded with a free book from Ulysses Travel Publications. All you have to do is write us at the following address and indicate which title you would be interested in receiving (see the list at the end of the guide).

Ulysses Travel Publications
4176 - rue Saint-Denis
Montréal, Québec
Canada H2W 2M5

LIST OF MAPS

Charlottetown	p 163
Downtown Fredericton	p 51
Downtown Saint John	p 66
Fredericton	p 49
Halifax	p 109
The Halifax Area	p 113
The Maritime Provinces	p 8
Moncton	p 69
New Brunswick	p 45
Tours A and B	p 53
Tour C	p 61
Tour D	p 73
Nova Scotia	p 105
Tours A, B, C and D	p 117
Tours E and F	p 129
Prince Edward Island (Tours A, B, C and D)	p 161
Saint John	p 64
Where are the Maritime Provinces?	p 7

TABLE OF SYMBOLS

☎	Telephone number
⇄	Fax number
≡	Air conditioning
⊗	Ceiling fan
≈	Pool
ℜ	Restaurant
⊛	Whirlpool
ℝ	Refrigerator
ℂ	Kitchenette
tv	Colour television

ATTRACTION CLASSIFICATION

★	Interesting
★★	Worth a visit
★★★	Not to be missed

HOTEL CLASSIFICATION

Unless otherwise indicated, accommodation prices are for one room, double occupancy, during the high season.

RESTAURANT CLASSIFICATION

$	less than $15
$$	between $15 and $25
$$$	more than $25

Restaurant prices are for a meal for one person not including taxes, drinks or tip.

Where are the Maritime Provinces ?

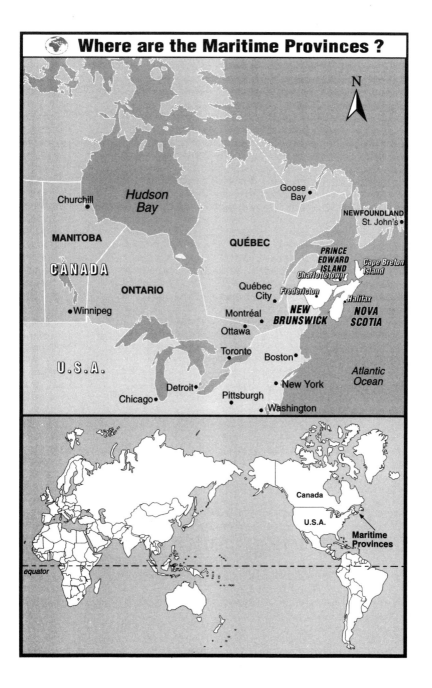

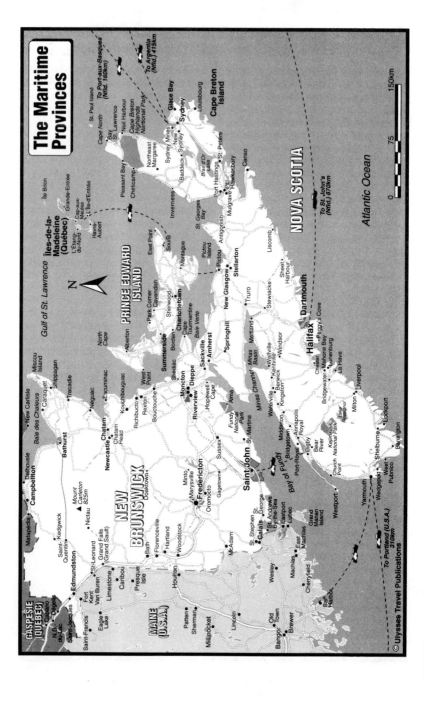

The Maritime Provinces

© Ulysses Travel Publications

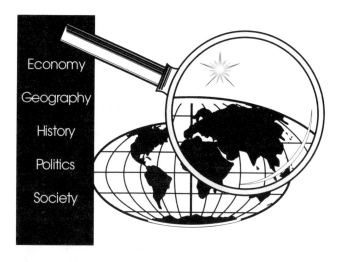

Economy

Geography

History

Politics

Society

A PORTRAIT OF CANADA'S MARITIME PROVINCES

New Brunswick, Nova Scotia and Prince Edward Island make up a picturesque region that combines thousands of kilometres of splendid coastal scenery with rich local tradition and a fascinating way of life. The Maritimes boast some of the most beautiful natural sites in eastern North America, including the spectacular Cape Breton Highlands, the magnificent sandy beaches on Prince Edward Island and the stunning landscape along the Bay of Fundy, sculpted by the highest and most powerful tides in the world. The area's unique charm, however, is also largely due to the simple scenes of everyday life, like the sight of a fleet of colourful ships heading out in the morning fog from a little fishing port along the coast.

The region, first inhabited by Amerindians of the Micmac and Malecite nations, was the birthplace of the original Acadia, founded in 1604, making it the first permanent colony in North America north of Florida. In the following centuries the Maritimes became the new world home of colonists of varying origins: American Planters, Loyalists, Scots, Irish, English, and more recently from all corners of the globe.

A trip to the Maritime Provinces thus offers visitors an opportunity to view the region's magnificent scenery, while getting to know the rich local culture and history. These are not the area's only pleasures, however. Among the most delightful memories will certainly be the beaches, washed by the warmest waters north of Virginia (U.S.A.), and the feasts of lobster and other fresh seafood.

Geography

Canada covers 9,959,400 km², stretching from the Atlantic Ocean in the east to the Pacific Ocean in the west. The Maritime Provinces lie in the eastern part of this immense country. These three provinces, New Brunswick, Nova Scotia and Prince Edward Island, all have shorelines along the Gulf of St. Lawrence, the Atlantic Ocean or the Bay of Fundy.

New Brunswick covers an area of 73,436 km² and shares a border with Québec to the west and Maine (U.S.A.) to the south; its coast is linked to Nova Scotia by the Chignecto Isthmus. To the northeast, the province is separated from Prince Edward Island by the Northumberland Strait. New Brunswick is bound by water on two sides; its northern and northeastern shores look out on Baie des Chaleurs and the Gulf of St. Lawrence, its southeastern shore on the Bay of Fundy. There are two major waterways, the St. John and Miramichi Rivers, running through the heart of the territory as well. New Brunswick also has highlands reaching up to 820 m, and its centre is studded by several hills. A dense forest consisting of mostly coniferous and some deciduous trees, covers approximately 85% of the territory and constitutes an important natural resource, enabling the province to become an exporter of pulp and paper.

Nova Scotia is only linked to the rest of Canada by a narrow strip of land, the Chignecto Isthmus. Its shores are washed by the Bay of Fundy to the southwest, the Atlantic Ocean to the east and the Gulf of St. Lawrence to the northwest. Everything in the province is within at least 49 km of the sea. The province also boasts no fewer than 3,000 lakes and many little streams and rivers. It covers an area of 54,565 km², about 10% of which is arable land. Like New Brunswick, Nova Scotia originally had a dense forest made up of both coniferous and deciduous trees, which has been greatly depleted by the forest industry. What little remains consists mainly of conifers. The forest covering the island of Cape Breton, which is part of the Nova Scotian territory, remains nearly untouched, however.

Prince Edward Island, which has an area of only 5,657 km², is the smallest but most densely populated province in Canada, with an average of 21 inhabitants per square kilometre (km²). Its economy, unlike that of the other two Maritime Provinces, is based largely on agriculture; nearly 50% of the territory is covered with extremely fertile soil. The potato is one of the island's most important crops. Vast fields stretch across land once occupied by a forest of beech, birch, maple, oak and pine trees. This island, separated from Nova Scotia and New Brunswick by the Northumberland Strait, lies in the Gulf of St. Lawrence. Its inland waters are limited to small ponds and narrow rivers.

History

The arrival of European explorers in the 15th and 16th centuries did not mark the beginning of human history in the region now known as the Maritime

Provinces. It was actually a moment of rupture, since the territory had already been inhabited for over 10,000 years by descendants of nomads who crossed the Bering Strait at the end of the ice age. Furthermore, John Cabot and Jacques Cartier were not the first Europeans to come to this part of North America. As far back as 1000 A.D., the Vikings took advantage of a general warming of the climate to explore the northern shores of the continent, fish in the local waters and establish a number of permanent settlements in the area. The voyages of Cabot and Cartier nevertheless represented a decisive moment in history, heralding an era of European colonization in the Maritimes and the rest of North America.

In 1497, after finding financial support in England, John Cabot (born Giovanni Caboto) set out from Bristol for Newfoundland. He was seeking a direct route to the riches of the Orient, an objective he never reached. The voyage would, however, be significant for another reason: upon returning to England, Cabot reported the existence of another form of riches—an apparently inexhaustible supply of cod off the northern shores of the New World. From that moment on, large numbers of English, French, Basque and Spanish fishermen started heading out from the ports of Europe to fish cod off the coast of Newfoundland and Nova Scotia.

In 1534, Breton navigator Jacques Cartier launched the first of his three voyages to North America. Commissioned by King Francis I of France to seek out gold and a passage to Asia, he found neither. These expeditions did, however, enable Cartier to discover the shoreline of a huge territory. On his first voyage, he explored the coast of the Maritimes, from the west point of

present-day Prince Edward Island to the mouth of the Miramichi River (in New Brunswick). Farther along, in Baie des Chaleurs (Québec), he met local Amerindians. He erected a cross here, symbolically claiming this land in the name of the King of France.

The Amerindians Cartier encountered in Baie des Chaleurs belonged to the Algonquian-speaking Micmac tribe. The Micmacs inhabited not only this region but also, in greater numbers, the Maritimes, a territory they shared with another Algonquian-speaking nation, the Malecites. The direct ancestors of these Amerindians settled in the Maritimes about 2,500 years ago. In the summer, the Micmacs and Malecites lived in fairly large groups along the coast, surviving mainly on fish. In winter, they would leave the coast and head into the forest to hunt game. This traditional way of life was greatly disrupted by the arrival of the explorers and European fishermen.

In the second half of the 16th century, the Europeans began doing more and more trading with the Amerindians. Fur garments were becoming fashionable in Europe and created an extremely lucrative market. In response to this trend many European fishermen became merchants, trading metal objects, for the most part, for furs. The Micmacs and the Malecites, who lived near the shore, profited the most from this activity. However, they were also the first to succumb to various illnesses transmitted by the Europeans, which their immune system could not combat. Before long, these diseases had claimed the lives of vast numbers of Amerindians. Around the year 1600, for example, it is estimated that a mere 3,500 Micmacs remained in the Maritimes; a century earlier, before their first contact with Europeans, their population was ten times that size.

■ Acadia

For the Europeans, the fur trade helped foster strong ties with Amerindian suppliers—so much so that it became necessary to establish permanent trading posts. Several fruitless attempts were made, namely on Sable Island (Nova Scotia) and in Tadoussac (Québec). Then, in 1604, one year after receiving authorization from King Henry IV of France, Pierre de Gua, Sieur de Monts, founded the first real French colony in North America. It was christened Acadia (*Acadie*), a term probably derived from the word Arcadia (the name of a region in ancient Greece), which the explorer Verrazano had already used to designate this part of the North American coast.

In March 1604, De Monts set out from the port of Le Havre, in France, for Acadia, accompanied by about 80 men, including Samuel de Champlain, who founded the settlement of Québec a few years later. De Monts and his men decided to spend their first winter on the little island of Sainte-Croix, at the mouth of the Sainte-Croix River (in the present-day state of Maine) in the Bay of Fundy. This proved to be an error in judgment, because as soon as winter set in, the men could no longer cross the strait between the island and the continent to go hunting, cut firewood or find potable water. At least 35 of the original colonists perished before spring arrived. As soon as the ice melted, the survivors hurried off to make another attempt at colonization somewhere else. They crossed the Bay of Fundy and settled at the mouth of the river now known as the Annapolis, where they founded the colony of Port-

Royal (in what is now Nova Scotia). The site had a safe, natural harbour and the advantage of being located on the territory of a Micmac tribe that welcomed the presence of French settlers. Its chief, Membertou, was in favour of trading with France, believing that his tribe could thereby increase its power by acting as a commercial intermediary between the Europeans and other Amerindian tribes and nations. Before long, a close personal relationship had developed between Membertou and one of the colony's most important officers, Baron Jean de Biencourt de Poutrincourt. Without this Micmac tribe's direct assistance, Port-Royal probably never would have existed.

In France, however, the settlers' efforts made little impression on Henry IV, who, in the spring of 1607, cancelled the fur-trading monopoly he had granted de Monts. In the wake of this royal decree, Port-Royal was temporarily abandoned, only to be re-inhabited some time later, mainly as a result of the Baron de Poutrincourt's efforts. In order to start colonizing Port-Royal again, De Poutrincourt joined forces with wealthy French Catholics, promising to try to convert the Amerindians to Christianity. In 1610, he left the French port of Dieppe, accompanied by a priest named Jessé Flesché and about twenty men. Upon arriving at Port-Royal in June, he found the settlement he had abandoned three years earlier almost entirely intact. In an effort to satisfy the baron's Catholic allies, Jessé Flesché baptised about twenty Micmacs, including Membertou, who were quite cooperative, apparently considering their conversion to be a mere adjunct to their own traditional religious beliefs. In France, however, news of the Amerindians' conversion was greeted with such great enthusiasm that Jesuit missionaries Pierre Biard and Edmond Massé, along with about 40 men, came to bolster the population of Port-Royal the following year.

Nonetheless, sustaining the French presence along this part of the North American coast was never an easy task. Due to its location, isolated from both France and New France (present-day Québec), the settlement was particularly vulnerable to attacks from Great Britain and its fledgling colonies farther south, along the Atlantic coast. In 1613, an adventurer from Virginia named Samuel Argall seized Port-Royal and drove out most of the colonists. It wasn't until 1632, with the Treaty of Saint-Germain-en-Laye, that France was able to regain possession of Acadia.

This episode was but the first of a long series, in which the Acadians were often the primary victims of the rivalry between the French and British empires. Acadia fell into British hands again in 1654, and was returned to the French in 1667 under the Treaty of Breda. The British seized Acadia once more in 1690, in the wake of a naval attack led by General Phips, and then again relinquished it to the French in 1697, under the Treaty of Ryswick. Finally, in 1710, Acadia was appropriated by the British once and for all. In 1713, its status as a British colony was confirmed by the Treaty of Utrecht.

During this entire time, the little colony continued to grow. Most of the original settlers, who arrived in the 1630s, 1640s and 1670s, came from the southern part of the Loire valley, mainly from Poitou. The Acadians quickly became self-sufficient, supporting themselves through farming, livestock, fishing and hunting as well as business. They remained in the immediate vicinity of Port-Royal at first, but were then attracted by the excellent farmlands along the Bay of Fundy, where they established new settlements in the 1670s and 1680s. The most important of these was Grand-Pré, on the Minas Basin. The Acadians were successful as farmers because they managed to develop an ingenious system of dykes and aboideaus , which made it possible to drain excellent farmlands and protect them from the tides in the Bay of Fundy.

■ **The Deportation**

With the signing of the Treaty of Utrecht in 1713, Acadia came under British rule once and for all. This loss, along with that of the port of Plaisance in Newfoundland and Britain's control of Hudson Bay, weakened France's position in North America considerably. To counterbalance the British presence on the Atlantic coast, French authorities decided to develop Île Saint-Jean (Prince Edward Island) and Île Royale (Cape Breton Island), which they still controlled. The first became a settlement devoted solely to agriculture. On Île Royale, however, France erected the largest network of fortifications in its North American possessions — the fortified city of Louisbourg, which had 5,000 inhabitants at its peak.

The struggle between Great Britain and France for control over North America put the Acadians in a difficult position. Having French roots, they were subjected to more and more pressure from colonial authorities anxious to make them swear an unconditional vow of allegiance to Great Britain. The Acadian leaders were willing to accept British authority, providing that they would be allowed to remain neutral in the event of a conflict between the two colonial powers. British governor Philips (1729-

1731) gave his verbal consent. Life went on under the British regime, and the Acadian population grew from about 2,500 inhabitants in 1713 to some 14,000 by 1755.

During this first half of the 18th century, however, there continued to be a great deal of tension between the two colonial powers, and a face-off for control of North America was clearly imminent. In 1745, troops from New England scored a decisive blow with the swift and stunning capture of the fortress of Louisbourg on Île Royale. To the great disappointment of British colonists, however, Louisbourg was returned to France three years later under the Treaty of Aix-la-Chapelle. In 1749, in an effort to reinforce their hold over Nova Scotia (the former Acadia), whose population was still mostly Acadian, 2,500 British soldiers landed on the Atlantic coast and built the citadel of Halifax. The French accelerated their own war preparations by erecting Fort Beauséjour (New Brunswick) on the Chignecto Isthmus in 1750. The British responded the following year by building Fort Lawrence just 3 km east of Fort Beauséjour.

Given the context, British authorities began to find the Acadians' neutrality more and more troubling. They feared that the Acadians would help the French in one way or another in the event of a conflict. In 1755, The Legislative Council of Nova Scotia, led by Charles Lawrence, decided to settle the issue once and for all by ordering the deportation of all Acadians. Between 1755 and 1762, the majority of Acadian villages were destroyed, the houses and churches burned and the livestock confiscated. About half of the 14,000 Acadians were put on boats and deported to England, France and other parts of North America. The others managed to escape, seeking refuge in the woods. When the signing of the Treaty of Paris brought the war between France and Britain to an end in 1763, Acadia had already been wiped from the map. Under the terms of the treaty, France ceded all of its North American possessions, including Île Saint-Jean and Île Royale, to Great Britain.

The Deportation scattered the Acadians and in many cases split up families. Many took up residence along the eastern and northeastern coast of New Brunswick, which now has the highest proportion of Acadians in the Maritimes. Others settled elsewhere in the Maritimes, in Québec, in Louisiana, where they would become the ancestors of today's Cajuns, and elsewhere in North America or Europe. It would take the Acadians of the Maritimes, especially those in New Brunswick, more than a century to establish their own institutions once again.

■ The Arrival of the Loyalists

Following the Franco-British wars for control of North America, another conflict, blazed up in the 13 British colonies to the south, and had significant repercussions on the Maritimes. The American Revolution, in the beginning at least, was a veritable civil war, which pitted supporters of independence against Loyalists wishing to preserve colonial ties with Great Britain. Over 350,000 of these Loyalists became active participants in the conflict by joining the British forces. In 1783, after a long, agonizing battle, the British had to admit defeat. The victory of the American revolutionary forces prompted about 100,000 Loyalists to seek refuge elsewhere. Of this number, approximately 35,000 chose the Maritimes as their new home. Within a few months, the impact of this massive influx of new colonists was felt all over the region, whose population had previously been no more than 20,000. The major ports of entry for the Loyalists were Shelburne, on the Atlantic coast of Nova Scotia, and the mouth of the St. John River, on the Bay of Fundy. Shelburne suddenly became one of the most populated towns in North America, with about 9,000 inhabitants. More than 14,000 Loyalists headed up the St. John River, most settling in the valley, on the fertile lands upriver. Several other ports, including St. Andrews, St. Stephen, Annapolis Royal and Halifax, were also flooded by large numbers of Loyalists.

The political and economic repercussions of this influx of Loyalists varied from one region to another, depending on the size of the local population. For example, the several hundred Loyalists who settled on Ile Saint-Jean (renamed Prince Edward Island in 1798) and Cape Breton Island quickly blended into the existing population, causing very few changes. In New Brunswick, however, the Loyalists represented more than three quarters of the population and soon occupied positions of political and economic power. In Nova Scotia, where they made up about half of the population, their integration caused a certain degree of friction for the first few years. These tensions arose because the Loyalists reproached the residents of Nova Scotia for not having participated actively enough in the war effort against the American revolutionaries. Be that as it may, the arrival of the Loyalists was a key moment in the history of the Maritimes and radically transformed the profile of region with a sudden increase in the local population.

■ The Golden Age and Canadian Confederation

For the first half of the 19th century, the Maritime Provinces experienced an economic boom, as well as a remarkable growth in population. In less than a century, the natural growth of the population, combined with substantial immigration (mainly from the British Isles) caused a ten-fold increase in the number of inhabitants. By 1861, the population of the region was no less than 672,000. This population explosion was sustained by a dramatic increase in the region's economic activity, due in large part to the export value of local products. Many people profited from this boom, but merchants, shipowners and shipbuilders were especially well-positioned to amass immense fortunes. Foreign markets were found for many local products, including agricultural produce from Prince Edward Island, coal ore from Cape Breton and the Chignecto Isthmus, wooden billets from the area around the Miramichi River and fish from Nova Scotia and other regions. All this exportation was made possible by the large fleet of the Maritimes' merchant navy, which crisscrossed seas all over the world. Shipyards could be found in many towns and villages along the coast. This was a glorious era for the Maritimes.

The second half of the 19th century, however, proved less prosperous for the region, whose economy gradually slowed down. This decline was caused by a number of different factors, an important one being the development of new technologies in the transport industry. Traditional vessels, until then one of the mainsprings of the local economy, began to face fierce competition from steamships. The era also witnessed the development of the railway, a new, highly efficient transportation network, in which the Maritimes played only a minor role. The decline of the Maritimes' economy and political powers was probably accentuated by the Canadian Confederation of 1867, which Nova Scotia and New Brunswick joined immediately, despite considerable controversy, followed by Prince Edward Island in 1873. Confederation soon led to the creation of a large domestic market stretching from the Atlantic to the Pacific. The central regions were at an advantage, since they served as transportation and communication centres for the entire country and were in a suitable position to produce manufactured goods that could easily be marketed in the Canadian west.

■ The 20th Century

The 20th century was marked by several bursts of economic growth, particularly during the two World Wars, in which the region played an important role. Most of the military convoys transporting Canadian troops to Europe set out from the city of Halifax, which is still the Canadian Navy's principal home port in the eastern part of the country. The period between the two wars was much more difficult for the Maritimes, however. The Great Depression of the 1930s dealt a crushing blow to the local economy, perhaps hitting harder here than elsewhere in the country, given the region's dependence on the decision-makers in central Canada.

The most significant political event in the post-war period took place in New Brunswick in the 1960s and 1970s, when the Acadian community was accorded more rights and began to advance economically. These changes were ushered in when Louis Robichaud was elected premier of the province in

1960. After serving an uneventful first term, Robichaud succeeded in getting re-elected in 1963 with a programme to promote equality by extending the provincial government's powers into the sectors of education, health and social services. This programme aimed to combat the great economic disparities that placed Acadians at a disadvantage. In 1968, in the heat of this campaign to promote equality, the provincial government passed the Official Languages Law, which required public services to be available in both French and English, thereby giving Acadians equal access to education, government agencies, the Legislative Assembly, etc. In 1970, Richard Hatfield became the province's new prime minister. Throughout his 17 years in power, Hatfield was extremely popular with Acadians and continued to promote their rights. The government's efforts had a concrete effect, for Acadians now play a very active role in the economy.

During the month of June, 1995 all eyes were on the Maritimes, Halifax, in particular, as it hosted the G-7 summit a meeting of the most powerful political leaders of the world.

Politics and the Economy

■ New Brunswick

Politically speaking, New Brunswick is different from the other Maritime Provinces because of its Official Languages Law, which makes it the only officially bilingual province in Canada. French-speakers make up about 33% of the province's total population, and government services are available here in both French and English. This law, along with the promotion of equality for Acadians in general, has been upheld by every provincial government since the 1960s. However, the Confederation of Regions, a political party opposed to official bilingualism in New Brunswick, has had eight deputies in the province's Legislative Assembly since 1991.

New Brunswick's economy revolves around forestry, the chemical and oil industries, farming, fishing, mining and tourism. First elected in 1987, the province's present premier, Frank McKenna, has managed to energize the economy through an effective public relations strategy aimed at foreign businesses. The province's extremely efficient telephone system and quality workforce have allowed McKenna to succeed in persuading several large companies to set up their telephone exchanges here. As well, in recent years, the province's Acadian community has demonstrated a dynamic entrepreneurial spirit.

■ Nova Scotia

Of the three Maritime Provinces, Nova Scotia is the most prosperous and has the most diversified economy. Its capital, Halifax, is the region's main seaport, as well as its most important financial and commercial centre. Halifax is also the Canadian Navy's principal home port on the east coast. The fishing, mining and shipbuilding industries, cornerstones of the local economy for many years, now represent only a small share of the province's gross national product. Today, the service and manufacturing industries predominate. In 1995, the city of Halifax was chosen to host the delegates of the G-7, a union of the seven most economically powerful countries in the world.

■ Prince Edward Island

Industrialization only began in Prince Edward Island at the end of the Second World War. Located far from the big urban centres and cut off from the major transportation networks, the island has always been slow to develop a strong manufacturing industry. The inhabitants of the island are nurturing the hope that the soon-to-be-completed bridge to New Brunswick will remedy some of their problems. Presently, a large portion of the economy is based on agriculture (especially potato farming) as well as the fishing, tourist and service industries.

Arts and Culture

Over the years, the three Maritime Provinces have established prestigious institutions in order to encourage local artistic expression and promote greater public awareness of the arts. Thanks to the patronage of Lord Beaverbrook, Fredericton was endowed in 1958 with the remarkable Beaverbrook Art Gallery, which houses the works of some of the greatest artists from the Maritimes, as well as from elsewhere in Canada and abroad. Particularly noteworthy is an impressive painting by Salvador Dalí. Fredericton also has a theatre, where the excellent New Brunswick Theatre Company performs regularly. In 1984, the Confederation Arts Centre, a large arts complex made up of theatres, an art gallery and a public library, was inaugurated in Charlottetown, the capital of Prince Edward Island. Concerts, plays and dance productions are presented here, and a number of works by local and national artists, including portrait artist Robert Harris, are exhibited in the gallery. In

1975, the Nova Scotia Art Gallery, housing the most impressive art collection in the Maritimes, was founded in Halifax. The city also boasts the Neptune Theatre and a symphony orchestra. The Maritimes have produced many artists, one of the most illustrious being the painter Alex Colville. Lucy Maud Montgomery, author of *Anne of Green Gables*, is doubtless the most widely renowned of local writers. Most of her stories take place on Prince Edward Island, where she was born.

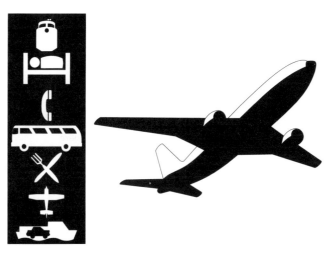

PRACTICAL INFORMATION

I nformation in this section will help visitors from English-speaking countries better plan their trip to the Maritimes.

Entrance Formalities

■ Passport

A valid passport is usually sufficient for most visitors planning to stay less than three months in Canada; visas are not required. American residents do not need a passport, but it is however a good form of identification. A three-month extension is possible, but a return ticket and proof of sufficient funds to cover this extension may be required.

Caution: some countries do not have an agreement with Canada concerning health and accident insurance, so it is advisable to have the appropriate coverage. For more information, see the section entitled **"Health"** on page 30.

European citizens who want to enter the United States will need a visa. It is best to apply for this visa from your home country, although it is obtainable abroad, usually without problems.

■ Extended Visits

Visitors must submit a request to extend their visit **in writing** and **before** the expiration of their visa (the date is usually written in your passport) to an Immigration Canada office. To make a request you must have a valid passport, a return ticket, proof of sufficient funds to cover the stay, as well as the $50 non-refundable filing-fee. In some cases (work, study), however, the request must be made **before** arriving in Canada.

Embassies and Consulates

■ Abroad

Australia
Canadian Consulate General
Level 5, Quay West
111 Harrington Road
Sydney, N.S.W.
Australia 2000
☎ (612) 364-3000
⇄ (612) 364-3098

Belgium
Canadian Embassy
2 Avenue de Tervueren
1040 Brussels
☎ 735.60.40
⇄ 732.67.90
Métro Mérode

Denmark
Canadian Embassy
Kr. Bernikowsgade 1,
DK = 1105 Copenhagen K,
Denmark
☎ 12.22.99
⇄ 14.05.85

Finland
Canadian Embassy
Pohjos Esplanadi 25 B,
00100 Helsinki, Finland
☎ 171-141
⇄ 601-060

Germany
Canadian Consulate General
Internationales Handelzentrum
Friedrichstrasse 95, 23rd Floor
10117 Berlin, Germany
☎ 261.11.61
⇄ 262.92.06

Great Britain
Canada High Commission
Macdonald House
One Grosvenor Square
London W1X 0AB
England
☎ 258-6600
⇄ 258-6384

Netherlands
Canadian Embassy
Parkstraat 25
2514JD The Hague
Netherlands
☎ 361-4111
⇄ 365-6283

Norway
Canadian Embassy
Oscars Gate 20,
Oslo 3, Norway
☎ 46.69.55
⇄ 69.34.67

Sweden
Canadian Embassy
Tegelbacken 4, 7th floor,
Stockholm, Sweden
☎ 613-9900
⇄ 24.24.91

Switzerland
Canadian Embassy
Kirchenfeldstrasse 88
3000 Berne 6
☎ 532.63.81
⇄ 352.73.15

United States
Canadian Embassy
501 Pennsylvania Avenue, N.W.
Washington, DC
20001
☎ (202) 682-1740
⇌ (202) 682-7726

Canadian Consulate General
Suite 400 South Tower
One CNN Center
Atlanta, Georgia
30303-2705
☎ (404) 577-6810 or 577-1512
⇌ (404) 524-5046

Canadian Consulate General
Three Copley Place
Suite 400
Boston, Massachusetts
02116
☎ (617) 262-3760
⇌ (617) 262-3415

Canadian Consulate General
Two Prudential Plaza
180 N. Stetson Avenue, Suite 2400,
Chicago, Illinois
60601
☎ (312) 616-1860
⇌ (312) 616-1877

Canadian Consulate General
St. Paul Place, Suite 1700
750 N. St. Paul Street
Dallas, Texas
75201
☎ (214) 922-9806
⇌ (214) 922-9815

Canadian Consulate General
600 Renaissance Center
Suite 1100
Detroit, Michigan
48234-1798
☎ (313) 567-2085
⇌ (313) 567-2164

Canadian Consulate General
300 South Grande Avenue
10th Floor, California Plaza
Los Angeles, California
90071
☎ (213) 687-7432
⇌ (213) 620-8827

Canadian Consulate General
Suite 900, 701 Fourth Avenue South
Minneapolis, Minnesota
55415-1899
☎ (612) 333-4641
⇌ (612) 332-4061

Canadian Consulate General
1251 Avenue of the Americas
New York, New York
10020-1175
☎ (212) 596-1600
⇌ (212) 596-1793

Canadian Consulate General
One Marine Midland Center
Suite 3000
Buffalo, New York
14203-2884
☎ (716) 852-1247
⇌ (716) 852-4340

Canadian Consulate General
412 Plaza 600
Sixth and Stewart Streets
Seattle, Washington
98101-1286
☎ (206) 442-1777
⇌ (206) 443-1782

■ **In the Maritimes**

Not all countries are represented in the
Maritimes. Those that are not generally
have offices in Montréal, Toronto or
Ottawa.

U.S. Consulate General
Suite 910
Cogswell Tower, Scotia Square
Halifax, Nova Scotia
B3J 3K1
☎ (902) 429-2480

Australian High Commission
50 O'Connor Street
Ottawa, Ontario
K1N 5R2
☎ (613) 236-0841

Consulate General of Belgium
999 Boulevard de
Maisonneuve Ouest
suite 1250
Montréal H3A 3C8
☎ (514) 849-7394

British Consulate General
1155 Rue University
Suite 901
Montréal H3B 3A7
☎ (514) 866-5863

Consulate General of Denmark
1 Place-Ville-Marie
35th Floor
Montréal H3B 4M4
☎ (514) 871-8977

Consulate General of Finland
800 Carré Victoria
Suite 3400
Montréal H4Z 1E9
☎ (514) 397-7600

Consulate General of Germany
3455 Rue de la Montagne
Montréal H3G 2A3
☎ (514) 286-1820

Consulate General of the Netherlands
1002 Rue Sherbrooke Ouest
Suite 2201
Montréal H3A 3L6
☎ (514) 849-4247

Consulate General of Norway
1155 Boul. René-Lévesque Ouest
Suite 3900
Montréal H3B 3V2
☎ (514) 874-9087

Consulate General of Sweden
800 Carré Victoria
34th Floor
Montréal H4Z 1E9
☎ (514) 866-4019

Consulate General of Switzerland
1572 Avenue Dr Penfield
Montréal H3G 1C4
☎ (514) 932-7181

Tourist Information

This guide is divided into three distinct regions: New Brunswick (N.B.), Nova Scotia (N.S.) and Prince Edward Island (P.E.I.). Within each province you will find tourist information offices which can provide brochures concerning attractions, restaurants and hotels of these regions. You can also pick up listings of bed and breakfasts in the area.

Information is available by mail for these three provinces by writing to the following addresses:

New Brunswick
Department of Economic Development and Tourism
P.O.Box 12345
Fredericton
E3B 5C3
☎ (506) 453-4283 or 1-800-561-0123

Nova Scotia
Department of Tourism
P.O.Box 130
Halifax
B3J 2M7
☎ (506) 424-4217 or 1-800-565-0000

Prince Edward Island
Visitors Centre
P.O.Box 940
Charlottetown
C1A 7M5
☎ (902) 368-4444 or 1-800-463-4734

Customs

If you are bringing gifts into Canada, remember that certain restrictions apply:

Smokers (minimum age is 16) can bring in a maximum of 200 cigarettes, 50 cigars, 400 g of tobacco, and 400 tobacco sticks.

Wine and alcohol: the limit is 1.1 litres; in practice, however, two bottles per person are usually allowed. The limit for beer is 24 cans or bottles, the 355 ml size.

Plants, vegetation, and food: there are very strict rules regarding the importation of plants, flowers, and other vegetation; it is therefore not advisable to bring any of these types of products into the country. If it is absolutely necessary, contact the Customs-Agriculture service of the Canadian embassy **before** leaving.

Pets: if you are travelling with your pet, you will need a health certificate (available from your veterinarian) as well as a rabies vaccination certificate. It is important to remember that the vacci-

nation must be carried out **at least** 30 days **before** your departure and should not have been administered more than one year ago.

Tax reimbursements for visitors: it is possible to get reimbursed for certain taxes paid on purchases made while in the Maritimes (see p 32).

 Finding Your Way Around

■ By Plane

European visitors will arrive in the Maritime provinces in Halifax, since it is the only airport that regularly receives international flights; in New Brunswick and Prince Edward Island, the airports occasionally receive flights from the United States. **British Airways** and **KLM** also offer direct connections from Europe, the former through London and the latter through Amsterdam. **American Airlines** (☎ 1-800-433-7300) offer flights through Montréal to Halifax, while **Delta Airlines** (☎ 1-800-221-1212) offer direct flights from Boston to Halifax (N.S.), with connections to St. John (N.B.). Charter flights to Montréal, and then a Montréal-Halifax flight can be cheaper. It is strongly recommended to compare prices several weeks before your departure.

Air Canada and its partner **Air Nova**: Air Canada and Air Nova offer direct flights from London, England to Halifax and from Newark, New Jersey to Halifax. Otherwise European and American travellers must stop-over in Montréal or Toronto. From Montréal, Air Canada and Air Nova offer direct flights to Halifax (N.S.), Fredericton (N.B.), Moncton (N.B.) and Saint John (N.B.), and a flight with a stop-over for Charlottetown (P.E.I.). For information: ☎ 1-800-361-8620.

Canadian and its partner **Air Atlantic:** Canadian and Air Atlantic do not offer direct flights between the airports in the Maritimes and Europe. European travellers must stop-over in Montréal or Toronto. From Montréal, Canadian and Air Atlantic offer direct flights to Halifax (N.S.), Fredericton (N.B.), Moncton (N.B.) and Saint John (N.B.), and a flight with a stop-over for Charlottetown (P.E.I.). For information: ☎ 1-800-426-7000.

Nova Scotia

Halifax Airport
40 km north of the city
Route 102, Exit 6
☎ (902) 873-2091

The Halifax airport is the largest airport in the Maritime provinces. There is an exchange office open everyday from 6 AM to 9 PM. Six car rental companies have offices in the airport. Taxis and limousines offer transportation to downtown for about $30. A shuttle bus makes the trip from the airport to downtown about once an hour ($11). The airport is mostly served by Air Canada-Air Nova (☎ 429-7111) and by Canadian-Air Atlantic (☎ 427-5500)

New Brunswick

Fredericton Airport
16 km from the city
Lincoln Road
☎ (506) 444-6202

The Fredericton airport does not have an exchange office. Four car rental companies have offices here. Taxis offer transportation to downtown. The airport is mostly served by Air Canada-Air Nova (☎ 458-8561) and by Canadian-Air Atlantic (☎ 458-4089)

Moncton Airport
12 km east of the city
Champlain Street
Dieppe
☎ (506) 851-2200

The Moncton airport does not have an exchange office. Four car rental companies have offices. Taxis offer transportation to downtown for less than $10. The airport is mostly served by Air Canada-Air Nova (☎ 857-1044) and by Canadian-Air Atlantic (☎ 857-0620).

Saint John Airport
4180 Loch Lemond
☎ (506) 636-3950

The Saint John airport does not have an exchange office. Five car rental companies have offices. Taxis offer transportation to downtown for less than $10. The airport is mostly served by Air Canada - Air Nova (☎ 652-1517) and by Canadian - Air Atlantic (☎ 696-2630).

Prince Edward Island

Charlottetown Airport
Sherwood
☎ (902) 566-7992

The Charlottetown airport does not have an exchange office. Four car rental companies have offices. Taxis offer transportation to downtown for less than $10. The airport is mostly served by Air Canada - Air Nova (☎ 894-8825) and by Canadian - Air Atlantic (☎ 892-5358).

Transportation

■ **By Car**

Considering the large distances to be covered, the easiest way to tour the Maritimes is by car. The roads are generally in good condition.

Things to Consider

Driver's License: As a general rule, foreign driver's licenses are valid for six months from the arrival date in Canada.

Pedestrians: Drivers in the Maritimes are very respectful of pedestrians, and willingly stop to give them the right of way even in the big cities, so be careful when and where you step off the curb. Crosswalks are usually indicated by a yellow sign. When driving pay special attention that there is no one about to cross near these signs.

Turning **right on a red** when the way is clear is permitted in the Maritimes.

When a **school bus** (usually yellow in colour) has stopped and has its signals flashing, you must come to a complete stop, no matter what direction you are travelling in. Failing to stop at the flashing signals is considered a serious offense, and carries a heavy penalty.

Wearing of **seatbelts** in the front and back seats is mandatory at all times.

There are no **tolls** on Maritime highways. There is an occasional toll for bridges.

The **speed limit** on highways is 100 km/h. The speed limit on secondary highways is 90 km/h, and 50 km/h in urban areas.

Gas Stations: Because Canada produces its own crude oil, gasoline prices are less expensive than in Europe. However, due to hidden taxes, gas prices are considerably higher than those in the United States and in Western Canada. Some gas stations (especially in the downtown areas) might ask for payment in advance as a security measure, especially after 11 p.m.

Car Rentals

The best way to get a good price for car rental is to reserve well in advance. Many travel agencies have agreements with the major car rental companies (Avis, Budget, Hertz, etc.) and offer good values; contracts often include added bonuses (reduced ticket prices for shows, etc.).

When renting a car, find out if:

● contract includes unlimited kilometres.
● insurance provides full coverage (accident, property damage, hospital costs for you and passengers, theft).

Caution:

To rent a car you must be at least 21 years of age and have had a driver's license for **at least** one year. If you are between 21 and 25, certain companies (for example Avis, Thrifty, Budget) will ask for a $500 deposit, and in some cases they will also charge an extra sum for each day you rent the car. These conditions do not apply for those over 25 years of age.

A credit card is extremely useful for the deposit to avoid tying up large sums of money, and can in some cases (gold

km	Charlottetown	Fredericton	Halifax	Moncton	Montréal	Québec City	Sydney
Charlottetown		373	280	175	1 200	960	367
Fredericton	373		415	200	835	585	695
Halifax	280	415		275	1250	982	422
Moncton	175	200	275		1 025	785	497
Montréal	1 200	835	1 250	1 025		270	1 520
Québec City	960	585	982	785	270		1 280
Sydney	367	695	422	497	1 520	1 280	

cards) cover the collision and theft insurance.

Most rental cars come with an automatic transmission, however you can request a car with a manual shift.

Child safety seats cost extra.

Accidents and Emergencies

If you run into trouble on the highway, pull onto the shoulder of the road and turn the hazard lights on. If it is a rental car, contact the rental company as soon as possible. Always file an accident report. If a disagreement arises over who was at fault in an accident, ask for police help.

If you are a member of an automobile association (Canada: Canadian Automobile Association; U.S.A.: American Automobile Association; Switzerland: Automobile Club de Suisse; Belgium: Royal Automobile Touring Club de Belgique; Great-Britain: Automobile Association; Australia: Australian Automobile Association), you have access to some free services provided in Canada by the C.A.A.

■ By Bus

Besides the car, travelling by bus is the best way to get around. Buses cover most of the Maritimes and are relatively inexpensive. Except for public transportation, there is no government run service; several companies service the region.

- Smoking is forbidden on almost all lines.
- Pets are not allowed.
- Generally children five years old or younger travel for free
- People aged 60 or over are eligible for discounts.

■ By Train

Travelling by train is not always the cheapest way to get around, however it is a comfortable alternative for long distances. VIA Rail Canada offers trips east to New Brunswick and Nova Scotia. A few years ago passenger train travel in Prince Edward Island became a thing of the past. The only way to get around the island these days is by bus or car.

When coming from the United States your best option is to take Amtrak to Montréal and then VIA Rail to the Maritimes since Amtrak does not provide service through Maine. Make your reservations through a travel agent that can reserve with both companies.

Travel Times

Montréal-Halifax: 20 hours
Moncton-Halifax: 5 hours
Toronto-Halifax: 25 hours

VIA Rail offers several discounts :

Reductions for certain days of the week, during the off-season and on reservations made at least five days in advance: up to 40 % off depending on the destination.

Discount for students and those 24 years of age or less: 10 % throughout the year or 40 % if the reservation is made five days in advance, except during the holidays.

Discount for people aged 60 and over: 10 % on certain days, not during peak travel times.

Special rates for children: children 2 to 11 travel for half-price; children under two accompanied by an adult travel free.

Another option, the *Canrailpass*, allows travel throughout Canada with only one ticket. Certain restrictions apply but the pass can prove very advantageous, particularly for visitors planning on visiting western Canada. The pass also entitles you to special rates for car rentals. The Canrailpass is only sold outside of Canada.

Finally, take note that first-class service is quite exceptional, including a meal, wine, and alcoholic beverages free of charge. Second-class is also quite adequate, often including a meal or snack depending on the length of the trip.

For additional information:

VIA Rail Halifax ☎ 429-8421
VIA Rail Moncton ☎ 857-9830
VIA Rail Montréal ☎ 871-1331
VIA Rail Toronto ☎ 366-8411
Amtrak ☎ 1-800-872-7245

■ By Plane

Flying is by far the most expensive mode of transportation; however, some airline companies, especially the regional ones, regularly offer special rates (off season, short stays). Once again, it is wise to shop around and compare prices.

■ Bicycling

Bicycling is very popular and is a great way to see the countryside. Tranquil backroads are numerous in each province but caution is always recommended, even on these quiet roads.

■ Hitchhiking

Hitchhiking is common, especially in summer, and much easier outside the big centres. Nevertheless do not forget that hitchhiking is actually illegal on the highways.

■ Ferries

The biggest ferry company is Marine Atlantic (☎ 1-902-794-5700, ⇄ 1-902-564-7480). It connects Cape Tourmentine (N.B.) to Borden (P.E.I.), Saint John (N.B.) to Digby (N.S.), Bar Harbor (Maine, USA) to Yarmouth (N.S.). Northumberland Ferries connects Wood Islands (P.E.I.) to Caribou (N.S.).

Time Difference

All the Maritime provinces (N.B., N.S., P.E.I.) are on Atlantic Time, one hour ahead of Eastern Standard Time, and four hours ahead of the West Coast. Continental Europe is five hours ahead, while the United Kingdom is four hours ahead. Be careful as the time switch to Daylight Savings Time is not the same as in Europe. In Canada, as in the United States, the clocks go back one hour the last Sunday in October and go ahead one hour the first Sunday in April. When it is 11 AM in Montréal and New York it is noon in Halifax, Nova Scotia.

Currency

The monetary unit is the dollar ($), which is divided into cents (¢). One dollar = 100 cents.

Bills come in 2, 5, 10, 20, 50, 100, 500 and 1000 dollar denominations, and coins come in 1 (pennies), 5 (nickels), 10 (dimes), 25 (quarters) cent pieces and in 1 (loonies) dollar coins.

Business Hours and Public Holidays

■ Business Hours

Stores

The law respecting business hours allows stores to be open the following hours:

Mon to Fri 10 AM to 6 PM;
Thu and Fri 10 AM to 9 PM;
Sat 9 AM or 10 PM to 5 PM;
Sun noon to 5 PM

Well-stocked convenience stores that sell food are found throughout the Maritimes and are open later, sometimes 24 hours a day.

Banks

Banks are open Monday to Friday from 10 AM to 3 PM. Most are open on Thursdays and Fridays, until 6 PM or even 8 PM. Automatic teller machines are widely available and are open night and day.

Post Offices

Large post offices are open from 9 AM to 5 PM. There are several smaller post offices throughout the Maritimes, located in shopping malls, convenience stores, and even pharmacies; these post offices are open much later than the larger ones.

■ Holidays and Public Holidays

Here is a list of public holidays in the Maritimes. Most administrative offices and banks are closed on these days.

January 1st and 2nd
Easter Monday
Victoria Day: the 3rd Monday in May
July 1st: Canada Day
Labour Day (1st Monday in September)
Thanksgiving (2nd Monday in October)
Remembrance Day (November 11; only banks and federal government services are closed)
December 25 and 26

Currency Exchange and Banks

■ Currency Exchange

Most banks readily exchange American and European currencies but almost all will charge **commission**. There are, however, exchange offices that do not charge commissions and have longer hours. Just remember to **ask about fees** and **to compare rates**.

Traveller's Cheques

Traveller's cheques are accepted in most large stores and hotels, however it is easier and to your advantage to change your cheques at an exchange office. For a better exchange rate buy your traveller's cheques in Canadian dollars before leaving.

Credit Cards

Most major credit cards are accepted at stores, restaurants and hotels. While the main advantage of credit cards is that they allow visitors to avoid carrying a large sums of money, using a credit card makes leaving a deposit for car rental much easier; also some cards, gold cards for example, automatically insure you when you rent a car (check with your credit card company to see what coverage it provides). In addition, the exchange rate with a credit card is generally better. The most commonly accepted credit cards are Visa, Master Card, and American Express.

■ Banks

Banks can be found almost everywhere and most offer the standard services to tourists. Visitors who choose to stay in Canada for a long period of time should note that **non-residents** cannot open bank accounts. If this is the case, the best way to have money readily available is to use traveller's cheques. Withdrawing money from foreign accounts is expensive. However, several automatic teller machines accept foreign bank cards, so that you can withdraw directly from your account. Money orders are another means of having money sent from abroad. No commission is charged but it takes time. People who have residence status, permanent or not (such as landed-immigrants, students), can open a bank account. A passport and proof of residence status are required.

Climate and Clothing

■ Climate

The sea air makes for milder temperatures, especially close to the Bay of Fundy which is warmed by the Gulf Stream. Temperature ranges are however quite significant. Summer temperatures are around 25°C, and in the winter around -2°C. Temperatures vary on the coasts where it is colder in summer and winter. Finally the coasts are often shrouded by a thick fog.

Winter

From December to March is the best season for skiing, snowmobiling, skating, snowshoeing and other winter sports. Temperatures remain low. Warm clothing (coats, scarves, hats, gloves or mittens, wool sweaters and boots). On the coast, it remains quite humid in winter.

Spring and Fall

Spring is short, lasting roughly from the end of March to the end of May. Everything thaws and streets are often slushy. In fall its time to watch the colours. it can get quite cool in both these seasons so be sure to pack a sweater, scarf, gloves, wind-breaker and of course an umbrella.

Summer

From the end of May to the end of August it can get very hot. Bring t-shirts, lightweight shirts and pants, shorts and sunglasses. A jacket or sweater will still come in handy in the evening. In certain regions of the Maritimes, notably near the Bay of Fundy and on the Atlantic Coast of Nova Scotia, rain and fog are frequent; an umbrella and raincoat are a good idea.

Health

■ General Information

Vaccinations are not necessary for people coming from Europe, the United States, Australia and New Zealand. On the other hand, it is strongly suggested, particularly for medium or long-term stays, that visitors take out health and accident insurance. There are different types so it is best to shop around. Bring along all medication, especially prescription medicine. Unless otherwise stated, the water is drinkable throughout the Maritimes.

In the winter, moisturizing lotion and lip balm are useful for people with sensitive skin, since the air in many buildings is very dry.

During the summer, always protect yourself against sunburn. It is often hard to feel your skin getting burned by the sun on windy days. Do not forget to bring sun screen!

■ Emergencies

The 911 emergency number is not available throughout the Maritimes. It is used in select cities in New Brunswick and Nova Scotia, but not at all in Prince Edward Island.

For other regions: dial 0 and an operator will tell you who to call.

 ## Shopping

■ What to Buy

Lobster and salmon: you'll find these provisions for sale on piers and docks for good prices. Most merchants can also sell you a hermetically sealed container (about $6) for transporting your catch on a plane.

Books: books by local authors are widely available, as well as books on the Acadian culture.

Local crafts: paintings, sculptures, woodworking items, ceramics, copper-based enamels, weaving, etc.

Native Arts & Crafts: There are beautiful native sculptures made from different types of stone that are generally quite expensive. Make sure the sculpture is authentic by asking for a certificate of authenticity issued by the Canadian government. Good quality imitations are widely available and are much less expensive.

Accommodation

A wide choice of types of accommodation to fit every budget is available in most regions of the Maritimes. Most places are very comfortable and can offer a number of extra services. Prices vary according to the type of accommodation and the quality/price ration is generally good, but remember to add the 7% G.S.T (federal Goods and Services Tax) and the provincial sales tax of 11% in Nova Scotia, 11% in New Brunswick and 10% in Prince Edward Island. The G.S.T. and the Nova Scotia sales tax are refundable for non-residents (see p 32). When reserving in advance, which is strongly recommended during the summer months, a credit card is indispensable for the deposit, as payment for the first night is often required.

■ Hotels

Hotels rooms abound, and range from modest to luxurious. Most hotel rooms come equipped with a private bathroom. The Maritimes has several internationally reputed hotels, four of them being part of the Canadian Pacific chain.

■ Inns

Often set up in beautiful historic houses, inns offer quality lodging. There are a lot of these establishments which are more charming and usually more picturesque than hotels. Many are furnished with beautiful period pieces. Breakfast is often included.

■ Bed and Breakfasts

Unlike hotels, rooms in private homes are not always equipped with a bathroom. Bed and breakfasts are well distributed throughout the Maritimes, in the country as well as the city. Besides the obvious price advantage, is the unique family atmosphere. Credit cards are not always accepted in bed and breakfasts.

The following associations can arrange accommodation in a bed and breakfast:

New Brunswick

N.B. Bed & Breakfast Association
Riverside, Albert County
New Brunswick
EOA 2RO
☎ (506) 882-2079

Nova Scotia

Annapolis Royal Tourist Bureau B&B Places
Box 2
Annapolis Royal, Nova Scotia
B0S 1A0
☎ (902) 532-5769

South Shore B&B Assocation
Box 82
Bridgewater, Nova Scotia
B4V 2W6
☎ (902) 476-9999

Northumberland Shore B&B Homes
Box 782
New Glasgow, Nova Scotia
B2H 5G2
Pictou County Tourist Association
☎ (902) 755-5180

Evangeline Trail Tourism Association
1153 Prospect Road
New Minas, Nova Scotia
B4N 3K6
☎ (902) 679-1645

Nova Scotia Farm Vacations
Newport Station
Hants County, Nova Scotia
B0N 2B0
☎ (902) 798-5864

Central Nova B&B
Parrsboro Tourist Office
Box 263
Parrsboro, Nova Scotia
B0M 1S0
☎ (902) 254-3266

Cape Breton B&B
Box 1750
Commerce Tower
Sydney, Nova Scotia
B1P 6T7 (Ray Peters)
☎ (902) 564-3629

Prince Edward Island

P.E.I. Farm Vacations
Bonshaw, Orwell
R.R. 2
P.E.I.
C0A 2E0 (Ivan Wood)
☎ (902) 651-2620

Visitors' Services P.E.I.
Box 940
Charlottetown, P.E.I.
C1A 7N5
☎ (902) 368-4444 or 1-800-565-0267

Kensington and Area Tourist
Association
R.R. 1
Kensington, P.E.I.
C0B 1M0
☎ (902) 836-3031 or 836-4206

■ Motels

There are many motels throughout the province, and though they tend to be cheaper they are also lacking in atmosphere. These are particularly useful when pressed for time.

■ Youth Hostels

Youth hostel addresses are listed in the "Accommodation" section for the cities in which they are located.

■ University Residences

Due to certain restrictions, this can be a complicated alternative. Residences are only available during the summer (mid-May to mid-August); reservations must be made several months in advance, usually by paying the first night with a credit card.

This type of accommodation, however, is less costly than the "traditional" alternatives, and making the effort to reserve early can be worthwhile. Visitors with valid student cards can expect to pay approximately $25 plus tax. Bedding is included in the price, and there is usually a cafeteria in the building (meals are not included in the price).

■ Camping

Next to being put up by friends, camping is the most inexpensive form of accommodation. Unfortunately, unless you have winter-camping gear, camping is limited to a short period of the year, from June to August. Services provided as well as prices vary considerably, from $8 to $20 or more per night, depending on whether the site is private or public.

Taxes and Tipping

■ Taxes

The ticket price on items usually **does not include tax**. There are two taxes, the G.S.T., federal Goods and Services Tax, of 7 % and the P.S.T., Provincial Sales Tax (New Brunswick, 11%; Nova Scotia, 11%; and Prince Edward Island, 10%) you must therefore add between 17 and 18% to the price of most items and to restaurant and hotel prices.

There are some exceptions to this taxation system, such as books, which are only taxed 7% and food (except for ready made meals), which is not taxed at all.

Tax Refunds for Non-Residents

Non-residents can obtain refunds for the G.S.T. paid on purchases. To obtain a refund, it is important to keep your receipts. Refunds are made at the border or by returning a special filled-out form.

For information, call:
☎ 1-800-668-4748.

Nova Scotia does refund its provincial tax, but only to Canadians residing in the other provinces.

For information, call:
☎ (902) 424-6300

■ Tipping

In general, tipping applies to all service at a table: restaurants, bars and nightclubs (therefore no tipping in fast-food restaurants). Tips are also given in taxis and in hair salons.

The tip is usually about 15 % of the bill before taxes, but varies of course depending on the quality of service.

Restaurants and Bars

■ Restaurants

There are several excellent restaurants in the Maritimes. The big specialty is without a doubt fish and seafood, notably lobster.

■ Bars and Discos

In most cases there is no cover charge, aside from mandatory coat-check occasionally. However expect to pay a few dollars to get into discos on weekends. Alcohol is not sold after 2 AM.

Wine, Beer and Alcohol

The legal drinking age is 19. Beer, wine and alcohol can only be purchased in liquor stores run by the provincial governments. Very little wine-producing goes on in the Maritimes. Several good beers however are brewed, including Moosehead.

Advice for Smokers

As in the United States, cigarette smoking is considered taboo, and it is being prohibited in more and more public places:

in most shopping centres;
in buses;
in government offices.

Most public places (restaurants, cafés) have smoking and non-smoking sections. Cigarettes are sold in bars, grocery stores, newspaper and magazine shops.

Safety

There is far less violence in the Maritimes, compared to the United States. A genuine non-violence policy is advocated throughout the area.

By taking the normal precautions, there is no need to worry about your personal security. If trouble should arise, remember that 911 is the emergency telephone number.

Children

As in the rest of Canada, facilities exist in the Maritimes that make travelling with children quite easy, whether it be for getting around or when enjoying the sights. Generally children under five travel for free, and those under 12 are eligible for fare reductions. The same rules apply for various leisure activities and shows. Find out before you purchase tickets. High chairs and children's menus are available in most restaurants, while a few of the larger stores provide a babysitting service while parents shop.

Weights and Measures

Although the metric system has been in use in Canada for more than 10 years, some people continue to use the Imperial system in casual conversation. Here a some equivalents:

1 pound (lb) = 454 grams
1 kilogram (kg) = 2.2 pounds (lbs)
1 foot (ft) = 30 centimetres
1 centimetre (cm) = 0.4 inch
1 mile = 1.6 kilometres

1 kilometres (km) = 0.63 miles
1 metre (m) = 40 inches

General Information

Illegal Drugs: are against the law and not tolerated (even "soft" drugs). Drug users and dealers caught with drugs in their possession risk severe consequences.

Electricity: Voltage is 110 volts throughout Canada, the same as in the United States.

Electricity plugs have two parallel, flat pins, and adaptors are available here.

Hairdressers: As in restaurants, a tip of 15% before taxes is standard.

Laundromats: are found almost everywhere in urban areas. In most cases, detergent is sold on site. Although change machines are sometimes provided, it is best to bring plenty of quarters (25¢) with you.

Movie Theatres: There are no ushers and therefore no tips.

Museums: Most museums charge admission, however it is rarely more than $2. Reduced prices are available for people over 60, for children, and for students. Call the museum for further details.

Newspapers: Each big city has its own local newspaper:
Fredericton: *Gleaner*
Saint John: *Telegraph Journal* and *Times-Globe*
Moncton: *Times-Transcript*
Halifax: *Chronicle Herald* and *Daily News*

Charlottetown: *The Guardian* and *Evening Post*
The larger newspapers, for example *The Globe and Mail*, are widely available. Many international newspapers are available in Halifax.

Pharmacies: In addition to the smaller drug stores, there are large pharmacy chains which sell everything from chocolate to laundry detergent, as well as the more traditional items such as cough drops and headache medications.

Religion: Almost all religions are represented. Most of the francophone population are Catholic and the anglophone, Protestant.

Restrooms: Public restrooms can be found in most shopping centres. If you cannot find one, it usually is not a problem to use one in a bar or restaurant.

Telephones: Long distance charges are cheaper than in Europe, but more expensive than in the U.S.. Pay phones can be found everywhere, often in the entrance of larger department stores, and in restaurants. They are easy to use and some even accept credit cards. Local calls to the surrounding areas cost $0.25 for unlimited time. Have a lot quarters on hand if you are making a long distance call. It is less expensive to call from a private residence. 1-800 numbers are toll free.

OUTDOOR ACTIVITIES

Parks

Nova Scotia, New Brunswick and Prince Edward Island all boast vast, untouched stretches of wilderness protected by national and provincial parks, which visitors can explore on foot or by bicycle. Red sand beaches and cliffs overhanging the sea (Prince Edward Island National Park), stretches of shoreline with tides reaching as high as 18 m (Fundy National Park) and steep mountains whose sides plunge into the rough waters of the Atlantic Ocean (Cape Breton Highlands National Park) all await discovery. The following pages contain a description of the various outdoor activities that can be enjoyed in these parks.

In the Maritimes, there are national parks, run by the federal government, and provincial parks, each administered by the government of the province in question. Most national parks offer services such as information centres, nature programmes, guides, accommodation (B&Bs, inns, equipped and primitive camping sites) and dining facilities. Not all of these services are available in every park (and some vary depending on the season), so it is best to contact park authorities before setting off on a trip. Provincial parks are usually smaller, with fewer services, but are still attractively located.

A number of parks are crisscrossed by marked trails stretching several kilometres, perfect for hiking, cycling and cross-country skiing. Primitive camping sites or shelters can be found along some of these paths. Some of the camping sites are very rudimentary, and a few don't even have water; it is therefore essential to be well equipped. Since some of the trails lead deep into the forest, far from all human habitation, visitors are strongly advised to heed all signs. Useful maps showing trails, camping sites and shelters are available for most parks.

■ National Parks

There are five national parks in the Maritimes: Fundy National Park (Alma, New Brunswick), Kouchibouguac National Park (along the Acadian coast of New Brunswick), Prince Edward Island National Park (Cavendish, Prince Edward Island), Cape Breton Highlands National Park (Baddeck, Nova Scotia) and Kejimkujik National Park (Maitland Bridge, Nova Scotia). In addition to these parks, the Canadian Park Service also oversees a number of national historic sites, which are described in the "Exploring" section of the chapters describing the various provinces.

For more information on national parks, contact:

Parks Canada Atlantic Regional Office
Upper Water Street
Halifax, Nova Scotia
B3G 1S9
☎ (902) 426-3436
⇄ (902) 426-6881

■ Provincial Parks

Each of the three provinces manages a wide variety of parks. Some of these are small, open only during the daytime, while the larger ones, offer a broader scope of activities. There are no fewer than 23 provincial parks in New Brunswick, 29 on Prince Edward Island and over a hundred in Nova Scotia. These parks provide visitors with access to beaches, camping sites, golf courses and hiking trails. Throughout this guide, the most important parks are described in the "Parks and Beaches" section of each relevant chapter. For more information on provincial parks, contact:

New Brunswick

New Brunswick Ministry of Natural Resources and Energy
Park Services
P.O. Box 6000
Fredericton
E3B 5H1

Nova Scotia

Department of Natural Resources
R.R. 1
Belmont
B0M 1C0

Prince Edward Island

Department of Economic Development and Tourism
R.R. 3
O'Leary
C0B 1D0

 Summer Activities

When the weather is mild, visitors can enjoy the activities listed below. Anyone deciding to spend more than a day in the park should remember that the nights are cool (often even in July and August) and that long-sleeved shirts or sweaters will be very practical in some regions. In June, an effective insect repellent is almost indispensable for an outing in the forest.

 Hiking

Hiking is an activity open to everyone, and it can be enjoyed in all national and most provincial parks. Before setting out, plan your excursion well by checking the length and level of difficulty of each trail. Some parks have long trails that require more than a day of hiking and lead deep into the wild. When taking one of these trails, which can stretch tens of kilometres, it is crucial to respect all signs.

To make the most of an excursion, make sure to bring along the right equipment. Remember a good pair of walking shoes, all appropriate maps, sufficient food and water and a small first-aid kit containing a pocket knife and bandages.

 Bicycling

Bicycling is practised throughout the Maritimes, whether it be along the usually quiet secondary roads or the trails crisscrossing the parks. The roads offer prudent cyclists one of the most enjoyable means possible of visiting these picturesque regions. Keep in mind, however, that even though the Maritimes are Canada's smallest provinces, distances can still seem very long here.

If you wish to bring your own bicycle, you are allowed to bring it on any bus; just be sure it is properly protected in an appropriate box. Another option is to rent one on site. For bike rental locations, look under the heading **"Bicy-**

cling" in the "Outdoor Activities" section of the chapters on each province, contact a tourist information centre or check under the "Bicycles-Rentals" heading in the *Yellow Pages*. Adequate insurance is a good idea when renting a bicycle. Some places include insurance against theft in the cost of the rental. Inquire before renting.

 Canoeing

Many parks are studded with lakes and rivers, that canoe-trippers could spend a day or more exploring. Primitive camping sites have been laid out to accommodate canoers during long excursions. Canoe rentals and maps of possible routes are usually available at the park's information centre.

 Beaches

White and red sand beaches, shores washed by 18 m tides, sand dunes inhabited by fascinating animal life, beaches stretching endlessly for several kilometres with no sign of human habitation and others located near charming villages... without question, these are some of the Maritimes' most precious natural attractions. Each province takes care to offer visitors clean, well maintained beaches that are perfect for swimming. A visit to the Maritimes would not be complete without a stop at one of the region's many beaches.

 Fishing

Fishing is permitted in Nova Scotia and New Brunswick, but visitors should remember that it is a regulated activity. Fishing laws are complicated, so it is wise to request information from the Ministry of Natural Resources of each province and obtain the brochure stating key fishing regulations (see p 38).

As a general rule, however, keep in mind that:

- it is necessary to obtain a permit from the provincial government before going fishing;
- a special permit is usually required for salmon fishing;
- fishing seasons are established by the ministry and must be respected at all times; the seasons vary depending on the species;
- fishing is permitted in parks, but it is necessary to obtain a permit from park officials beforehand; for more information, look under the "Fishing" heading in the "Outdoor Activities" section of the relevant chapter.

Bird-watching

The shores of the Maritime provinces attract all sorts of birds, which can easily be observed with the help of binoculars. Among the species frequenting this region, are cormorants, kingfishers, a wide variety of ducks (including the mallard) and great blue herons. If you're lucky, you might catch a glimpse of an Atlantic puffin, a piping plover or a bald eagle. For help identifying them, get a copy of *Peterson's Field Guide: All the Birds of Eastern and Central North America*, published by Houghton Mifflin. Although parks are often the best places to observe certain species, bird watching is an activity that can be enjoyed all over the Maritimes.

Whale-watching

Whales swim near the coasts of the Maritimes, in the Gulf of St. Lawrence and the Bay of Fundy. Visitors wishing to catch a closer view of these impressive but harmless sea mammals can take part in a whale-watching cruise. The most commonly sighted species is the humpback. These excursions usually start near St. Andrews in New Brunswick and Digby and Cape Breton in Nova Scotia.

■ Seal-watching

Seals swim off the coasts of Nova Scotia, New Brunswick and Prince Edward Island, and anyone wishing to observe them from close up can take part in an excursion designed for that purpose. Occasionally, attracted by the boat, these curious mammals will pop their heads out of the water right nearby, gazing at the passengers with their big black eyes. Other times, they can be spotted lying on a deserted beach. The best place for seal watching is along the eastern shore of Prince Edward Island.

Golf

All over the Maritimes, there are magnificent golf courses, renowned for their remarkable natural setting. Stretched along the seashore, they offer stunning views. Golf lovers can enjoy unforgettable vacations here, since some courses lie in the heart of provincial parks, in the most tranquil surroundings imaginable, with luxurious hotels just a short distance away.

Winter Activities

In winter, the Maritimes are covered with a blanket of snow. Most parks with summer hiking trails adapt to the climate, welcoming cross-country skiers. New Brunswick also features an extensive network of snowmobile trails. Finally, although there are only a few mountains in this region, visitors can enjoy downhill skiing in both New Brunswick and Nova Scotia.

 Cross-Country Skiing

Some parks, such as Kejimkujik and Cape Breton Highlands, as well as Mount Sugarloaf and Kouchibouguac in New Brunswick, are renowned for their long cross-country ski trails. Daily ski rentals are available at a number of resorts.

 Downhill Skiing

Although this region is not really known for downhill skiing, there are a few noteworthy mountains here. New Brunswick has some lovely ski resorts, most importantly Mount Sugarloaf and Mount Crabbe. Although the mountains in Nova Scotia are lower, Keltic Cape Smokey is worth mentioning.

 Snowmobiling

There are a large number of snowmobilers in New Brunswick and Nova Scotia, both of which are crisscrossed by trails. Visitors can explore these two provinces by snowmobile, but should take care to heed all regulations. Don't forget, furthermore, that a permit is required. It is also advisable to take out liability insurance.

The following rules should always be obeyed:

- stay on the snowmobile trails;
- always drive on the right side of the trail;
- wear a helmet;
- all snowmobiles must have headlights.

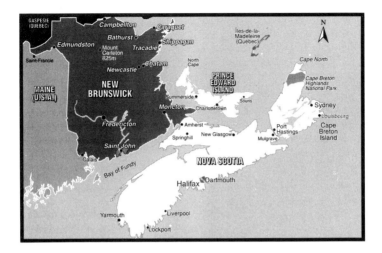

NEW BRUNSWICK

New Brunswick, gateway to the Maritimes, is enchanting in its diversity. Geographically, it is remarkably varied, combining more than a thousand kilometres of shoreline and seascapes with picturesque farmlands and endless stretches of often mountainous wilderness. Forests cover a full 85% of the territory, which is traversed from north to south by the majestic St. John River, whose source lies in the Appalachian foothills. This river has always been essential to the province's development, and charming town and villages have sprung up along its richly fertile banks. Among these are Fredericton, New Brunswick's pretty capital, with its aura of a bygone era, and Saint John, the province's chief port city and industrial centre. After winding its way through a pastoral landscape, the St. John River empties

into the Bay of Fundy, whose often spectacularly steep shores mark the southern border of New Brunswick. An amazing natural phenomenon occurs in this bay twice a day when the highest, most powerful tides in the world surge up onto the shores, reshaping the landscape in sometimes unusual ways, and actually reversing the current of the rivers! Without question, the Bay of Fundy's giant tides constitute one of the greatest natural attractions in the eastern part of the continent. The bay's shoreline, furthermore, is of incomparable beauty. Be that as it may, New Brunswick's other coast, on the Atlantic Ocean, has charms of its own. It is here, from the border of Nova Scotia to that of Québec, that visitors will find the province's most beautiful sandy beaches, washed by uncommonly warm waters that are perfect for swimming. Most importantly, however, this is the Acadian coast. It is here, in towns and villages like Caraquet, Shippagan and Shediac, that visitors can learn about Acadia and its warm, hospitable inhabitants.

In addition to its varied scenery, New Brunswick offers a rich medley of strong, distinct cultures. In fact, after a past scarred by rivalry between the French and British empires for control of the continent in the 18th century, New Brunswick is now Canada's only officially bilingual province. Originally inhabited by Amerindians of the Micmac and Malecite Nations, the territory corresponding to present-day New Brunswick was first visited by envoys of the King of France. In 1604, a trading post was established on Île Sainte-Croix, right near the city of St. Stephen, marking the birth of Acadia. The following year, the French moved the trading post to the opposite shore of the Bay of Fundy, founding Port-Royal in what is now Nova Scotia. For a century and a half, Acadia developed mainly along the shores of the Bay of Fundy. In 1755, however, the British decided to put an end to Acadia, and a tragic event took place: the Deportation of the Acadians. Approximately half of the 14,000 Acadians were put on boats and deported, while the others hid or escaped into the woods. Many of these eventually took up residence on the Atlantic coast of New Brunswick. A little more than two decades later, another event, the end of the American Revolution, would have a tremendous influence on the course of history in this region. From 1783 on, when American revolutionary forces finally defeated the British, thousands of soldiers and civilians wishing to remain loyal to Great Britain sought refuge in the Maritimes; many settled on the banks of the St. John River. Later, a heavy flow of immigrants from the British Isles added to the province's population. Today, English is the mother tongue of the majority of New Brunswick's inhabitants, although French-speakers still make up a third of the population. The Acadians still live, for the most part, on the Atlantic coast, while another group of French-speakers, known as Brayons, may be found along the St. John and Madawaska Rivers, in the northwestern part of the province.

 Finding Your Way Around

During a trip to New Brunswick, visitors can explore pretty rural landscapes, towns and villages steeped in history and the coasts along the Bay of Fundy and the Atlantic Ocean. The following four tours embrace the wide range of tourist attractions found in this province: **Tour A: Fredericton ★★★; Tour B: The St. John River Valley ★★; Tour C: The Fundy Shore ★★★; Tour D: The Acadian Coast ★★.**

■ **Tour A: Fredericton**

The city of Fredericton grew up on either side of the St. John River, but the downtown area and most tourist attractions lie on the west bank. Visitors will have no difficulty finding their way around the small city centre, which may be explored on foot. The two main downtown arteries are Queen and King Streets, both of which run parallel to the river. Most attractions, as well as many restaurants and businesses, lie on one or the other of these streets.

Bus Terminal: At the corner of Brunswick and Regent Streets, ☎ 458-6000.

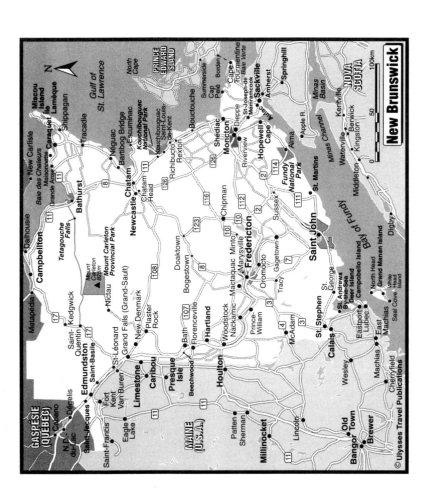

Airport: Located about 16 km southeast of the city, on Lincoln Road (☎ 444-6100), Fredericton's airport is served mainly by Air Canada (☎ 468-4561) and its partner, Air Nova, and Canadian Airlines (☎ 459-4089) and its partner, Air Atlantic. Visitors can take a taxi to the downtown area.

■ Tour B: The St. John River Valley

From the Québec border, visitors can take Highway 2 (the TransCanada Highway) or any other parallel road to the province's capital, Fredericton. After passing through Fredericton, take Highway 7, then Route 102 to Gagetown, the last stop on the tour. By continuing south, visitors will soon reach the city of Saint John, on the shores of the Bay of Fundy.

Edmundston

Bus Terminal: Victoria Street, near Hébert Boulevard, ☎ 739-8309.

■ Tour C: The Fundy Shore

From St. Stephen to Saint John, and then on to Sussex, the major road is Highway 1. In Sussex, Highway 1 connects with Highway 2, which leads to Moncton and Aulac, at the border of Nova Scotia, where the tour ends. To reach Deer Island, take the exit for St. George from Highway 2, then follow the signs to the tiny village of Letete. A ferry crosses from there to Deer Island. It is possible to reach Campobello Island from the state of Maine by taking the road from Calais to Lubec. To go to Grand Manan Island, visitors must take the ferry from Blacks Harbour.

Saint John

Bus Terminal: 300 Union Street, at the corner of Carmarthen Street, ☎ 648-3555.

Train station: Station Street, ☎ 642-2916.

Airport: About ten kilometres east of the city. A shuttle carries passengers from the large downtown hotels to the airport several times a day. The airport is served mainly by Air Canada (☎ 652-1517) and its partner, Air Nova, and Canadian Airlines (☎ 698-2630) and its partner, Air Atlantic.

Ferry: A ferry makes the crossing from Saint John to Digby, Nova Scotia three times a day, setting out from a dock on the west bank of the St. John River; ☎ 636-4048.

Moncton

Bus Terminal: Well-located downtown, at 960 Main Street, ☎ 859-5060.

Train station: Downtown, on the west side, near Main Street, ☎ 382-7892.

Airport: Located on Champlain Street, in Dieppe. The downtown area may be reached by taxi. The airport is served mainly by Air Canada (☎ 857-1044) and its partner Air Nova, and Canadian Airlines (☎ 857-0620) and its partner, Air Atlantic.

■ Tour D: The Acadian Coast

Except for a small section between Cape Tourmentine and Shediac, Highway 11 is the main road used on this tour. The highway passes through most of the towns and villages on the coast, skirts around the peninsula, then runs alongside Baie des Chaleurs to the

Québec border. From Newcastle, visitors can cross New Brunswick from east to west on Highway 1, which runs through the Miramichi River valley.

Cape Tourmentine

Ferry: Several times a day, a ferry makes the crossing between New Brunswick and Prince Edward Island; ☎ 538-7312.

 Practical Information

New Brunswick Area Code: 506.

Tourist Information Centre: ☎ 1-800-561-0123.

■ Tour A:Fredericton

Tourist Information Centre: On the TransCanada Highway, ☎ 458-8331. City Hall, Queen Street, ☎ 452-9616.

■ Tour B: The St. John River Valley

Saint-Jacques

Tourist Information Centre: On the TransCanada Highway, ☎ 735-2747.

■ Tour C: The Fundy Shore

St. Stephen

Tourist Information Centre: King Street, ☎ 466-7390.

Saint John

Tourist Information Centre: Highway 3, ☎ 658-2940. Near the Reversing Falls, ☎ 863-2937. Downtown, near the market, ☎ 658-2855.

Moncton

Tourist Information Centre: Main Street, facing Boreview Park, ☎ 856-4390. City Hall, 774 Main Street, ☎ 853-3596.

■ Tour D: The Acadian Coast

Campbellton

Tourist Information Centre: Highway 11, ☎ 789-2367.

 Exploring

■ Tour A: Fredericton ★★★

Fredericton is definitely one of the most precious jewels in the province's crown. Capital of New Brunswick, it has managed to preserve the remarkable historical legacy and architectural harmony handed down to it from the previous century, giving it a subtle elegance and old-fashioned character. Adorned with magnificent churches and government buildings, as well as large green spaces, some of which lie alongside the St. John River, Fredericton is one of those cities that charms visitors at first sight. Its quiet streets, lined with stately elms, are graced with vast, magnificent Victorian residences. These pretty houses, with their invariably well-tended front gardens, abound in Fredericton, contributing greatly to the city's charm. The site now occupied by the city was originally an Acadian trading post named Sainte-Anne, which was founded in the late 17th century. Acadians lived here until 1783, when they were driven away by the arrival of the Loyalists. The city of Fredericton was founded the following year. It became the provincial capital and was named Fredericton in honour of the second son of George III, Great Britain's king at the time. Over the years, very few industries have set up shop here, opting instead for Saint John. Today, Fredericton's chief employers are the provincial government and the universities.

Downtown

The best place to start off a tour of downtown Fredericton is the excellent tourist office located inside City Hall *(at the corner of Queen and York Streets, ☎ 452-9616)*, which also offers very good guided bus tours of the city. The oldest part of **City Hall ★ (1)** *(free admission; mid-May to early Sep, everyday 8 AM to 7:30 PM; early Sep to mid-May, by appointment)* was built in 1876, at which time it included not only the municipal offices and council rooms, but also an opera house, a farmer's market and a number of prison cells. The fountain in front of City Hall dates from 1885, while the building's second wing was erected between 1975 to 1977. The Council Chamber, open to the public during summer, makes for an interesting visit.

On the other side of York Street, visitors will see the **Courthouse (2)** *(no tours; at the corner of Queen and York Streets)*, a large stone building erected in the late 1930's. The edifice was used as a high-school before being adopted for its present purpose in 1970. Right next to the Courthouse stands the **New Brunswick College of Craft and Design (3)** *(no tours)*, the only post-secondary school in Canada to offer a program devoted entirely to training artisans.

A little farther, visitors will see the **Military Compound and Guard House ★★ (4)** *(free admission; Jun to*

early Sep, everyday 10 AM to 6 PM; at the corner of Queen and Carleton Streets, ☎ 453-3747). These stone buildings, erected in 1827 as replacements for the city's original, wooden military buildings, served as barracks for British troops until 1869. One room has been restored to illustrate the building's initial use, and a soldier in period dress serves as a guide. A sundial was reconstructed on the barracks wall. Up until the beginning of this century, residents of Fredericton could check the time by referring to devices such as this one.

Head up Carleton Street to the corner of King Street, where **Wilnot United Church ★★ (5)** *(at the corner of Carleton and King Streets)* is located. Its rather austere façade conceals a superb, exceptionally colourful interior abounding in hand-carved woodwork. This church was built in 1852, although the Fredericton Methodist Society, which joined the United Church of Canada in 1925, was founded back in 1791.

Back on Queen Street, turn right in order to reach the **New Brunswick Power and Electricity Museum** *(free admission; Jul and Aug, Mon to Fri 9 AM to 9 PM, Sat 10 AM to 5 PM, Sun 12 PM to 4 PM; Sep to Jun, Mon to Fri 9 PM to 4:30 PM; 514 Queen Street)*. This informative little museum displays a collection of objects illustrating the history of electricity in New Brunswick.

Immediately opposite the Electricity Museum stands a beautiful Second Empire style building erected in 1881. This edifice houses the **National Exhibition Centre ★ (7)** *(free admission; Jun to early Sep, everyday 10 AM to 6 PM; Sep to early Jun, Tue to Sun noon to 5 PM; at the corner of Queen and*

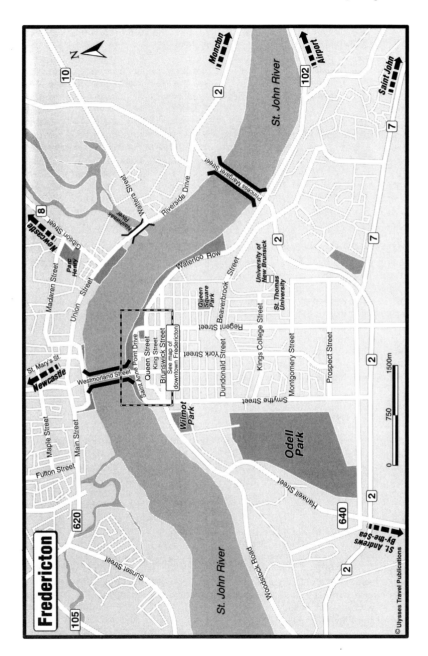

Fredericton

N

St. John River

Moncton

Airport

Saint John

Princess Margaret Street

Riverside Drive

Waterloo Row

University of New Brunswick

St. Thomas University

Queen Square Park

Beaverbrook Street

Regent Street

Kings College Street

York Street

Dundonald Street

Montgomery Street

Prospect Street

Smythe Street

Saint Anne Point Drive

Queen Street

King Street

Brunswick Street

See map of downtown Fredericton

Westmorland Street

Wilmot Park

Odell Park

Hanwell Street

Woodstock Road

St. John River

St. Andrews By-the-Sea

Newcastle

Newcastle

St. Mary's St.

Maclaren Street

Union Street

Gibson Street

Waters Street

Nashwaak River

Pac Henry

Maple Street

Main Street

Fulton Street

Sunset Street

St. John River

© Ulysses Travel Publications

0   750   1500m

10
2
102
7
8
7
2
620
640
105
2
2
7

Carleton Streets, ☎ 453-4737), which presents exhibits on history, crafts, the arts, sciences and technology. The second floor of the building is occupied by the **New Brunswick Sports Hall of Fame** *(free admission; ☎ 453-3747)*, dedicated to New Brunswick's finest athletes.

Also on Queen Street, **Officer's Square ★★ (8)** *(adults $1; May to Jun, Mon to Sat 10 AM to 6 PM; Jul and Aug, Mon, Wed, Fri and Sat 10 AM to 6 PM, Tue and Thu 10 AM to 9 PM, Sun 12 PM to 6 PM; Sep to mid-Oct, Mon to Fri 9 AM to 5 PM; mid-Oct to Apr, Mon, Wed and Fri 11 AM to 3 PM; Queen Street, near Regent Street, ☎ 455-6041)* is an attractive park. Facing it is the building once used as officers' quarters, erected in two stages, from 1839 to 1840 and in 1851. Its bow-shaped stone columns, railings and iron stairs are typical of architecture designed by royal engineers during the colonial era. The former quarters now house the **York-Sunbury Museum**, devoted to the province's military and domestic history.

Continue along Queen Street to the pretty **York County Courthouse ★ (9)** *(no tours; Queen Street, after Regent Street)*, erected in 1855. In those years, there was a market on the ground floor. Today, the building houses the services of the Ministry of Justice, as well as a courtroom.

A little farther along Queen Street, on the opposite side of the street, stands the **Playhouse (10)** *(Queen Street, at the corner of St. John Street)*, built in 1964. Since 1969, it has served as home base for the only English-speaking theatre company in the province, The New Brunswick Theatre. Construction of the Playhouse was financed by

Lord Beaverbrook, a British newspaper tycoon who lived in New Brunswick as a child.

Not far from the Playhouse, visitors will see the **Provincial Legislature ★★ (11)** *(free admission; Jun to Aug, everyday 9 AM to 8 PM; end of Aug to early Jun, Mon to Fri 9 AM to 4 PM; Queen Street, at the corner of St. John Street, ☎ 453-2527)*, seat of the provincial government since 1882. Inside, an impressive spiral staircase made of wood leads to the library, which contains over 35,000 volumes, some very rare. Of particular interest are the Assembly Chamber, where the members of Parliament gather, and the portraits of King George III and Queen Charlotte, by British painter Joshua Reynolds.

Across from the Legislative Building stands the **Beaverbrook Art Gallery ★★★ (12)** *(adults $3; Jul and Aug, Sun to Wed 10 AM to 5 PM, Thu to Sat 10 AM to 7 PM; Sep to Jun, Tue to Sat 10 AM to 5 PM, Sun and Mon noon to 5 PM; Queen Street, ☎ 458-8545)*, another of Lord Beaverbrook's gifts to the city of Fredericton. The gallery houses, among other things, a superb collection of works by highly renowned British painters, as well as a number of other lovely canvases by Canadian artists such as Cornelius Krieghoff and James Wilson Morrice. Without question, however, the most impressive piece on display is Catalan artist Salvador Dali's *Santiago el Grande*.

After touring the fascinating Beaverbrook Art Gallery, summer visitors can enjoy a delightful stroll on Fredericton's splendid **Green ★**, which stretches 4 km alongside the St. John, enabling both walkers and cyclists to explore the banks of the river. The Green con-

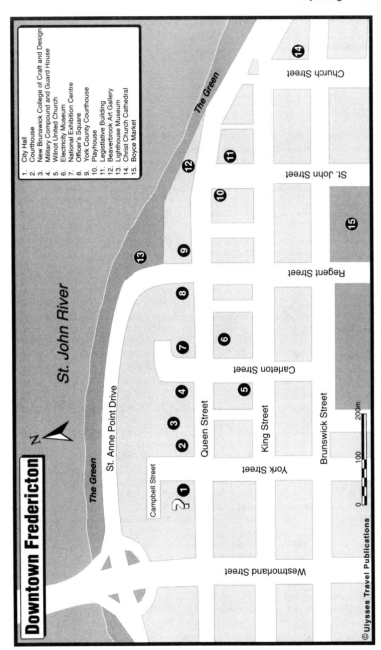

Downtown Fredericton

St. John River

The Green

St. Anne Point Drive

Campbell Street

Queen Street

York Street

King Street

Carleton Street

Brunswick Street

Regent Street

St. John Street

Church Street

The Green

Westmorland Street

N

1. City Hall
2. Courthouse
3. New Brunswick College of Craft and Design
4. Military Compound and Guard House
5. Wilmot United Church
6. Electricity Museum
7. National Exhibition Centre
8. Officer's Square
9. York County Courthouse
10. Playhouse
11. Legislative Building
12. Beaverbrook Art Gallery
13. Lighthouse Museum
14. Christ Church Cathedral
15. Boyce Market

0   100   200m

© Ulysses Travel Publications

tributes greatly to the quality of life in the city. Visitors can stop at the **Lighthouse Museum (13)** *(adults $2; Oct to May, Mon to Fri 9 AM to 4 PM; Jun to Sep, Mon to Fri 9 AM to 4 PM, Sat and Sun noon to 4 PM; Jul and Aug, everyday 10 AM to 9 PM; ☎ 459-2515)*, which presents a historical exhibit.

Take Queen Street to Church Street in order to visit the Gothic style **Christ Church Cathedral ★★ (14)** *(at the corner of Queen Street and Church Street)*, whose construction, completed in 1853, was largely due to the efforts of Fredericton's first Anglican bishop, John Medley.

From the cathedral, take Brunswick Street to Regent Street. On the left-hand side stands **Boyce Market (15)** *(at the corner of Brunswick and Regent Streets)*, a public market where farmers, artisans and artists sell their products every Saturday morning. Right next door, on the left side of Brunswick Street, lies Fredericton's **Old Loyalist Cemetery**. It was here that the most notable figures in Fredericton's early history were buried from 1787 to 1878.

Outside the Downtown Area

The **University of New Brunswick** *(at the end of University Street)*, founded in 1785 by newly arrived Loyalists, is made up of several different edifices. Its arts building is the oldest university building still in use in Canada.

On the same site, visitors will also find **St. Thomas University**, a Catholic institution originally located in Chatham, on the Miramichi River. The two universities are attended by a total of 8,000 students each year. This is a wonderful spot from which to view the city below.

Odell Park ★ *(Rookwood Avenue, northwest of the city)* covers over 175 ha and includes 16 km of trails. This beautifully preserved, peaceful natural area has been enhanced by the addition of an enclosure for deer, duck ponds, picnic tables and a play area for children.

■ Tour B: The St. John River Valley ★

From the *République de Madawaska*, in the northwestern part of the province, to the industrial city of Saint John, where it empties into the Bay of Fundy, the majestic St. John River is the keystone of New Brunswick's most continental region. Each bend in the river reveals new scenery and different facets of a land full of contrasts. Around Edmundston and Grand Falls (Grand-Sault) — French-speaking areas adorned with flamboyant Catholic churches — visitors will discover a lovely, gently rolling landscape, where the local economy centres on lumbering and potato farming. Farther south, as the valley widens, the rivers runs through an entirely different region, studded with towns and villages boasting a rich architectural heritage. Among these is Fredericton, the province's capital. Two centuries ago, this entire portion of the St. John valley became a veritable "promised land" for thousands of Loyalists (American colonists wishing to remain allegiant to the British crown after the Revolutionary War). In spite of these cultural and social differences, the valley is united by one force: an endless fascination with the mighty St. John, from its source to its estuary.

Saint-Jacques

This is the first village that many travellers (or at least those arriving from Québec) will encounter on their tour of

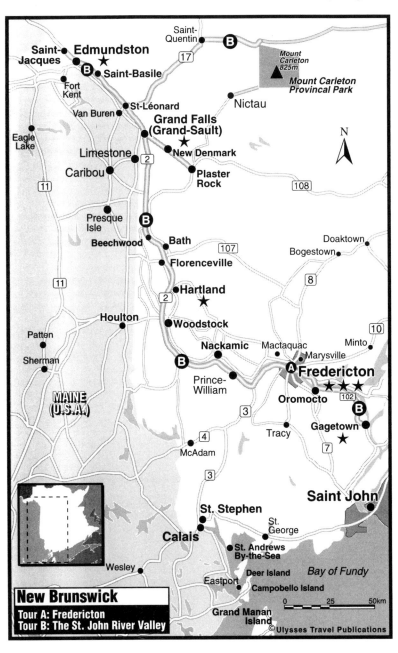

Saint-Quentin

Mount Carleton 825m

Mount Carleton Provincal Park

Saint-Jacques

Edmundston

Saint-Basile

Fort Kent

Van Buren

St-Léonard

Nictau

Grand Falls (Grand-Sault)

Eagle Lake

Limestone

New Denmark

Caribou

Plaster Rock

N

Presque Isle

Beechwood

Bath

Doaktown

Bogestown

Florenceville

Hartland

Houlton

Woodstock

Patten

Sherman

Nackamic

Mactaquac

Marysville

Minto

Fredericton

MAINE (U.S.A.)

Prince-William

Oromocto

Gagetown

McAdam

Tracy

St. Stephen

Saint John

St. George

Calais

St. Andrews By-the-Sea

Wesley

Deer Island

Bay of Fundy

Eastport

Campobello Island

New Brunswick
Tour A: Fredericton
Tour B: The St. John River Valley

0   25   50km

© Ulysses Travel Publications

Grand Manan Island

New Brunswick. It is therefore no coincidence that Saint-Jacques is home to one of the province's largest tourist information centres, as well as a provincial park, **Les Jardins de la République**, which includes two interesting attractions.

The **New Brunswick Botanical Garden ★★** *(adults $3; Jun to Sep; Highway 2, Exit 8, ☎ 739-6335)*, destined to become one of the region's greatest draws, is worth visiting for a number of reasons. Some 50,000 plants have been distributed over a well laid-out area of 7 ha, which offers a lovely panoramic view of the region's gentle, wooded valleys. The garden's designers had the clever idea of installing an unobtrusive sound system, enabling visitors to explore the garden with the music of Bach, Chopin or Mozart in the background.

The **Antique Automobile Museum ★** *(adults $2.50; end of May to mid-Sep; right beside the Garden, ☎ 735-2525)* grew up around the private collection of Edmundston resident Melvin Louden. It displays a lovely selection of antique cars, some of which are very rare nowadays, including the Bricklin—the only automobile made in New Brunswick—and the 1933 Rolls Royce Phantom.

Edmundston ★

The region's largest urban area, Edmundston is naturally the heart of northwestern New Brunswick's French-speaking community, which refers to it affectionately as the capital of the mystical *République de Madawaska*. The driving force behind the city's prosperity is immediately evident in the urban landscape—the pulp and paper industry, which has flourished due to

---

The République de Madawaska

The origins of the mythical République de Madawaska date back to the region's early colonization, a time when the British and the Americans were continuously redefining the border between Maine and New Brunswick after skirmishes and tortuous political negotiations. Tired of being mere pawns in all of this, the people of Madawaska, scorning the authorities, eventually decided to "found" their own republic, which had the very vaguest of borders, but more or less encompassed the French-speaking population in this part of the country. Pushing the fantasy even further, they decided that the republic would have its own president, namely, the mayor of Edmundston. Behind this peculiar historical legacy lies a very strong cultural bond between French-speakers on both sides of the border, which can best be appreciated during Edmundston's Foire Brayonne, a festival held each year at the end of July.

---

the richness of the neighbouring forests and the city's highly advantageous location at the confluence of the Madawaska and St. John Rivers. While Edmundston's industrial character is unmistakable, the city is also very proud of its festive spirit and cultural life, at their peak during the **Foire Breyonne** *(☎ 739-6608)*, the largest French-speaking event in the country to be held outside of Québec. It is during

The Brayons

Inhabitants of the République *are known as Brayons, a term whose origins remain obscure. The word might come from brayer, meaning "crush," since crushing flax was a common chore for Madawaskan women. The Brayons are descendants of both Quebecois and Acadians. The former came to New Brunswick in the 18th and 19th centuries seeking new land to settle, while the latter were driven from the lower St. John by an influx of Loyalist colonists at the end of the 18th century.*

this period, at the end of each July, that visitors can best discover the richness and generosity and of the local population.

The impressive **Cathedral of the Immaculate Conception ★** *(145 Rice Street)* towers over the city of Edmundston. It was built during the dark years of the Great Depression with materials from all over the world—Africa, India, Italy, France, etc. The stained-glass windows are superb.

Visitors interested in learning about the history of the area and its inhabitants can stop by the **Madawaska Museum** *(adults $1; mid-Jun to Sep; 195 Hébert Boulevard)*, which houses a permanent collection of artifacts linked to the region's development. The museum also includes a gallery devoted to the work of contemporary Madawaskan artists.

Saint-Basile

For many years, colonists from Québec and Acadians who came here seeking refuge formed only a small community, served for more than four decades by a single parish, Saint-Basile. Founded in 1792, the parish originally stretched from the Saint-François River to the present-day city of Grand Falls. Saint-Basile has therefore been dubbed the "Cradle of Madawaska." Visitors can learn a bit about the region's history at the **Chapel Museum** *(free admission; end of Jun to Aug; Rue Principale)*, while the **Convent Museum** *(adults $2, Jun to early Sep, everyday 10 AM to 8 PM; 409 Rue Principale)* deals with the history of medicine. Saint-Basile has recently become known for an entirely different reason as well: popular singer Roch Voisine was born here.

Saint-Léonard

Without a doubt, Saint-Léonard offers the clearest possible illustration of the arbitrary nature of Canadian-American border, which has separated the town from Van Buren (on the American side) since 1842. In any case, these two communities, linked by both history and language, still bear allegiance to the same republic: Madawaska!

Not far from Saint-Léonard's lovely church, the **Madawaska Weavers** *(739 Rue Principale, ☎ 423-6341)* company offers tours of its facilities. This company, founded in 1939 by Rolande and Fernande Gervais, produces a wide range of handmade clothing and fine woolen goods.

From Saint-Léonard, visitors can either go to Mount Carleton Provincial Park or head to the northeastern part of the province on Route 17.

Grand Falls (Grand-Sault) ★★

A charming little town on the banks of the St. John, at the point where the river plunges 23 m, Grand Falls is a dynamic, engaging community whose mostly French-speaking population has Québecois and Acadian roots. This pretty spot was frequented by Malecite Indians for many years before becoming a British military post in 1791. The city was finally established in 1896. In addition to its attractive location, Grand Falls has a charming town centre. Its wide boulevard, flanked by low houses facing right onto the street, gives it a slightly midwestern character. It is worth noting that Grand Falls is the only town in Canada with an officially bilingual name—Grand Falls-Grand Sault. With its field-covered valleys, the surrounding region, known for its potatoes, makes for a lovely outing.

The magnificent **waterfall** ★★ that inspired the town's name is the largest and most impressive to be found in the Maritimes. The waters of the St. John plunge 23 m, then rush for about 2 km through a gorge whose sides reach as high as 70 m. At the far end of the gorge, the turbulent water has eroded the rock, creating cavities known here as "wells," since water stays in them after the river rises. Visitors can start off their tour by dropping by the **Malobiannah Centre** *(on Chemin Madawaska, alongside the falls)*, which is both an interpretive centre and a regional tourist information centre. From here, there is a splendid **view** ★ of the falls and the hydroelectric dam. A footpath heading out from the centre makes it possible to observe the falls and the gorge from all different angles. At the **Centre La Rochelle** *(adults $1; Centennial Park)*, on the opposite bank, right in the centre of town, there is a staircase that leads down to the river bed, offering a lovely **view** ★★ of the gorge, the wells and the waterfall.

To learn more about Grand Falls and its surrounding area, visitors can head to the little **Grand Falls Museum** *(free admission; Jun to Aug; Rue Church, ☎ 473-5265)*, which displays an diverse assortment of objects linked to the region's history.

Route 108 leads to New Denmark, Plaster Rock and finally the Miramachi River, which flows into the Atlantic.

New Denmark

New Denmark is a small rural community similar in every way to other towns in the region, except that it also happens to be the hub of the largest Danish colony in North America. Its origins date back to 1872, when the provincial government invited a handful of Danes to settle at the confluence of the Salmon and St. John Rivers. These people were promised good, arable land, but instead inherited uneven, rocky soil. The provincial authorities apparently chose this precise spot along the river so that the Danes would act as a buffer between the French-speakers in the north and the English-speakers in the south. The settlers ended up staying anyway, and their descendants, who now number just under two thousand, hold an annual festival on June 19 to commemorate their ancestors' experience.

Beechwood

Visitors can stop in this tiny hamlet to examine its **hydroelectric power station** or enjoy a picnic in the park by the river.

Bath

The pretty, peaceful village of Bath, located on the east bank of the St. John River, has no sights per se, but is graced with a few lovely white residences, which are owned by local notables. Visiting here is like stepping back into another era, far from the hustle and bustle of modern cities.

Florenceville

This little village witnessed the humble origins of the McCain company, now an international frozen food empire known especially for its potatoes and french fries. The family is the second wealthiest in New Brunswick, after the Irvings. At the edge of Florenceville stands an imposing factory, which still processes tons of locally-grown potatoes each year. In the centre of the village, visitors can stop at the **Andrew & Laura McCain Gallery ★** *(free admission; open all year; McCain Street; ☎ 392-5294)*, which displays works by New Brunswick artists, artisans and photographers, and also presents the occasional international exhibit.

Hartland ★

Home town of Richard Hatfield, the province's eccentric former prime minister, Hartland is an adorable village typical of the St. John River Valley. It is known for its remarkable **covered bridge ★★**, the world's longest. Stretching 390 m across the river, the structure was built in 1899, at a time when simply covering a bridge made its skeleton last up to seven times longer. Today there are more covered bridges in New Brunswick than anywhere else on Earth. Visitors who would like to stop for a picnic and admire the local scenery will find an attractive park on the west bank of the river.

Woodstock

After the Revolutionary War, tens of thousands of American citizens who had fought on the British side took refuge in Canada, a territory Great Britain had wrested from France two decades earlier. In 1784, one of these Loyalists, Captain Jacob Smith, sailed up the St. John to the mouth of the Meduxnekeak River, where British authorities had granted him a piece of land. A few decades later, Woodstock was founded on that spot. Now a medium-sized town, it is the seat of Carleton County. Although known for being somewhat conservative, Woodstock takes pride in living up to its nickname, "Hospitality Town". At the end of July, the town holds an annual festival known as **Old Home Week**, which celebrates family and tradition.

Woodstock's Main and Connell Streets are graced with several pretty historic buildings, including **Connell House** *(free admission; Jul and Aug; 26 Connell Street, ☎ 328-9706)*, an impressive upper-class residence. Neoclassical in style, it belonged to the honorable Charles Connell, a local politician who also served as New Brunswick's postmaster until he had to resign in the wake of a controversy that erupted when he issued a stamp in his own honour.

Built in 1833, the **Old Carleton County Courthouse ★** *(free admission; Jul and Aug; Route 560, Upper Woodstock, north of the town centre, ☎ 328-9706)* is a two-story wooden building whose modest façade conceals an interior adorned with lovely, sober woodwork. The building served as the Courthouse for over 75 years, until a new Courthouse was inaugurated in the centre of town. A local farmer then used the building as a barn for nearly half a century before the Carleton County Historical Society finally purchased and renovated it in 1960.

Nackawic

Visitors can make a brief stop in Nackawic to see its **giant axe**. A tribute to the region's lumberjacks, it is the largest in the world.

Prince-William

A wonderful open-air museum covering 120 ha on the banks of the St. John, **Kings Landing** ★★★ *(adults $6; Jun to mid-Oct, everyday 9 AM to 5 PM; along the TransCanada Highway in Prince-William, ☎ 363-5805)* is a reproduction of an early 19th century Loyalist village. It includes more than 20 historic buildings and about 30,000 objects that help illuminate the area's past, including furniture, clothing and tools. To enliven the atmosphere, there are people dressed in period clothing, who perform the daily tasks of 19th century villagers, as well as answering visitors' questions. There is no more pleasant, effective means of learning about Loyalist history than a visit to Kings Landing, the best museum devoted to that subject.

Mactaquac

Mactaquac is the site of a very popular **provincial park**, which offers outdoor activities all year round. The park is located alongside the river, whose waters are regulated by the largest **hydroelectric dam** in the Maritimes.

Fredericton ★★★ (see p 47)

Oromocto

A somewhat dreary place, Oromocto is home to the soldiers stationed at Gage-town, a very important Canadian military base. It features a **military museum** *(free admission; open all year; on the Canadian base; ☎ 422-2530)*, which displays weapons from the 18th, 19th and 20th centuries.

Gagetown ★

After winding its way through the fields of a prosperous farming region, the little road heading out from Oromocto leads to Gagetown, a tiny village on the banks of the majestic St. John. Everything here—the church, the general store, the handful of houses, the very location—is so pretty that it appears to have come straight out of a fairy tale. This peaceful spot has retained the old-fashioned character of a Loyalist village, as well as an atmosphere that couldn't possibly be more Anglo-Saxon. With all that charm, it is hardly surprising that each year Gagetown attracts artists seeking inspiration, as well as vacationers looking for a place to relax. Sailors stop here, too, tying their yachts or sailboats to the village wharf. Although Gagetown is a tiny village, it nevertheless boasts several bed & breakfasts, a very good inn, an art gallery and several craft shops. There is also a free ferry service, enabling visitors to cross over to the other side of the river.

The **Tilley House** ★ *(adults $2, mid-Jun to mid-Sep, everyday 10 AM to 5 PM; Front Street, ☎ 488-2066)* was built in 1786, making it one of the oldest residences in New Brunswick. It now houses the Queens County Museum, which displays all sorts of objects relating to local history and the life of the house's most illustrious owner, Samuel Leonard Tilley, one of the Fathers of Canadian Confederation (1867).

At the **Loomcrofter Studio** ★ *(south of the village, near the school, ☎ 488-2400)*, visitors will find the studios of various designers and weavers of tartan cloth. The building itself is one of the oldest in the St. John River Valley.

■ **Tour C: The Fundy Shore ★★**

All along the coastal road that leads from the border of the United States to that of Nova Scotia, the landscape, villages and towns are marked by one of the most incredible natural phenomena on Earth: the tides of the Bay of Fundy. Twice a day, these tides, the highest in the world, storm the shores of the bay at lightning speed. In some places, the water can reach as high as 16 m (the equivalent of a four story building) in just a few hours, transforming the landscape in remarkable ways over the years. The tides are so powerful that they actually reverse the flow of a waterfall in Saint John and create a tidal bore (a small tidal wave) on the Petitcodiac River. Then, receding just as rapidly, they leave behind endless beaches perfect for clam-digging, that may be explored until the next massive rise in the water level. Adding to the pleasure of visiting this magnificent coastal region, the shores of the Bay of Fundy are studded with picturesque villages boasting a rich architectural heritage. Saint John, the province's largest city, and Moncton, its most dynamic, are also located here. Finally, the bay is one of the best places in the world for whale watching, since more than twenty different species come here to feed in the summer.

St. Stephen

The most important border town in the Maritimes, St. Stephen is a small, lively community, which was founded in 1784 by American colonists wishing to remain loyal to the British crown after the Revolutionary War. Today, ironically, St. Stephen and Calais, its twin town in the state of Maine, could easily be mistaken for a single town if it weren't for the St. Croix River, which forms a natural border. This lively community is celebrated on both sides of the border each year during the **International Festival**, which takes place at the end of August. In early August, another festival, this time dedicated to **chocolate**, is held only in St. Stephen, which has the distinction of being the birthplace of the chocolate bar, invented here in 1910 by the Ganong company. The ever successful **Ganong Chocolatier** *(73 Milltown Boulevard, ☎ 465-5611)* shop is a must for anyone with a sweet tooth.

The **Charlotte County Museum** *(free admission; Jun to Aug, Mon to Sat 9:30 AM to 4:30 PM; 443 Milltown Boulevard, ☎ 466-3295)* is set up inside a Second Empire style residence built in 1864 by a prosperous local businessman. It now houses a collection of objects related to local history, especially the period when St. Stephen and the small neighbouring villages were known for shipbuilding.

The **Crocker Hill Garden & Studio** *(2.4 km east of St. Stephen, on Ledge Road, ☎ 466-4251)* is a magnificent garden looking out on the St. Croix River.

St. Andrews By-the-Sea ★★

The most famous vacation spot on the Fundy shore, St. Andrews is a lovely village facing the bay. It has managed to benefit from its popularity by highlighting its astonishingly rich architectural heritage. Like many other communities in the area, St. Andrews was founded by Loyalists in 1783, and then enjoyed a period of great prosperity during the 19th century as a centre for shipbuilding and the exportation of billets. A number of the opulent houses flanking its streets, particularly **Water Street** ★, date back to that golden era. At the end of the century, St. Andrews began welcoming affluent visitors, who came here to drink in the invigorating sea air. St. Andrews' new vocation was clearly established in 1889 with the construction of a magnificent hotel, the **Algonquin** ★★ on a hill overlooking the village. In addition to the picturesque charm of its many historic buildings and its location alongside the bay, with its giant tides, St. Andrews now boasts a wide selection of accommodations and fine restaurants, numerous shops and a famous golf-course. All of this makes St. Andrews By-the-Sea a perfect place to stay during a tour of the region and its islands.

Erected in 1820, **Sheriff Andrews' House** ★ *(free admission; end of Jun to early Sep 9:30 AM to 4:30 PM; 63 King Street, ☎ 520-4270)* is one of the town's best-preserved homes from that era. It was built by Elusha Shelton Andrews, sheriff of Charlotte County and son of a distinguished Loyalist, Reverend Samuel Andrews. Since 1986, it has belonged to the provincial government, which has turned it into a museum. Guides in period costume explain the sheriff's life and times.

A sumptuous 19th century neoclassical residence, the **Ross Memorial Museum** ★ *(free admission, end of May to early Oct, Tue to Sat 10 AM to 4:30 PM, Sun 1:30 PM to 4:30 PM; 188 Montague Street, ☎ 529-1824)* contains an antique collection, which Henry Phipps Ross and Sarah Juliette Ross, an American couple who lived in St. Andrews from 1902 until they died,

assembled over their lifetime. The Rosses had a passion for travelling and antiques, and acquired some magnificent pieces of Chinese porcelain and other now priceless imported objects, as well as some lovely furniture made in New Brunswick.

There are several remarkable churches in St. Andrews. The most flamboyant is **Greenock Church** ★★ *(at the corner of Montague and Edward Streets)*, a Presbyterian church completed in 1824. Its most interesting feature is its pulpit, a good part of which is made of Honduran mahogany.

Until very recently, the **St. Andrews Blockhouse** *(on the west end of Water Street)*, a national historic site, was the last surviving blockhouse from the War of 1812. It was unfortunately damaged by fire, but necessary repairs have been completed. Pretty **Centennial Park** lies opposite.

The **Sunbury Shores Arts & Nature Centre** *(139 Water Street, ☎ 529-3386)* houses a small art gallery, where visitors can admire the work of New Brunswick artists. The centre is better known, however, for its summer courses on art, crafts and nature, which are open to groups of children and adults.

At the **Huntsman Marine Science Centre and Aquarium** ★★ *(adults $4; May to Oct 10 AM to 4:30 PM; Brandy Cove Road; ☎ 529-1202)*, visitors can learn about the bay's natural treasures. Several animal species may be observed here, including seals, who are fed every day at 11 AM and 4 PM There is also a touch-tank, where visitors can touch various live species of shellfish. This is an important research centre.

The **Ministers Island Historic Site** ★ *($5 per car includes tour of house; Jun to*

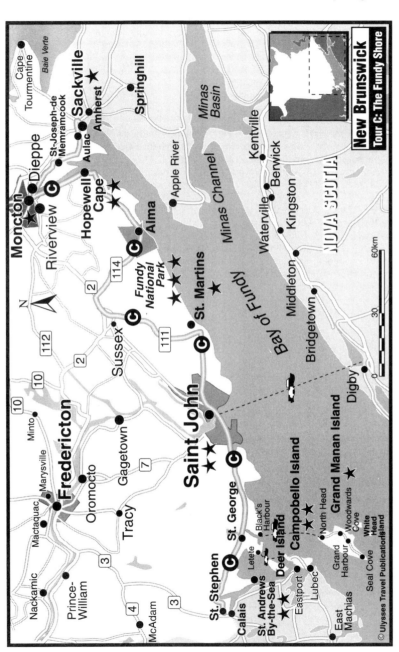

mid-Oct; Mowat Drive Road, take Bar Road only at low tide until the end) was originally, back at the very beginning of the 19th century, the property of Reverend Samuel. It was purchased in 1890 by Sir William Van Horne, a Montréal resident famous for building the first railroad linking Montréal to Vancouver. On this large estate, Van Horne erected an immense summer home with about 50 rooms. Minister's Island is only accessible at low tide. To arrange a visit, contact the tourist information office *(☎ 529-3000 or 529-5081)*.

At the **Atlantic Salmon Centre** *(adults $1; Chamcook, 8 km from St. Andrews on Route 127, ☎ 529-4581)*, visitors can learn about the life cycle of the Atlantic salmon, most importantly by viewing the fish in its natural environment through a window.

St. George

St. George, nicknamed Granite Town because of the rich granite deposits found in this area, is a small town with a Loyalist heritage, located alongside a pretty **waterfall ★** on the Magaguadavic River. A small overlook at the town entrance, beside the bridge on Brunswick Street, offers a lovely view of the waterfall, the gorge, the former dam of the St. George Pulp & Paper Company and the ladder built to help salmon swim upriver in summer. Like many towns and villages founded on the shores of the bay in the late 18th century, St. George has its share of interesting buildings, such as the **post office** *(Brunswick Street)*, with its red granite façade, and several churches, including the **Kirk Presbyterian** *(on Brunswick Street, at the east exit of the village)*, the oldest church of its denomination in Canada. From St. George, visitors can head to Letete, where a free ferry service takes passengers to Deer Island between 7 AM and 10 PM every day.

Deer Island

After cruising through a scattering of little islands covered with birds, the free ferry from Letete lands at Deer Island, with its wooded landscape, untouched beaches and tiny fishing villages. Three hours before high tide each day, visitors can view an interesting natural phenomenon from the southern point of the island—one of the largest whirlpools in the world, known locally as the **Old Sow ★**. In summertime, a private ferry makes the crossing between Deer Island and Campobello island about once an hour.

Campobello Island ★★

Campobello, the beloved island of former American president Franklin D. Roosevelt (1882-1945), is a good place for fans of history and the great outdoors to unwind. People come here to enjoy the lovely untouched beaches, go cycling on the quiet roads or walk along the well-maintained trails that follow the shoreline. On the eastern tip, the picturesque lighthouse at **East Quoddy Head ★** occupies a magnificent site on the bay, from which it is sometimes possible to spot whales and other sea mammals. In the early 19th century, Campobello's beauty began to attract the attention of wealthy families living in the northeastern cities of the United States, who built lovely summer homes here. The most famous of these families was that of Franklin D. Roosevelt, whose father, James, purchased 1.6 ha on the island in 1883. Franklin himself, and then his own family, spent most of his summers here from 1883 to 1921, the year he contracted polio. He returned on several occasions later to visit his friends on the island while serving as President of the United States. Although Campobello lies within Canadian lines, it is most easily accessible from the border town of Lubec, Maine. During the summer months, a private ferry also shuttles back and forth from Deer Island to Campobello about once an hour.

Roosevelt-Campobello International Park ★★ *(free admission; end of May to early Oct, 10 AM to 6 PM; Route 774, ☎ 752-2922)* is a joint project of the Canadian and American governments, launched in 1964 with the aim of increasing public awareness of Roosevelt's special attachment to Campobello Island and his magnificent property there. The visitors' centre shows a short film on Roosevelt's sojourns on the island. Afterward, visitors can tour the extraordinary **Roosevelt House**, most of whose furnishings belonged to the former American president, then stop at the **Prince House**, the site of the **James Roosevelt House** and the **Hubbard House**. The park also includes a beautiful natural area, south of the visitors' centre, where lovely hiking trails have been cleared along the shore.

Grand Manan Island ★

For many years, Grand Manan attracted mainly scientists, including the famous James Audubon in the early 19th century, due to the 275 or so species of birds that land here each year and the island's unique rock formations. More recently, however, Grand Manan has begun to benefit from the current craze for ecotourism, since the island obviously has a lot to offer nature lovers. It is a pleasant place to explore by bicycle, and even better on foot, thanks to the excellent network of trails running alongside the jagged shoreline with its often spectacular scenery. Without question, one of the most picturesque places on the island is the lighthouse known as **Swallowtail Light ★**, which stands at the tip of a peninsula at North Head. From here, whales can be seen regularly swimming off the shores of the island. Grand Manan also features a **museum** *(Grand Harbour, ☎ 662-3524)* and serves as the point of departure for numerous whale watching excursions and expeditions to **Machias Seal Island ★**, a remarkable bird sanctuary. To reach Grand Manan Island, visitors must take the ferry from Blacks Harbour *(☎ 662-3724)*, which makes five or six trips a day.

Saint John ★★

New Brunswick's largest city, Saint John occupies a hilly area on either side of the St. John River, at the point where it flows into the Bay of Fundy. A perfect example of the old, industrial port cities in the eastern part of North America, it has a unique, slightly mysterious charm. Lofty cranes and warehouses line the docks, which look strangely like wooden fences rising high out of the river at low tide. To add to its mysterious character, Saint John is often blanketed with a thick fog that can envelop the city at any moment, and then disappear just as quickly. The growth of the city's industries is due largely to its port, which is ice-free all year long. The site itself was scouted out for the first time on June 24, 1604 by explorer Samuel de Champlain, who christened the river St. John (Saint-Jean) in honour of the patron saint of that day. Later, in 1631, Charles de La Tour established a trading post here. The city's history didn't really start, however, until 1783, under the English regime. That year, from May 10 to May 18, about 2,000 Loyalists landed in Saint John, seeking a fresh start in life

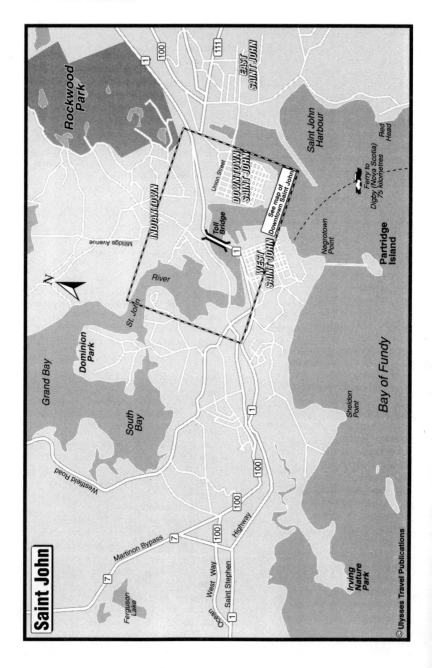

© Ulysses Travel Publications

after the defeat of British forces by American revolutionaries. More arrived before winter, doubling the population of Saint John. The city then absorbed a large number of immigrants, most from the British Isles. In those years, Partridge Island, in the port, was Canada's chief point of entry and quarantine station for immigrants. Today, Saint John has a higher concentration of Irish-Canadians than any other city in the country. It is a pleasant place to visit, particularly in mid-July during **Loyalist Days**, which commemorate the arrival of the Loyalists in 1783. The excellent **By-the-Sea Festival**, in August, celebrates the performing arts, while the **Franco-Frolic**, held in June, honours Acadian culture and traditions.

Downtown Saint John ★★, with its narrow streets lined with historic buildings and houses, lies on a hill on the east side of the river. A tour of the area usually starts at **Market Square (1)**, laid out a little more than a decade ago as part of an effort to revitalize the city centre. The square includes a shopping mall, a convention centre, several restaurants and a hotel, which combines modern construction with 19th century buildings. On the south side of the square stands **Barbour's General Store (2)** *(free admission; mid May to mid Oct; ☎ 658-2939)*, a small brick building displaying consumer goods typically available in this type of shop during the 19th century. From there, visitors can head up Union Street to the **Loyalist House National Historic Site (3)** *(adults $2; open all year; 120 Union Street, ☎ 652-3590)*, a very simple house built in the first decade of the 19th century, which is decorated with elegant period furniture. Union Street later intersects with Charlotte Street, where visitors can turn right to reach **King's Square (4)**, a pretty urban park marking the centre of Saint John. The paths in the

park are laid out in the pattern of the Union Jack; what better way for the inhabitants of Saint John to express their attachment to their mother country? Standing opposite the park on Charlotte Street is the **Old City Market (5)** *(free admission; open all year, Mon to Thu 7:30 AM to 6 PM, Fri 7:30 AM to 7 PM, Sat 7:30 AM to 5 PM; 47 Charlotte Street, ☎ 658-2820)*, dating back to 1876, where shoppers can still purchase fresh produce from local farms. On another side of the park, visitors will find the sumptuous **Imperial Theatre (6)** *(24 King Street, ☎ 634-8355)*, built in 1913 and restored in 1994, which is dedicated to the performing arts.

The **Aitken Bicentennial Exhibition Centre** ★ **(7)** *(free admission; Jun to Sep, everyday 10 AM to 5 PM; Sep to Jun, Tue to Sun 11:30 AM to 4:30 PM; 20 Hazen Avenue, ☎ 633-4870)* presents exhibits on both science and art. One of the five exhibition rooms was specifically designed to teach children about various facets of science in a dynamic fashion.

The **Reversing Falls** ★★ **(8)** *(on Route 100, at the river)* is a unique natural phenomenon that occurs twice a day at high tide. The current of the river, which, at this point drops 4 m at low tide, is reversed at high tide when the water level of the bay is several metres higher than that of the river. This counter-current is felt as far up-river as Fredericton.

The **New Brunswick Museum** ★ *(adults $2; changing schedule; 277 Douglas Avenue, ☎ 658-1842)*, the oldest museum in Canada, is devoted not only to the work of New Brunswick artists, but also to the history of the province's inhabitants—Amerindians, Acadians, Loyalists, and others. The permanent

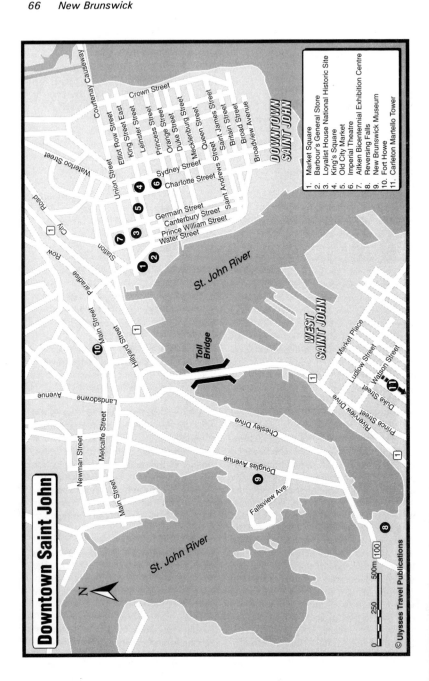

Downtown Saint John

DOWNTOWN SAINT JOHN

WEST SAINT JOHN

St. John River

1. Market Square
2. Barbour's General Store
3. Loyalist House National Historic Site
4. King's Square
5. Old City Market
6. Imperial Theatre
7. Aitken Bicentennial Exhibition Centre
8. Reversing Falls
9. New Brunswick Museum
10. Fort Howe
11. Carleton Martello Tower

© Ulysses Travel Publications

collection features certain imported objects as well, including pieces of Chinese porcelain. There is also a room designed specially for children.

For an excellent **view ★** of the city, head to the site of **Fort Howe (9)** *(Main Street, ☎ 658-2090)*. At the same location, there is a wooden blockhouse, which was built in Halifax and moved here in 1777 to protect the port of Saint John in the event of an American attack.

The **Carleton Martello Tower ★ (10)** *(free admission; Jun to Oct 9 AM to 5 PM; on the west bank, Charlotte Street, ☎ 636-4011)* is a circular tower built during the War of 1812 to protect the port from American attacks. It was also used as a command post for the Canadian army during the Second World War. Guides in 19th century dress explain the history of both the tower and the city of Saint John. From the top, visitors can enjoy a magnificent panoramic view of the city, the port and the bay.

If Saint John were a person, **Rockwood Park** *(main entry on Mt. Pleasant Avenue)* would be its lungs. Covering 890 ha, it is Canada's largest city park. All sorts of outdoor activities may be enjoyed here, including hiking, swimming, fishing, canoeing and pedal-boating. A number of other activities are organized just for children. In the north section of the park, is the **Cherry Brook Zoo** *(adults $3.25; open all year 10 AM to nightfall; Sandy Point Road, in the north part of Rockwood Park, ☎ 634-1440)*, the only zoo in the Maritimes featuring exotic animals. Some one hundred or so different species may be found here.

For many years, **Partridge Island ★** *(adults $10; May to Nov; from the port of St. John, for information ☎ 635-0782)* was the main point of entry for immigrants coming to Canada from the British Isles and the European continent. Between 1785 and 1942, it was the transition point and quarantine station for some three million immigrants who then settled in Saint John or, more commonly, elsewhere in Canada or the United States. About 2,000 of these individuals, having survived the often difficult journey across the Atlantic, never had the chance to see anything beyond Partridge Island. They died and were then buried in one of the six cemeteries located here. The island is also the site of New Brunswick's oldest lighthouse, as well as a historical museum.

The perfectly marvelous **Irving Nature Park ★★** *(free admission; at the end of Sand Cove Road, ☎ 632-7777)* has a great deal to offer nature lovers. Located just a few kilometres west of the industrial city of Saint John, this magnificent park covers a 225 ha peninsula trimmed with untouched beaches. The city seems a million miles away from here. Visitors can also enjoy a pleasant stroll along one of the park's trails, communing with nature and observing the plant and animal life along the Fundy shore.

St. Martins ★

St. Martins is one of New Brunswick's best kept treasures. An idyllic fishing village looking out on the Bay of Fundy, St. Martins is adorned with numerous houses built in the last century, when it was known as a major producer of large wooden ships. Today, the village is very picturesque, with the boats of local fishermen moored in its little port. It also has two covered bridges, one of which leads to the famous **echo caves ★**, cavities created in local cliffs by the action of the tides in the Bay of Fundy. Nature lovers will find long, untouched beaches in St. Martins, as well as the attractive **Lions Park**, which is a good place to take a walk or go swimming. As home to two of the province's best inns (see p 89), the village also has something to offer connoisseurs of fine cuisine. Finally, to enjoy a **spectacular view ★** of the local red cliffs, head to the **Quaco Head lighthouse**, located several kilometres west of St. Martins.

Fundy National Park ★★★

This national park covers a densely-wooded, mountainous area of 206 km² along the Bay of Fundy (see p 79).

Alma

Alma, a small fishing village located at the entrance of the park, features a variety of accommodations and numerous restaurants. When the tide is at its lowest, vast stretches of the sea bed are exposed, offering an interesting place for a stroll. From Alma, Route 915 leads to a peninsula with the evocative name of **Cape Enrage**, then runs alongside the bay to **Mary's Point ★**, a water-bird sanctuary where hundreds of thousands of semipalmated sandpipers alight between mid-July and mid-August.

Hopewell Cape ★★

Hopewell Cape's rock formations, nicknamed the **flower pots ★★**, are one of the province's most famous attractions. All by themselves, they symbolize the massive force of the tides in the bay. At high tide, they look like small wooded islands right off the coast. As the waters recede at low tide, they expose lofty rock formations sculpted by the endless coming and going of the tides. When the tide is at its lowest, visitors can explore the sea bed.

Moncton ★

Due to its location in the heart of the Maritimes, as well as its qualified, bilingual workforce, Moncton is now New Brunswick's rising star. Up until the Acadians were expelled from the region, this site on the banks of the Petitcodiac River was a small Acadian trading post. Colonists from the United States then settled here and founded the city, which thrived in the mid-19th century as a shipbuilding centre and later as a transportation hub for the Intercolonial Railway. The economy is now based chiefly on commerce and the service sector. For Acadians, who constitute 35% of the population, Moncton offers a unique opportunity to face the challenges and savour the pleasures of city living. Despite their minority status, they have made Moncton a base for their most important economic and social institutions and the home of the province's only French-speaking university, the Université de Moncton. Ironically, the city and by extension the university were named after officer Robert Monkton, commander of the British forces during the capture of Fort Beauséjour in 1755, an event that heralded the fall of the French Empire in North America. In any case, Moncton is now the centre of Acadian rebirth and the vibrant energy in the air here is due in good part to the entrepreneurial spirit that characterizes today's Acadians. Moncton's immediate surroundings include such varied communities as **Dieppe**, most of whose inhabitants are Acadian, and the very anglophone **Riverview**. An excellent time to visit the city is in early July, when the atmosphere is enlivened by the **Moncton Jazz Festival**.

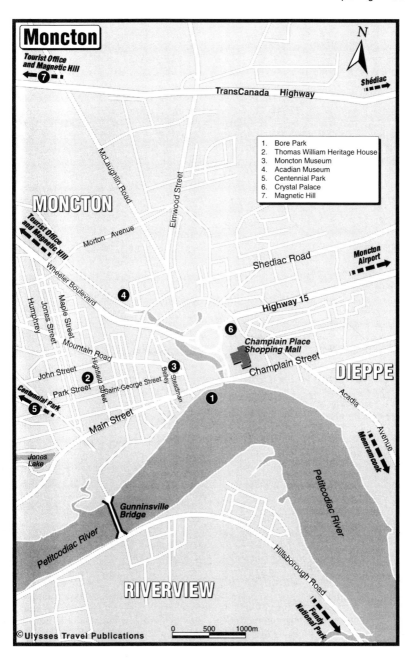

Moncton

Tourist Office
and Magnetic Hill
← 7 ▪▪

N

Shédiac ▪▪▪▶

TransCanada Highway

1. Bore Park
2. Thomas William Heritage House
3. Moncton Museum
4. Acadian Museum
5. Centennial Park
6. Crystal Palace
7. Magnetic Hill

McLaughlin Road

Elmwood Street

MONCTON

Tourist Office
and Magnetic Hill
◀

Morton Avenue

Wheeler Boulevard

Shediac Road

Moncton Airport ▶

Highway 15

Maple Street

Humphrey
Jones Street

Mountain Road

Highfield Street

4

6

Champlain Place Shopping Mall

John Street

2

Saint-George Street

Bailey

3

Steadman

Park Street

DIEPPE

Centennial Park
◀
5 ▪▪

1

Champlain Street

Acadia

Memramcook Avenue

Main Street

Jones Lake

Gunninsville Bridge

Petitcodiac River

Petitcodiac River

Hillsborough Road

Fundy National Park

RIVERVIEW

0   500   1000m

© Ulysses Travel Publications

The Petitcodiac River, known locally as the Chocolate River because of the colour of its waters, empties and then fills back up again twice a day, in accordance with the tides in the Bay of Fundy. The rise in the river's water level is always preceded by an interesting phenomenon known as a **tidal bore** ★, a wave up to several dozen centimetres high that flows upriver. The best spot to watch this wave is **Bore Park (1)** *(downtown on Main Street)*. To know what time of the day the tidal bore will occur during your stay, contact Moncton's tourist information office *(at the corner of Main Street, facing Bore Park, ☎ 856-4399)*.

The Second Empire style **Thomas Williams House** ★ **(2)** *(free admission; May, Mon, Wed and Fri 10 AM to 5 PM; Jun, Tue to Sat 10 AM to 5 PM, Sun 1 PM to 5 PM; Jul and Aug, Mon to Sat 9 AM to 5 PM, Sun 1 PM to 5 PM; Sep, Mon, Wed and Fri 10 AM to 5 PM; 103 Park Street, ☎ 857-0590)* is a 12-room residence built in 1883 for the family of Thomas Williams, who was an accountant for the Intercolonial Railway at the time. His heirs then lived here for nearly a century. Today, the house is a museum where visitors can learn about the lifestyle of the Moncton bourgeoisie during the Victorian era. Back in 1883, Moncton was no more than a tiny village, and the house lay outside its boundaries, in the middle of the countryside.

The **Moncton Museum** ★ **(3)** *(free admission; Jul and Aug, Mon to Sat 10 AM to 5 PM, Sun 1 PM to 5 PM; Sep to Jun, Tue to Fri 1 PM to 5 PM, Sat 10 AM to 5 PM, Sun 1 PM to 5 PM; 20 Mountain Road, ☎ 856-4383)* houses a lovely collection of objects linked to the history of the city and its surrounding area. During summertime, the museum often presents large-scale temporary exhibits. The sumptuous façade was salvaged from the city's former City Hall. Moncton's oldest building, dating back to 1821 and very well preserved, stands right next door.

The **Musée Acadien** ★ *(free admission; Jun to Sep, Mon to Fri 10 AM to 5 PM, Sat and Sun 1 PM to 5 PM; Oct to May, Tue to Fri 1 PM to 4:30 PM, Sat and Sun 1 PM to 4 PM; Université de Moncton, Clément Cormier Bldg., ☎ 858-4088)* displays over 30,000 objects, including a permanent collection of Acadian artifacts dating from 1604 up to the last century. The museum was founded in Memramcook in 1886 by Père Camille Lefebvre of the Collège Saint-Joseph, and was moved to its present location in 1965. In the same building as the museum, visitors will find the **Centre d'Art de l'Université de Moncton** ★★, where works by Acadian artists are exhibited.

On the west side of the city, the **Centennial Park** *(St. George Boulevard)* is a place where the whole family can come to relax any time of the year. The area includes hiking trails, a small beach, tennis courts and a playground. Canoe and pedalboat rentals are also available.

The **Crystal Palace** *(499 Rue Paul, Dieppe, beside Place Champlain)* hotel complex is a family entertainment centre featuring carousels, games, miniature golf, a swimming pool, movie theatres and a science centre intended for children.

The **Magnetic Hill** ★ *($2 per car; west of Moncton, Exit 88 from the Trans-Canada Highway)* is an intriguing optical illusion, which gives people the impression that their car is climbing a slope. The staff ask drivers to stop their engines at what seems to be the bottom of a very steep hill. Then, as if by miracle, the car seems to climb the slope. This remarkable illusion is a must for families. Other family attractions have sprung up around the Magnetic Hill, including a terrific water park, a zoo, a mini-train, a go-kart track and a miniature golf course, as well as shops, restaurants and a hotel.

Saint-Joseph-de-Memramcook

A small rural town in the pretty Memramcook valley, Saint-Joseph is of great symbolic importance to the Acadian people. This is the only region on the Bay of Fundy where Acadians still live on the farmlands they occupied before the Deportation. It thus serves as a bridge between pre- and post-Deportation Acadia. Collège Saint-Joseph, where the Acadian elite was educated for many years, was founded here in 1864. The college hosted the first Acadian national convention in 1881. At the **Acadian Odyssey National Historic Site** ★ *(free admission; Jun to early Sep, everyday 9 AM to 5 PM; Monument Lefebvre,* ☎ *758-9783)*, visitors can learn about Acadian history by viewing an exhibition on the key factors and pivotal moments leading to the survival of the Acadian people.

Sackville ★

A subtle aura of affluence and a unique awareness of the past emanate from Sackville, whose beautiful residences lie hidden behind the stately trees that flank its streets. The city is home to **Mount Allison University**, a small, highly reputable institution whose lovely buildings stand on beautiful, verdant plots of land in the centre of town. On campus, visitors will find the **Owens Art Gallery** ★ *(on campus,* ☎ *364-2574)*, which displays a large collection of paintings by New Brunswick artists, including several works by master Alex Colville.

Waterfowl Park ★★ *(free admission; every day until nightfall; entrance on East Main Street)* is an interpretive centre focusing on the plant and animal life in salt-water marshes. Thanks to two kilometres of trails and wooden footbridges, visitors can enter a world of unexpected richness and diversity. In addition to being exceptionally informative, this park is a wonderful place to relax.

Aulac

After British forces captured Fort Beauséjour in 1755, that tragic event in Acadian history, the Deportation, was initiated in Aulac. Built in 1751, Fort Beauséjour occupied a strategic location on Chignecto Bay, on the border of the French and British colonial empires. The **Fort Beauséjour National Historic Site** ★ *(free admission; mid-May to mid-Oct; Highway 2, Exit 550A,* ☎ *536-0720)* includes an interpretive centre, which deals with Acadian history and the Deportation. Visitors can also stroll around several of the star-shaped structure's remaining fortifications. The view of the bay, New Brunswick and Nova Scotia is excellent from here.

■ Tour D: The Acadian Coast ★★

Post-Deportation Acadia lies mainly here, all along the east coast of New Brunswick, which is studded with a string of villages and towns whose inhabitants are mostly of Acadian descent. It was here that the majority of Acadians fleeing deportation or returning from exile sought refuge two centuries ago, aiming to keep a low profile and build a new Acadia. Because the soil was so poor, the Acadians, who were once skilled farmers, adopted fishing as their livelihood. Although this vast region is known chiefly for the simple beauty of its landscape and the candid hospitality of its inhabitants, it also evokes all sorts of other images—long, white sand beaches washed by incredibly warm waters, fresh lobster to be enjoyed at any time of the day, fishing ports bustling with activity and a population with an inherently festive spirit. In short, the Acadian coast offers visitors a wealth of delightful activities, as well as an opportunity to discover not only the legacy of 18th and 19th century Acadia, but also modern Acadia, which is marching resolutely forward, more confident than ever.

Cape Tourmentine

A tiny coastal village, Cape Tourmentine is known mainly as the boarding point for the ferry to Prince Edward Island. It is from here that travelers can reach P.E.I. the fastest (at least until the bridge that will finally link the smallest Canadian province to the rest of the country is completed!). From Cape Tourmentine northward, the road running alongside the coast passes through a number of small towns.

Cap-Pelé ★

Cap-Pelé offers visitors a wonderful opportunity to discover the fascinating world of fishing. Founded at the end of the 18th century, this Acadian community still depends on the riches of the sea for its survival, as may be gathered from its large fleet of fishing boats. The village is also home to about a dozen *boucanières* (smokehouses), barn-like buildings where fish is smoked before being exported. Near both Cap-Pelé and tiny **Robichaud**, the coast is graced with lovely **beaches**, which are

often uncrowded. Farther along the same road, visitors will reach **Barachois**. In the centre of the village stands the oldest Acadian church in the Maritimes, the **historic church of Saint-Henri-de-Barachois ★** *(free admission; Jul and Aug; Route 133, ☎ 532-2976).*

Shediac ★

The town of Shediac is the best-known vacation spot on the east coast of New Brunswick. Its popularity is due largely to the magnificent beach in **Parlee Beach Provincial Park ★★** *(Route 15)*, whose surprisingly warm waters are perfect for swimming. Because of this popularity, a number of recreational facilities have sprung up in and around Shediac, including a lovely golf course and some amusement parks. The town's reputation, however, is also due in good measure to the abundance of lobster found off its shores, which can be savoured fresh any time. The town has even proclaimed itself the lobster capital of the world and holds an annual **lobster festival** in mid-July. Shediac was founded as a fishing port in the 19th century. A handful of lovely buildings have endured from that era, contrasting sharply with the chaotic atmosphere that characterizes the town during the busy summer season. Heading northward along the coast, visitors will pass through several tiny Acadian communities, which survive mainly on fishing.

Bouctouche ★

A pleasant little town looking out on a large, calm bay, Bouctouche was founded at the end of the 18th century by Acadians driven from the Memramcook valley. It has the distinction of being the birthplace of two celebrated New Brunswickers, Antonine Maillet and

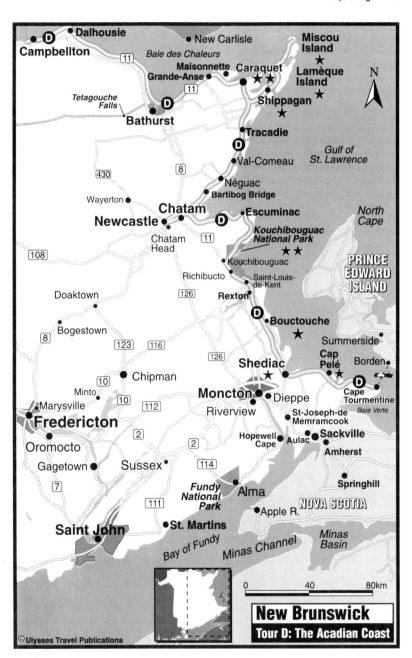

Campbellton
D ● Dalhousie
● New Carlisle
Baie des Chaleurs
Miscou Island ★
Maisonnette
Caraquet ★ ★
Grande-Anse ●
Lamèque Island ★
11
Shippagan ★
Tetagouche Falls
D
Bathurst
Tracadie
D
Val-Comeau ●
Gulf of St. Lawrence
8
430
Néguac ●
Bartibog Bridge
Wayerton ●
Chatam
Newcastle ●
D ● Escuminac
Chatam Head
11
Kouchibouguac National Park ★ ★
North Cape
108
Kouchibouguac ●
Richibucto ●
Saint-Louis-de-Kent
126
PRINCE EDWARD ISLAND
Doaktown ●
Rexton
D ●Bouctouche
Bogestown ●
8
123
116
126
★
Summerside ●
Cap Pelé
Borden ●
Chipman ●
10
Shediac ★
Minto ●
10
112
Moncton ●
Dieppe ●
D
Cape Tourmentine
Marysville ●
Riverview
St-Joseph-de-Memramcook
Baie Verte
Fredericton
2
Oromocto ●
Hopewell Cape
Aulac ●
Sackville ●
Gagetown ●
Sussex ●
2
114
Amherst ●
7
Fundy National Park
Alma ●
Springhill ●
111
Apple R. ●
NOVA SCOTIA
Saint John
●St. Martins
Bay of Fundy
Minas Channel
Minas Basin

N

0   40   80km

New Brunswick
Tour D: The Acadian Coast

© Ulysses Travel Publications

The 1994 Congrès Mondial Acadien

A large-scale event known as the Congrès Mondial Acadien was held in the towns and villages of southeastern New Brunswick from August 12-22, 1994. During this period, Acadians and their descendants from around the world came together at festivals and celebrations. The high point of the festivities took place on the evening of August 15, the Acadian national holiday, when a huge show entitled L'Acadie Parle au Monde (Acadia Speaks to the World) was presented on the beach in Shediac and broadcasted on television in French-speaking countries worldwide. The Congrès provided an opportunity to review the status of today's Acadians through a series of conferences. The Secretary General of the United Nations, Mr. Boutros Boutros Ghali, made a short, salient speech on the occasion, referring to the "Acadian nation."

K.C. Irving. Winner of the 1979 Prix Goncourt for her novel *Pélagie-la-Charrette*, Antonine Maillet has gained more international recognition than any other Acadian author. She first came into the public eye in the 1960's with *La Sagouine*, a remarkable play that evokes the lives and spirit of Acadians at the beginning of the century. K.C. Irving, who died recently, built a colossal empire with widely diversified operations, most importantly in the oil indus-

try. He started out with nothing and died one of the wealthiest individuals in the world.

The brand new **Pays de la Sagouine** ★★ (adults $6.50; mid-Jun to early Sep, everyday 10 AM to 6 PM; at the southern entrance of the village on Route 134; ☎ 743-1400, ⇄ 743-1414) is an effort to recreate early 20th century Acadia, drawing inspiration from Antonine Maillet's highly successful play, *La Sagouine*. Its creators cleverly decided to enliven the atmosphere with characters from the famous play, who perform theatrical and musical pieces. The highlight is Île-aux-Puces, in the centre of the bay. It is here that the Pays de la Sagouine is the liveliest, and visitors can learn what they wish about the lifestyle of early 20th century Acadians by talking with the characters on site. The restaurant l'Ordre du Bon Temps, located at the entrance, serves tasty, traditional Acadian cuisine.

The **Kent County Museum** ★ (adults $2; end of Jun to early Sep; on the east side of the village, 150 Convent Street, ☎ 743-5005) is one of the most interesting regional museums in the province. The building itself was used as a convent until 1969. Its various rooms contain period furniture and pieces of sacred art, evoking the history of the convent and the daily life of the nuns and their students. The museum's friendly guides give interesting tours.

Rexton

The English-speaking village of Rexton is the birthplace of Bonar Law (1858-1923), the only prime minister of Great Britain to be born outside of the United Kingdom. The **Bonar Law Historic Site** (free admission; Jul to end of Sep;

Route 11 or 116, in the centre of Rexton, ☎ 1-800-561-0123) pays homage to that famous New Brunswicker, while offering visitors an idea of how people lived at the time of his birth. The site includes the farm and house where Bonar Law spent his early years.

Kouchibouguac National Park ★★ (see p 79)

Escuminac

Visitors with a taste for pretty, isolated beaches will find several in the **Escuminac Provincial Park** *(5 km east of Escuminac)*. Those who stop in the village can see a **monument** dedicated to 35 fishermen who lost their lives at sea during a storm in 1939.

Chatham

Chatham, like Newcastle on the other side of the Miramichi, owes its existence to the forest industry, the most important activity in this region for nearly two centuries now. Both communities were settled mainly by Irish and Scottish colonists, which sets them apart from the rest of the Acadian coast. Chatham was the birthplace of Joseph Cunard, founder of Cunard Lines, a large fleet of ocean liners.

Newcastle

Another predominately English-speaking town, Newcastle is the gateway to the Miramichi River, a river renowned for its Atlantic salmon. The Miramichi flows through a lovely landscape whose dense vegetation consists mainly of conifers. On the way to Fredericton, visitors can stop at the **Miramichi Salmon Museum ★** *(adults $3; Jun to end of Sep; Route 8, in Doaktown, ☎ 365-7787)*, whose exhibit deals with both fishing and the

life cycle of the salmon itself. Farther along in the same direction, visitors will reach the **Central New Brunswick Woodmen's Museum** *(adults $3, end of May to Sep; Highway 8, in Boiestown, ☎ 369-7214)*, which stands on the site of a lumber camp and examines the lives of its inhabitants and the arduous line of work they pursued.

Bartibog Bridge

In addition to offering an excellent view of the Miramichi River, this tiny community is home to the very interesting **MacDonald Farm Historic Site** *(adults $2.25; end of Jun to end of Sep; Route 11, ☎ 773-5761)*. Born in Scotland in 1762, Alexander MacDonald served as a private in the British army during the American Revolution. In 1784, after the war had ended, MacDonald took up residence on the banks of the Miramichi River. MacDonald Farm, now open to the public, includes a lovely Georgian-style stone house and several other buildings dating back to the early 19th century.

Tracadie-Sheila

After passing through the villages of **Néguac** and **Val-Comeau**, each of which has beaches and a provincial park, Route 11 leads to Tracadie-Sheila, a little town with numerous restaurants and hotels, as well as an attractive wharf. As the institutional buildings attest, the town's history was marked for many years by the presence of the *Religieuses Hospitalières de Saint-Joseph* (Sisters of Mercy), who nursed the sick—especially lepers— here from 1868 to 1965. Every year in late June and early July, Tracadie-Sheila hosts the **Festival International de la Francophonie**, which highlights French-language music and arts.

The **Tracadie Historical Museum** ★ *(free admission; Jun to mid-Aug; on the 3rd floor of the Académie Sainte-Famille, Rue du Couvent,* ☎ *395-2212)* houses an exhibit on the various stages in the history of Tracadie and its surroundings. Visitors will find a selection of Micmac artifacts, religious objects and 19th century tools. Not far from the museum lies the **leper cemetery**, where about sixty identical crosses stand in rows.

Shippagan ★

Protected by the strait that separates it from Île Lamèque, the site now occupied by Shippagan was originally a trading post, which gave way to a sea port at the end of the 18th century. Now a bustling little community, Shippagan boasts several industries and, more importantly, a port that accommodates one of the largest fishing fleets on the Acadian peninsula. Its charm lies not only in its seaside location, but also in the unique atmosphere created by its port. Anyone interested in learning more about the fishing industry—the mainspring of the Acadian economy for over two hundred years now—should stop in Shippagan, explore the town, stroll along the wharf and visit the marine centre. In addition, each year around the third week of July, the town holds a **Fisheries Festival**, made up of a number of fishing-related activities, including the blessing of the boats.

Most Acadians who succeeded in avoiding deportation fled from the fertile shores of the Bay of Fundy through the woods to the province's east coast. Since the soil there was much poorer, they turned to the sea for survival, taking up fishing, an economic activity that has long been an integral part of Acadian culture. To discover the fascinating world of modern fishing in Acadia and the Gulf of St. Lawrence, especially the rich animal life inhabiting the sea bed in this region, visitors can head to the **Marine Centre and Aquarium** ★★ *($4; mid-May to Sep; near the Shippagan wharf,* ☎ *336-3013)*. This complex is also used for scientific research.

Île Lamèque ★

A ramp connects Shippagan to Île Lamèque. With its flat landscape and handful of tiny hamlets made up of pretty white or coloured houses, this island is a haven of peace where time seems to stand still. A visit to the **Église Sainte-Cécile** ★ in Petite-Rivière-de-l'île is a must. This charming, colourful wooden church provides an enchanting setting for the **International Baroque Music Festival**, a wonderful event held each year during the third week of July.

Île Miscou ★

Just a short ferry ride from Île Lamèque lies Île Miscou, another sparsely populated haven of peace, renowned for its lovely, often deserted beaches. At the far end of the island stands the **Île Miscou Lighthouse** ★ *(at the end of Route 133)*, one of the oldest in New Brunswick and a marvelous spot from which to view the ocean. A few kilometres before the lighthouse, on the same road, visitors will find an **interpretive site** ★ *(Route 133)* with a path and footbridges leading through a peat bog.

Caraquet ★★

Caraquet's charm lies mainly in the warmth and vitality of its inhabitants. The largest town on the peninsula, equipped with a number of hotels and restaurants, Caraquet is also considered the cultural hub of Acadia —

and with good reason. It is probably this town and its residents' lifestyle that best illustrate modern Acadian culture, which draws on a variety of influences without, however, renouncing its rich past. August is by far the best time to visit Caraquet, since August 15 is the Acadian national holiday, the culmination of the **Festival Acadien**, a series of about ten different events. The Tintamarre and Frolic (August 15) alone make for a memorable experience. At other times, visitors can attend performances by the excellent theatre company of the **Théâtre Populaire d'Acadie** *(276 Boulevard Saint-Pierre Ouest,* ☎ *727-0920)*, relax on one of the town's little beaches or set off on a cruise from the **Carrefour de la Mer** *(51 Boulevard Saint-Pierre Est)*.

The **Acadian Museum** ★ *(free admission; mid Jun to mid Sep; 15 Boulevard Saint-Pierre Est,* ☎ *727-1713)* houses a small collection of everyday objects from the past two centuries.

An important place of pilgrimage in a lovely natural setting, the **Sanctuaire Sainte-Anne-du-Bocage** ★ *(free admission; everyday, all year round; Boulevard Saint-Pierre Ouest)* includes a small wooden chapel, the Stations of the Cross and a monument to Alexis Landry, ancestor of most of the Landrys in Acadia.

No history book on Acadia could ever be as an effective an educational tool as the **Village Historique Acadien** ★★★ *(adults $7.50; mid-Jun to early Sep; on Route 11, about 10 km west of Caraquet,* ☎ *727-3467)*. Here, on a vast piece of land, visitors will find a reconstructed village, including about twenty houses and other buildings, most of which are authentic, dating from 1780 to the end of the 19th century. The atmosphere is enlivened by

performers in period costume, who carry out everyday tasks using traditional methods and gladly inform visitors about the customs of the past. A film at the interpretive centre presents a brief history of the Acadian people.

Maisonnette

This hamlet, known for its oysters, is graced with one of the most beautiful beaches on the Acadian peninsula: the beach at **Maisonnette Provincial Park** *(take Route 11 to Route 303)*.

Grande-Anse

At Grande-Anse, another tiny coastal village, visitors will find pretty **Ferguson Beach**, which lies at the foot of a cliff, and the unique **Pope Museum** ★ *(adults $2; Jun to Sep; 184 Rue Acadie,* ☎ *732-3003)*. The museum's exhibit includes a model of Saint Peter's in Rome, clothing and pieces of sacred art, as well as a collection of papal iconography. A number of these objects are both rare and interesting. The museum serves as a reminder of the important role religion has played in Acadian history.

Bathurst

An industrial town situated at the mouth of the Nepisiquit River, Bathurst is the largest urban centre in the northeastern part of the province. Accordingly, all sorts of services are available here. For visitors, however, Bathurst's interest lies mainly in the numerous natural sites located nearby. Right after the port, northeast of town, visitors can observe the plant and animal life in the salt marshes, wooded areas and fields encompassed by the **Pointe Daly Reserve** *(Route 11, toward the Acadian peninsula)*, a haven of peace stretching 40 ha. Nature lovers can also admire nearby **Papineau Falls** *(several kilometres from town on Route 430)* and **Tetagouche Falls** *(11 km from town on Route 180).*

Dalhousie

Dalhousie, like Campbellton, was founded by Scottish settlers at the beginning of the 19th century, although a large segment of the present population of both towns is of Acadian descent. A pleasant little community, Dalhousie has a beach and a pretty marina, which serves as the boarding point for cruises on Baie des Chaleurs. A visit here also offers an interesting opportunity to learn more about local history, from the Amerindian period to the present day, at the **Restigouche Regional Museum** *(free admission; open all year; 437 George Street).* A ferry makes a daily crossing between Dalhousie and Misquasha, in Québec.

Campbellton

Located alongside the estuary of the Restigouche River, Campbellton is the largest town in this lovely region. It is renowned for fishing, especially salmon. In fact, salmon fishing is so closely linked to Campbellton's history that a **giant salmon** was erected here. Furthermore, the town holds a **Salmon Festival** each year in late June and early July. Visitors can discover another side of the region at the **Restigouche Gallery** *(39 Andrew Street).* Because of its proximity to the Québec border, Campbellton is also home to a provincial tourist information centre.

From Campbellton, visitors can head to Mount Carleton Provincial Park by taking Route 17 to Saint-Quentin and then picking up the 180.

Parks

New Brunswick is a paradise for nature lovers, for those with a passion for fresh air and exploring vast stretches of wilderness; from north to south and east to west, the province stretches no less than 74,437 km², 85% of which is covered with forests. New Brunswick also boasts about a thousand kilometres of coastline along the Bay of Fundy and the Atlantic Ocean, countless lakes and magnificent rivers, the most important being the St. John and the Miramichi. The province offers a great escape for those who know how to appreciate the beauty of nature. Two national parks top the list of the province's most stunning natural sites: Fundy National Park, on the shores of the Bay of Fundy, and Kouchibouguac National Park, on the Acadian coast. These parks were laid out with the aim of preserving two remarkable sites and encouraging the public to enjoy them. The government of New Brunswick has also developed a large network of provincial parks, which extends to all different parts of the territory. These parks vary greatly in size. The largest, Mount Carleton Provincial Park, is the site of New Brunswick's highest peak.

■ Tour B: The St. John Valley

Saint-Jacques

Les Jardins de la République Provincial Park *(off of Route 2, ☎ 735-2525)* has campgrounds, a swimming pool and playgrounds, as well as hiking trails and bike paths.

Longs Creek

As well as being the natural habitat of about thirty different animal species,

Woolastook Provincial Park *(near Kings Landing, off of Route 2,* ☎ *363-5410)* has 200 campings sites, a miniature golf course, a flume and a beach, making it a popular destination for families.

Mactaquac

Visitors can enjoy activities year-round at **Mactaquac Provincial Park** *(off of Route 2,* ☎ *363-3011)*, which features beaches, hiking trails, campgrounds, a marina, a golf course and also a trail for cross-country skiing.

■ Tour C: The Fundy Shore

Saint John

The perfectly marvelous **Irving Nature Park** ★★ *(free admission; at the end of Sand Cove Road,* ☎ *632-7777)* has a great deal to offer nature lovers. Located just a few kilometres west of the industrial city of Saint John, this magnificent park covers a 225 ha peninsula trimmed with untouched beaches. The city seems a million miles away from here. Visitors can also enjoy a pleasant stroll along one of the park's trails, communing with nature and observing the plant and animal life along the Fundy shore.

Fundy National Park

Fundy National Park ★★★ *(Route 114, near Alma,* ☎ *887-6000 or 887-2005)* is the ultimate place to explore the shores of the bay, observe its plant and animal life and grasp the power of its tides. It covers a densely wooded, mountainous territory of 206 km^2, abounding in spectacular scenery, lakes and rivers and nearly twenty kilometres of shoreline. All sorts of athletic activities can be enjoyed here. The park is a hiker's paradise, with its 120 km of trails running through the forest, near lakes and alongside the magnificent bay. Visitors can also enjoy fishing, camping on one of many equipped or natural sites, playing a game on the excellent golf course or swimming in the heated pool. Travellers pressed for time should make sure at the very least to visit **Pointe Wolfe** ★★, where nearby trails offer spectacular views of cliffs plunging straight into the waters of the bay. At each entrance to the park, employees offer information on the various activities available.

■ Tour D: The Acadian Coast

Kouchibouguac National Park

Blanketed by a forest of cedars and other conifers and studded with peat bogs, magnificent **Kouchibouguac National Park** ★★ *(Route 11 or 134,* ☎ *876-2443)*, boasts over 26 km of spectacular coastline made up of salt-water marshes, lagoons, dunes and golden, sandy beaches. It is the natural habitat of several hundred animals, including the extremely rare piping plover. The park is laced with hiking trails and bicycle paths, and may also be explored by canoe or rowboat. All equipment necessary for these sports is available on site, along with a campground. The park is a perfect place for salt-water swimming, especially at Lagoon Beach, which is washed by the warmest salt-water in the province, and the excellent Kelly's Beach and Collanders Beach.

Saint-Quentin

Mount Carleton Provincial Park ★ *(Route 180 from Saint-Quentin,* ☎ *235-2025 or 735-2525)* lies in the heart of New Brunswick, in the province's wildest region. At 820 m, Mount Carleton is the highest peak in the Maritimes.

This park is frequented mainly by hiking buffs. Campings sites are available.

Beaches

It is worth taking a trip to New Brunswick for the beaches alone. The lovely white sand beaches of the Acadian coast, particularly in the southeastern portion of the province, near Shediac, are especially popular—and with reason. In addition to being beautiful, they are lapped by the warmest salt waters north of Virginia, making them ideal for swimming and water sports.

■ Tour D: The Acadian Coast

Murray Corner

Murray Beach Provincial Park *(Route 955)* has a lovely beach, a campground and various games.

Cap Pelé

Aboiteau Beach *(Route 15)* stretches 2.5 km and features lovely sand dunes. This is an excellent spot for swimming. Between Cap Pelé and Shediac, there are three more pretty beaches along the coast.

Shediac

Parlee Beach Provincial Park ★★ *(near Exit 17 on Route 15)* is probably New Brunswick's most famous beach. It is patrolled by life guards and stretches several kilometres. Visitors can camp nearby.

Saint-Louis-de-Kent

Some of the most beautiful beaches in the province are to be found in **Kouchi-bouguac National Park** *(Route 134 and 11)*. Visitors can also rent a canoe or rowboat, go hiking or cycling and, in winter, enjoy cross-country skiing here. There are campings sites as well.

Escuminac

Escuminac Provincial Park *(Route 117)* has a lovely beach with magnificent sand dunes. There are campgrounds in the neighbouring villages.

Île Miscou

Île Miscou Beach *(Route 113, 14 km from the crossing)* is well laid-out and equipped with a campground and cottages.

Caraquet

The **Downtown Beach** *(Route 11, downtown)* and the **Caraquet Park Beach** *(Route 11, west of Caraquet)* are two spots where visitors can go swimming or enjoy other water sports. No lifeguards.

Maisonnette

Maisonnette Provincial Park *(8 km east of Route 11, on the 303)* has a beautiful beach with shallow waters.

Grande-Anse

Peaceful **Ferguson Beach** *(Route 11)* lies tucked away in a pretty spot at the foot of a cliff.

Outdoor Activities

 Hiking

Hiking is a very popular activity in New Brunswick, and there are all sorts of places where visitors can enjoy pleasant excursions in the wilderness. The best spots, featuring the largest number of trails and the most interesting settings, are Fundy National Park, Kouchibouguac National Park, Irving Nature Park in Saint John and Mount Carleton Provincial Park.

 Bicycling

Bicycling is not only a great sport, but also a fantastic means of exploring New Brunswick, which abounds in peaceful roads and bike paths. Fredericton, the pretty provincial capital, is a marvellous city to tour by bicycle. In addition to its often quiet streets, Fredericton has a magnificent bicycle trail that runs along the river for 4 km. The islands in the Bay of Fundy, especially Campobello and Grand Manan, also feature excellent bike paths. Both the St. John River Valley and the Acadian coast are very interesting regions, but the distances between villages can be quite long. One solid word of advice: avoid the roads in the middle of the province (along the Miramichi River, for example), as these are long and monotonous.

Bicycle Rentals

Freewheeling Adventure
Saint John
☎ 857-3600

Covered Bridge Bicycle Tour
Saint John
☎ 849-9028

Savages Bicycle
Fredericton
☎ 458-8985

Kouchibouguac National Park
Rental Centre
☎ 876-2571

 Whale-watching

Because of its rich feeding grounds, the Bay of Fundy is one of the best places in the world to observe certain species of whales. Whale-watching excursions are organized throughout the summer, starting from the following places: St. Andrews By-the-Sea, Deer Island, Campobello Island and Grand Manan Island, in the southwestern part of the province. Contact Cline Marine Inc.

Departures from St. Andrews, Deer Island and Campobello Island
☎ 529-4188 or 747-2287

Atlantic Marine Wildlife Tours Ltd
Departures from St. Andrews
☎ 459-7325

Island Coast Boat Tours
Departures from Grand Manan Island
☎ 662-8181

Ocean Search
Departures from Grand Manan Island
☎ 662-8488

Seawatch
Departures from Grand Manan Island
☎ 662-8552

Starboard Tours
Departures from Grand Manan Island
☎ 662-8545 or 663-7525

Bird-watching

Both of the province's national parks (Fundy and Kouchibouguac) are excellent places for bird-watching. Kouchibouguac is frequented by shorebirds, including the piping plover (see p 175).

Both Grand Manan Island and Machias Seal Island (located mid-way between Grand Manan Island and Machias) are veritable bird sanctuaries, where nearly 275 different species, including the Atlantic puffin and the Arctic tern, can be observed.

  Canoeing and Kayaking

Numerous rivers, both fast- and slow-moving, wind through the territory of New Brunswick. A number of these lie within parks, and may be explored by canoe. Visitors can set off on this type of excursion with their own canoe or kayak, or a rented one.

Kouchibouguac National Park
Rental Centre
☎ 876-2571

Saint-Quentin
Centre de Plein Air du Vieux Moulin
☎ 235-1110

Fredericton
A to Z Rentals
☎ 452-9758

Grand Manan Island
Adventure High Seas Kayaking
☎ 662-3563

St. Andrews
Seascape Kayak Tours
☎ 529-4866

 Fishing

Fans of this sport can try their luck in several rivers that are teeming with all different types of fish. The Miramichi, for example, is famous for its salmon, while Fundy National Park is known for angling. Those interested in casting their lines into the province's rivers will need a permit.

 Cross-country Skiing

During winter, when the province is blanketed with snow, the parks convert their hiking paths into cross-country trails and then welcome the public. At **Mount Sugarloaf Provincial Park** *(P.O. Box 629, Atholville, tel. 789-2366)*, skiiers have use of 25 km of trails. Both national parks (Fundy and Kouchibouguac) feature trails studded with shelters where skiiers can rest during their outings. Another option is Mount Carleton Provincial Park.

 Downhill Skiing

New Brunswick has several noteworthy peaks, including **Mount Sugarloaf** *(P.O. Box 629, Atholville,* ☎ *789-2366, skiing conditions,* ☎ *789-2392,* ⇄ *753-7275)*, which maintains eight trails for skiiers of all levels; six are open in the evening. **Mount Farlagne** *(P.O. Box 61, Edmunston,* ☎ *735-8401, skiiing conditions,* ☎ *735-6617)* has a vertical drop of 182 m and features 17 trails of all different levels of difficulty. The mountain is also open for night skiing.

 Snowmobiling

6000 km of snowmobile trails criss-cross New Brunswick, enabling visitors to discover another side of the province. There are more than 60 skimobile clubs in the province. Visitors can thus set off to conquer the province and its vast stretches of wilderness. To plan your trip properly, contact:

F.C.M.N.B.
Box 536
Newcastle
E1V 3T7

Ministry of Economic Development and Tourism
Box 12345
Fredericton
E3B 5C3
☎ 1-800-561-0123

 Accommodation

■ **Tour A: Fredericton**

Set up in an old school, the **Youth Hostel** *($12 per person; 193 York Street,* ☎ *454-1233)* is well maintained and well located downtown. Its dormitories can accommodate up to thirty people. Open in summer only.

During the summer, student residence rooms can be rented at the **University of New Brunswick** *(at the end of University Avenue,* ☎ *453-4891)*. Expect to pay around $40 for a double occupancy room, or a bit more than half that for a single room.

It would be difficult to find a more boring decor scheme than the one used in the rooms of the **City Motel** *($54; 56 rooms, tv,* ℜ, *≈; 1216 Regent Street, E3B 3Z4,* ☎ *450-9900 or 1-800-268-2858,* ⇄ *452-1915)* located next to the TransCanada. For visitors aiming to see the main sights of Fredericton, this

hotel is a little out of the way. Nevertheless, it is clean, not too expensive and lies adjacent to a good seafood restaurant.

The charm of Fredericton is due to the many opulent Victorian residences lining its streets. The **Carriage House Inn** *($55; 10 rooms, tv; 230 University Avenue, E3B 4H7,* ☎ *452-9924 or 1-800-267-6068)* is one of these magnificent houses, which has been transformed into an inn with a unique atmosphere that transports guests to another era. There are several large rooms including a ballroom, a library and a solarium, as well as ten guest rooms furnished with antiques. The inn looks out onto a quiet, well-to-do street shaded by large elm trees and lies just a few minutes walk from downtown. It is best to reserve in advance, regardless of the season.

Located just outside the downtown area, and close to several shopping malls, along the TransCanada, the **Fredericton Inn** *($57; 200 rooms, tv,* ℜ, *≈; 1315 Regent Street, E3B 1A1* ☎ *455-1430,* ⇄ *458-5448)* offers a large choice of rooms, from suites to motel-style accommodation. The latter offer a good quality/price ratio.

The elegant **Sheraton Inn** *($65; 223 rooms, tv,* ℜ, *≈; 225 Woodstock Road, E3B 2H8,* ☎ *457-7000 or 1-800-325-3535,* ⇄ *457-4000)* is beautifully located on the shores of the St. John River, just outside of downtown Fredericton. It is by far the most luxurious hotel in the capital and one of the nicest in the province. The architects made the most of the location including a superb terrace looking out over the river, the ideal spot for cocktails, a dip in the pool or a relaxed meal while taking in the scenery. The rooms are very comfortable, pretty and functional, and several offer great views. Built recently, the Sheraton is of course equipped with an indoor pool and exercise facilities, a very good restaurant, a bar and conference rooms. It has clearly been designed to please both business people and travellers.

You won't find a hotel more centrally located than the **Lord Beaverbrook Hotel** *($89; 175 rooms, tv, ℜ, ≈; 659 Queen Street, E3B 5A6, ☎ 455-3371 or 1-800-561-7666, ⇄ 455-1441)* which has been a landmark in downtown Fredericton for half a century. With its back to the St. John River, it faces the Legislative Assembly of New Brunswick. The hotel's prestigious history is evident in the richly decorated entrance hall and the aristocratic air about the Governor's Room, a small dining room tucked away. Despite renovations, the rooms are a bit disappointing.

■ **Tour B: The St. John River Valley**

Edmundston

Due to its proximity to the borders of Québec and the United States, Edmunston is a town most people simply pass through on their way to somewhere else. It therefore has quite a few hotels, whose clean, functional, but non-descript rooms are suitable for short stays. One of these is the **Auberge Wandlyn Inn** *($62; 132 rooms, tv, ℜ, ≈; 919 Canada Road, E3V 3K5, ☎ 735-5525 or 1-800-561-0000, ⇄ 739-6243)*, located close to the highway, towards the Québec border.

The convention centre of the "capital" of Madawaska, the province's second largest, is located right downtown. Adjoining it is the **Howard Johnson Hotel** *($85; 103 rooms, tv, ℜ, ≈; 100 Rice Street, E3V 1T4, ☎ 739-7321 or 1-800-654-2000, ⇄ 735-9101)*, which offers the most comfortable lodging in Edmunston. Designed for both business people and vacationers, the hotel features a wide range of services, two restaurants and a bar.

Grand Falls (Grand-Sault)

The **Hill Top Motel** *($44; 21 rooms, tv, ℂ, 131 Madawaska Road, E3Y 1A7, ☎ 473-2684)* distinguishes itself from the competition on two counts: first, it is the only motel located in the heart of Grand Falls, just a few hundred metres from the Interpretive Centre; second, its rooms are the least expensive in the area. As its name implies, the Hill Top is located atop a promontory offering a view of the city's hydroelectric dam. The rooms are clean but decorated with little imagination.

An excellent bed and breakfast located in downtown Grand Falls, the **Maple Tourist Home** *($45; 3 rooms, tv; 142 Main Street, E3Z 1E8, ☎ 473-1763)* has three spotless rooms. Guests can also relax in a comfortable common room.

Along the TransCanada Highway, 2.5 km north of Grand Falls the **Motel Léo** *($56; 34 rooms, tv, ℜ; 2.5 km north of Grand Falls, E0J 1M0, ☎ 473-2090 or 1-800-661-0077, ⇄ 573-6614)* rents inexpensive well-appointed rooms. It is a fairly typical motel, where most guests only stop for one night to take a break on a long trip. The staff is very friendly.

Not far from Lake Pirie, about 5 km south of Grand Falls, the **Lakeside Lodge & Resort** *($70; 15 rooms, ℂ, tv, △; Lake Pirie, E0J 1V0, ☎ 473-6252)* offers nature-lovers an excellent alternative to the local motels. Seven cottages with fireplaces and kitchenettes are available, as well as eight rooms, two of which have a fireplace and a sauna.

Right next door to the Motel Léo is the **Motel Près du Lac** *($74; 100 rooms, tv, ℜ, ≈; 2.5 km north of Grand Falls, E0J 1M0, ☎ 471-1300 or 1-800-528-1234, ⇄ 473-5501)*, offering quality lodging in the area. The complex includes motel rooms as well as cottages on the shores of an artificial lake. Guests can choose a standard room or a wedding suite. Activities ranging from pedal-boating on the lake, to mini-golf, basketball, working out and swimming in the indoor pool make this a popular spot for families.

Plaster Rock

Set back from the road, the **Tobique View Motel & Restaurant** *($55; 18 rooms, tv, C, ℜ; a few kilometres before Plaster Rock, E0J 1W0, ☎ 356-2684 or 356-8413 or 356-2683)* is beautifully located on the shores of the peaceful Tobique River. Due to its ideal location and the tranquility of the surroundings, this motel is popular with travellers out to explore the wilderness around Plaster Rock.

Hartland

It is hard to imagine a more peaceful spot than **Campbell's Bed & Breakfast** *($35; 3 rooms, tv, C; 1 km north of Hartland, E0J 1N0, ☎ 375-4775)*, a farmhouse built along the St. John River near the town of Hartland. Sitting on the large porch, it is easy to appreciate the tranquility of Richard Hatfield country. The rooms are comfortable, although a bit over-decorated, and guests have use of a fully-equipped kitchen at all times. Mrs. Campbell doesn't actually live in the B&B, but rather in a little house about 200 m away on the same property.

Woodstock

Just like the numerous other motels along the TransCanada on the outskirts of Woodstock, the **John Gyles Motor Inn** *($42; 20 rooms, tv, ℜ; on the TransCanada 8 km south of Woodstock, E0J 2B0, ☎ 328-6682)* offers rooms at a good price. The quality of its restaurant, which serves various German specialties, distinguishes the John Gyles from the others.

The only motel located inside the city limits of Woodstock, the **Stiles Motel Hill View** *($55; 30 rooms, tv; 827 Main Street, E0J 2B0, ☎ 328-6621)* gives visitors the opportunity to discover a small anglophone community typical of the St. John River valley. The rooms were recently renovated; this isn't luxury but its still very comfortable and clean. The motel includes a small restaurant serving family-style cuisine.

The nicest accommodations in the immediate area of Woodstock are at the **Auberge Wandlyn Inn** *($62; 50 rooms, tv, ℜ, ≈; Houlton Exit off the TransCanada, E0J 2B0, ☎ 328-8876 or 1-800-561-0000 from Canada or 1-800-561-0006 from the U.S., ⇄ 328-4828)*. There are 50 well-appointed rooms as well as a heated indoor pool and a dining room. For those in a hurry this motel is ideally located along the TransCanada and Route 95 towards the United States.

Kingsclear

The **Mactaquac Inn** *($69; 81 rooms, tv, ℜ, ≈, ⊘, ⊛; Exit 274 off the TransCanada, ☎ 363-5111 or 1-800-561-5111, ⇄ 363-3000)* is a large hotel complex overlooking Lake

Mactaquac, a widening of the St. John River caused by a dam downstream. Besides 74 rooms, the luxurious complex includes six cottages each equipped with a kitchenette and a dining room. Several activities are organized for vacationers, including various types of fishing. Extensive facilities make this is a prized spot for conferences and business meetings in a relaxed setting.

Gagetown

The small hamlet of Gagetown features a rather interesting-looking inn, the **Loaves & Calico Country Inn** *($40; 4 rooms, tv; Second Street, E0G 1V0, ☎ 488-3018)* which occupies a commercial style building that apparently served as an automobile showroom at the beginning of the century. The four rooms are modest but clean, and are located on the second floor along with a common room. There is a cafe on the first floor.

A rather austere house in the heart of town along the shore of the St. John River, the **Steamers Stop Inn** *($45; 7 rooms, tv; ℜ; Front Street, E0G 1V0, ☎ 488-2903)* fits right in with the pastoral charm that characterizes Gagetown. There is definitely no better place to get a real feel for this little vacation spot, since everything is close by. Rooms are well appointed, and five of them provide a view of the river. The inn also has a decent restaurant.

■ **Tour C: The Fundy Shore**

St. Stephen

A lovely period house, built in the middle of the last century for an eminent Loyalist family, the **Blair House Bed & Breakfast** *($40; 3 rooms, tv; 38 Prince William Street, E3L 2W5, ☎ 466-*

2233, ⇄ 466-2233) stands on a beautifully landscaped lot in the heart of St. Stephen. Comfortable rooms and a copious English breakfast are offered.

In the heart of the community, the **St. Stephen Inn** *($55; 51 rooms, tv; 99 King Street, E3L 2C6, ☎ 466-1418 or 1-800-565-3068, ⇄ 466-4168)* is a pleasant spot with typical inexpensive motel-style rooms.

St. Andrews By-The-Sea

Even though St. Andrews is a rather posh vacation spot, visitors can still find inexpensive motel-style accommodations with clean and simple rooms. One option is the **Greenside Motel** *($45; 16 rooms, tv, ℂ 242 Mowatt Drive, E0G 2X0, ☎ 529-3039)*, located just outside of St. Andrews near the golf course. Some rooms have kitchenettes.

The **Seaside Beach Resort** *($50; 24 rooms, tv, ℂ 339 Water Street, E0G 2X0, ☎ 529-3039)* consists of 10 wood cottages ideally located on the shores of the bay. It is not the most luxurious spot, but the rooms are clean and include a kitchenette. Though this is a "resort", the mood is relaxed and guests will feel right at ease.

St. Andrews Motor Inn *($65; 33 rooms, tv, ℜ; 111 Water Street, E0G 2X0, ☎ 529-4571)*, right on the bay, offers comfortable, modern rooms with a balcony or terrace. Some rooms even have a kitchenette. The outdoor pool behind the building looks out over the bay.

Considered one of the oldest hotels in the country, in operation since 1881, the **Best-Western Shiretown Inn** *($70; 26 rooms, tv, ℜ, ℂ 218 Water Street, E0G 2X0, ☎ 539-8877 or 1-800-528-*

1234) is centrally located near the St. Andrews pier. This picturesque historic building has cosy rooms, an excellent restaurant and a beautiful front balcony where guests can dine or enjoy drinks. Nicely-appointed apartments with kitchenettes can also be rented close by.

Set in the middle of a large property overlooking the surrounding countryside, the **Rossmount Inn** *($75; 17 rooms, tv, ≈; a few kilometres from St. Andrews on Hwy 127 heading east, EOG 2XO, ☎ 529-3351, ⇄ 529-1920)* is a magnificent old inn with antique furniture in each room. The Rossmount Inn also offers an excellent dining room.

Dominating the quaint setting of St. Andrews By-The-Sea is the best and most reputed hotel in the Maritimes, the **Algonquin Hotel** *($121; 240 rooms, tv, ℜ, C, ≈; EOG 2XO, ☎ 529-8823 or 1-800-268-9410, ⇄ 529-4194)*. A majestic neo-Tudor grouping in the centre of a large property, this dream hotel has withstood the test of time by carefully preserving the aristocratic refinement and Anglo-Saxon character of an elite resort of the late 1800s. Built in 1889, the Algonquin was completely devastated by fire in 1914. Most of it was rebuilt the next year. Then, in 1991, a new convention centre was added, followed by a new wing with 54 rooms and suites in 1993. The Algonquin offers superb, modern and very comfortable rooms and suites, excellent food at the Passamaquoddy Veranda dining room, flawless service and a whole slew of activities. If the nightly rate is beyond your budget, do at least visit the hotel and treat yourself to Sunday brunch, lunch or supper, a drink in the Library Bar or stop at the gift shop.

St. George

The **Town House Bed & Breakfast** *($50; 3 rooms, tv; 8 Main Street, EOG 2YO, ☎ 755-3476)* was built in the 1840s by politician and businessman A. H. Gillmor. The stately house, set on a beautiful lot in the centre of the town, is maintained by a friendly pre-retirement couple, Pat and Dan Gillmor, who are the fifth generation of their family to live in the house. The rooms are spacious, clean and furnished in a classic English style. You'll be warmly welcomed by your hosts.

The **Granite Town Hotel** *($66; 32 rooms, tv, ℜ, C; 15 Main Street East, EOG 2YO, ☎ 755-6415, ⇄ 755-6009)* provides a conventional level of comfort. It is a good address to remember mainly because it is clean and ideally located for guests wanting to visit the islands in the bay.

Campobello Island

Well situated near the park, the **Lupin Lodge** *($55; 10 rooms, tv; EOG 3HO, ☎ 752-2555)* offers relatively comfortable accommodation. The neighbouring restaurant is busy during the summer season, all day long until evening falls.

Grand Manan Island

Lots of families spend at least a few days of their vacation on Grand Manan Island. A popular option for such vacationers is to rent a cottage like the ones offered at **Fisherman's Haven Cottages** *($65; 5 rooms, Grand Harbour, ☎ 662-8919, ⇄ 652-2389)* which have two or three bedrooms. Weekly rates are available.

Saint John

Saint John unfortunately has no youth hostel. For those in search of accommodation under $20 per person, there are two options. Men are welcome at the **YMCA** *(25 Hazen Avenue, ☎ 634-7720)*, and women can go to **Evangeline Home** *(260 Prince William Street, ☎ 634-1950)*.

In the immediate surroundings of Saint John, numerous motels offer reasonably-priced accommodation in simple but clean rooms. The **Park Plaza Motel** *($48; 96 rooms, tv, ℜ, 607 Rothesay Avenue, E2H 2G9, ☎ 633-4100 or 1-800-561-9022, ⇄ 648-9494)* is one of these. To get there take Exit 117 off of Route 1.

Just a short distance from the pier where the ferry for Digby, Nova Scotia docks, in Saint John West is the **Five Chimneys Bed and Breakfast** *($50; 2 rooms, tv; 238 Charlotte West, E2M 1Y3, ☎ 635-1888, ⇄ 635-1888)*. It is set up in an upper-class house dating from the middle of the 19th century and offers quality accommodation for the price.

For an inexpensive hotel with clean but no-nonsense rooms, located within a short distance from downtown Saint John and the major highways, **Keddy's Fort Howe Hotel** *($60; 135 rooms, tv, ℜ, ≈; at the corner of Portland and Main Streets, E2K 4H8, ☎ 654-7320 or 1-800-561-7666, ⇄ 693-1146)* is your best bet. The staff is courteous, and as an added bonus, there is a bar and restaurant on the top floor.

If you don't see Saint John as an idyllic spot to take a relaxing and revitalizing vacation it must be because you've never come across the **Inn on the Cove** *($45-85 and more; 5 rooms, tv; 1371 Sand Cove Road, E2M 4X7, ☎ 672-7799, ⇄ 635-635-5455)*, probably one of the best inns in the province. Located in a quiet setting with a spectacular view of the Bay of Fundy, the inn is actually only 5 minutes by car from downtown. Nature-lovers will find beautiful wild beaches to explore close by and trails leading to Irving Nature Park. The house is furnished with taste and a particular attention to detail, and the comfortable rooms are decorated with antiques. All of the rooms are nice, but the two located on the second floor and facing over the back of the house are even better: they are larger, have their own bathrooms and offer a stunning view of the bay. The owners are friendly but discreet, and prepare excellent breakfasts.

In the heart of downtown on the busiest street, the **Delta Brunswick Hotel** *($100; 255 rooms, tv, ℜ, ≈; 39 King Street, E2L 4W3, ☎ 648-1981 or 1-800-268-1133, ⇄ 658-0914)* is the largest hotel in Saint John, with 255 deluxe rooms and suites. Attached to a shopping mall, the building itself lacks a bit of charm. The hotel is best known for its comfort and for the gamut of services for vacationers and business people.

The Saint John **Hilton** *($135; 197 rooms, tv, ℜ, ≈; 1 Market Square, E2L 4Z6, ☎ 693-8484 or 1-800-561-8282, ⇄ 657-6610)*, offering high quality accommodation, lies in a beautiful setting at the edge of the pier close to the market. It is a great spot to enjoy the singular beauty of this sea port whose activity is dictated by the continuous ebb and flow of the tides. The Hilton has a good restaurant and a pleasant bar, the Brigandine Lounge, with a view of the piers.

St. Martins

The tiny coastal town of St. Martins offers a wide choice of quality accommodation. One of these is the reputed **Quaco Inn** *($55; 6 rooms, tv; EOG 2ZO, ☎ 833-4772, ⇄ 833-2531)* which provides comfortable lodging in the refined atmosphere of a Victorian house. Beautifully-furnished and including a dining room with a well-established reputation, this inn is among the best in the province.

The divine **St. Martins Country Inn** *($57; 12 rooms, tv; R. R. 1, EOG 2ZO, ☎ 633-4534 or 1-800-565-5257, 833-4725)* is situated in the enchanting setting of a large property overlooking the town. Built in 1857 for the most important shipbuilder in St. Martins, it has maintained the serene and perhaps slightly snobby atmosphere befitting the residence of a highly-visible member of the Anglo-Saxon upper class of that era. Everything to satisfy the discerning tastes of the epicurean traveller is in place: beautifully decorated rooms filled with period furniture, a highly-reputed kitchen, three splendid dining rooms and impeccable service. Reserve in advance.

Fundy National Park

Besides the camping ground, visitors have only two other options for accommodation in Fundy National Park. The **Fundy Park Chalets** *($47; 29 rooms, tv, C, EOA 1BO, ☎ 887-2808)* offer somewhat rustic lodging near the coast, right after entering the park when coming from Alma.

The other choice is the **Caledonia Highlands Inn & Chalets** *($60; 44 rooms. tv. C, EOA 1BO, ☎ 887-2939)*, which is more centrally, located on the side of a hill by the road, is more isolated. Motel-style rooms and chalets with kitchenettes are offered.

Alma

The **Captain's Inn** *($59; 10 rooms, tv; Main Street, EOA 1BO, ☎ 887-2017, ⇄ 887-2074)* is just one of the numerous places to stay in Alma, gateway to Fundy National Park. The inn is simple, comfortable, well maintained and well located.

Moncton

The **YWCA** *(35 Highfield, ☎ 855-4349)* is located in a beautiful building, ideally located in downtown Moncton. A dormitory bed costs about $10 per person, per night, but only women can stay here. For a few dollars more, both men and women are welcome during the summer in the student residence of the **University of Moncton** *(☎ 858-4008)*.

The **Colonial Inn** *($59; 61 rooms, tv, ℜ, ≈; 42 Highfield, E1C 8T6, ☎ 382-3395 or 1-800-561-4667, ⇄ 858-8991)* offers motel-style accommodation right in the heart of Moncton. The rooms are well kept, the service is excellent and guests have use of a pool. This is a good spot for families.

The years have taken their toll on the grandeur that once was **Keddy's Brunswick Hotel** *($60; 193 rooms, tv, ℜ, ≈; 1005 Main Street, E1C 8N6, ☎ 854-6340 or 1-800-561-7666, ⇄ 382-8973)*. This is particularly evident in the outdated furniture and decor, not to mention the unpredictable elevator service. There remain, however, several good reasons to stay here, namely the affordable price and the central location.

As a member of the heritage association of inns, the **Canadiana Inn** *($65;*

17 rooms, tv; 46 Archibald Street, E1C 5H9, ☎ 382-1054) offers its visitors the charm and atmosphere of an opulent, turn-of-the-century house just a short distance from the city's liveliest streets. The quiet comfortable rooms are decorated with old-fashioned furniture.

For those travellers in need of some pampering and in search of elegance and comfort, there is the **Hotel Beauséjour** ($80; 314 rooms, tv, ℜ, ≈; 750 Main Street, E1C 1E6, ☎ 858-8584 or 1-800-561-3328, ⇄ 858-9057), Moncton's finest establishment and a member of the Canadian Pacific hotel chain. The quality of service that has made the reputation of this chain is here, as well as beautifully-decorated and spacious rooms, an excellent restaurant and piano bar and a rooftop swimming pool where it is easy to put the bustle of urban life behind, or perhaps below, you. Right in the heart of Moncton, the hotel could not be more suitably located for business people and travellers hoping to take advantage of the nearby restaurants and bars.

Sackville

The cheapest accommodation in Sackville is in the residences of **Mount Allison University** (☎ 364-2251), but only during the summer. A double room costs about $35. The campus lies right in the middle of this small town.

Borden's Restaurant & Motel ($42; 8 rooms, tv; at the southern end of town, E0A 3C0, ☎ 536-1066), a small red brick building at the edge of town, has a few inexpensive, clean rooms.

Set up in a spacious Victorian house from the last century is the excellent bed and breakfast, the **Different Drummer** ($48; 8 rooms, tv; 83 West Main Street, E0A 3C0, ☎ 536-1291). All of the rooms are comfortable and furnished with real antiques. The healthy breakfast is generous and delicious.

The charm of Sackville is due in good part to the multitude of large, beautiful houses from the 1800s. One of these has been converted into the outstanding **Marshlands Inn** ($53; 21 rooms, tv; 59 Bridge Street, E0A 3C0, ☎ 536-0170, ⇄ 536-0721), once a sumptuous residence offered as a wedding gift by William Crane, an important man of that era, to his daughter. The inn has more than 20 rooms, each one impeccably furnished; several have private bathrooms.

■ Tour D: The Acadian Coast

Shediac

Out towards the provincial park and the beach, the **Four Seas Motel** ($42; 42 rooms, tv, ℜ, ℭ; 762 Main Street, E0A 3G0, ☎ 532-2585) is a good choice for families and for travellers on a budget. The service is efficient and friendly, the restaurant is very good and the rooms are clean and well furnished, mostly with modern pieces. During the summer season, it is best to reserve early in the morning if you want one of the less expensive rooms since they go fast.

Also towards the park is the **Neptune Motel** ($45; 34 rooms, tv, ℭ; East Main Street, E0A 3G0, ☎ 532-4299), offering accommodation similar in price and quality to the Four Seas. Several of the rooms also have kitchenettes.

Located on a beautifully-maintained piece of property in the heart of Shediac, **Chez Françoise** ($47; 19 rooms, tv; 93 Main Street, E0A 3G0, ☎ 532-4233) is a wonderful inn. Built at the turn of the century, it was originally the residence of a wealthy family. The elegant interior, with its wood trim and sumptuous staircase, and the large front porch, ideal for coffee or an apéritif, make for a charming little spot. The dining room is a virtual institution. Be sure to reserve well in advance.

Seely's Motel *($55; 34 rooms, tv, ℂ; East Main Street, EOA 3GO, ☎ 532-6193)*, also towards the park, offers plainly-decorated rooms that are nonetheless comfortable and clean.

The **Belcourt Inn** *($60; 7 rooms, tv; 112 Main Street, EOA 3GO, ☎ 532-6098)* occupies a pretty house built at the beginning of the century. With its beautiful, spacious front porch, it is surprisingly peaceful, even though it is located on the town's busiest street. The rooms are nicely furnished and tastefully decorated. When it comes to charm, the Belcourt Inn is right up there with Chez Françoise. The rates are a bit higher, however.

Bouctouche

Besides a terrific view of the bay, the **Bouctouche Bay Inn** *($30; 27 rooms, tv, ℜ; at the entrance to town, EOA 1GO, ☎ 743-2726)* offers clean motel-style rooms, some of which are very competitively priced. It is not far from the entrance to the *Pays de la Sagouine* (see p 74).

The **Old Presbytery of Bouctouche** *($55; 22 rooms, ℜ; 157 Chemin du Couvent, EOA 1GO, ☎ 743-5568)* actually occupies a presbytery constructed at the end of the 19th century. Today it is a superb family inn just outside the centre of Bouctouche, with a beautiful view of the bay. The atmosphere is first-rate, ideal for relaxation, and the building, which has been reno-

vated several times is full of charm. An old chapel has been converted into a reception hall. The restaurant has an excellent reputation as well.

Richibucto

The **Motel Habitant** *($54; 29 rooms, tv, ≈; R.R. 1, EOA 2MO, ☎ 523-4421, ⇄ 523-0155)* is located a bit more than ten kilometres south of the entrance to Kouchibouguac National Park (see p 79). It is a nice looking motel with clean rooms and a pool. This is one of the more comfortable motels near the park.

The **Pack Woodland Motel & Restaurant** *($45; 7 rooms, tv, ℜ, right at the entrance to Kouchibouctou Park, ☎ 876-2407)* has the obvious advantage of being located right at the entrance to the park, on a secluded site by the side of the road.

Tracadie-Sheila

The **Motel Boudreau** *($52; 79 rooms, tv, ℜ, ≈; Route 11, EOC 2BO, ☎ 395-2244 or 1-800-563-2242, ⇄ 395-6868)* is a fine establishment that rents very comfortable, modern rooms. The clientele is made up mostly of business people.

Shippagan

Just on the outskirts of Shippagan, the **Maison Touristique Mallet** *($25; 4 rooms; Haut Shippagan, EOB 2PO, ☎ 336-4167)* is a small residence offering well-maintained rooms. The owner seems to have forgotten long ago to raise the prices.

Amongst the other possibilities of accommodation, the **Motel Shippagan** *($52; 51 rooms, ℜ, tv; centre of Shippagan, EOB 2PO, ☎ 336-2276)*, with its clean comfortable rooms, is worth a mention.

Caraquet

For economical accommodation, nothing beats the **Youth Hostel** (577 St. Pierre Blvd West, ☎ 727-1712) which has beds for around $10 per night per person. The hostel is actually quite nice and looks out over the sea.

At the beginning of the century, a number of hotels sprang up in Caraquet when the town was linked to the Canadian railway system. One of these was the **Dominion Hotel** ($20; 5 rooms, tv; 145 St. Pierre Blvd West, EOB 1KO, ☎ 727-4275), which is still in operation today. Though it is well situated in the heart of town and its rooms are very inexpensive, the Dominion has seen better days.

At the western edge of Caraquet is the **Maison Touristique Dugas B&B** ($29; 18 rooms, tv; 638 St. Pierre Blvd West, EOB 1KO, ☎ 727-3195), located in a building constructed in the twenties. There is something for all tastes here: rooms, suites, cottages and camping sites.

Also part of the Caraquet skyline for many years, the **Hôtel Paulin** ($45; 9 rooms, tv, ℜ; 143 St. Pierre Blvd West, EOB 1KO, ☎ 727-9981) is actually a pleasant inn run by the Paulin family for the last three generations. The rooms vary in quality: some have recently been nicely renovated while others are quite out of date but still very clean; in all cases, however, the quality/price ratio is very good. There is a very pretty suite at the back of the building with a view of the ocean. Guests can relax in the sitting room and enjoy the restaurant's excellent food.

The **Auberge de la Baie** ($64; 54 rooms, tv, ℜ; 139 St. Pierre Blvd West, EOB 1KO, ☎ 727-3485) provides comfortable and modern motel-style accommodation. Strangely enough, most of the rooms open onto an interior hallway instead of outdoors. There is a good restaurant with polite, friendly and attentive service. Finally the ample grounds affer access to a small deserted beach located behind the inn.

Bathurst

Slightly on the outskirts of downtown Bathurst, the **Best Western Danny's Inn** ($59; 40 rooms, tv; Route 134, EOB 1HO, ☎ 546-6621, ⇄ 548-3260) offers spotless modern rooms.

Campbellton

The modern and well located **Maritime Inn** ($48; 58 rooms, tv; 36 Duke Street, E3N 3G9, ☎ 753-7699 or 1-800-561-1881) offers adequate comfort and clean rooms, some of which are among the least expensive in Campbellton.

A beautiful example of Campbellton's architectural heritage, the **Aylesford Inn** ($56; 6 rooms, tv; 8 MacMillan Avenue, E3N 1E9, ☎ 759-7672) is a magnificent stately Victorian residence built at the turn of the century. The house is set on a beautifully landscaped property. Adding to the character of the place, the rooms are all decorated in period furniture. Breakfast is served each morning.

 **Restaurants**

■ **Tour A: Fredericton**

The **Café du Monde** *($; 608 Queen Street)* is a cosy café-style restaurant close to the main attractions of Fredericton. Light dishes, sandwiches and a small choice of breads and buns are served. This is the perfect spot for an afternoon break, an inexpensive meal or a good cup of coffee to start off the day.

Without a doubt the best spare ribs in town are at the **Bar-B-Barn** *($$; 640 Queen Street)*; equally good are their steaks and barbecued chicken. The wood panelling in this family restaurant is reminiscent of an English pub. Good quality/price ratio.

Rye's Deli & Pub *($$; King Street)* is a favourite with smoked meat fans, and according to their advertisements they follow the original Montreal recipe. What the decor lacks in atmosphere is more than made up for by the terrace when the warm weather arrives. Rye's is particularly popular among employees of the neighbouring offices and shops.

Mexicali Rosa's *($$; King Street)* is the perfect spot for fans of spicy food. Servings are usually quite large, and a small terrace allows for outdoor dining.

Open 24 hours a day, seven days a week, the **Diplomat** *($$; next to the Sheraton)* is a favourite perch for night owls. The menu is varied but simple, consisting essentially of typical delicatessen fare.

The **Lobster Hut** *($$; 1216 Regent Street, City Motel)* could almost be listed as a Fredericton attraction, due to its bizarre, almost psychedelic decor, made up of an eclectic collection of photos, posters and gadgets all having to do with maritime life. The restaurant is as friendly as can be, and as you may have guessed specializes in fish and seafood. The food is good and relatively inexpensive.

The Lord Beaverbrook Hotel (see p 84) is endowed with a dining room and a terrace looking out over the St. John River. For a fancier dinner, however, make reservations at the **Governor's Room** *($$$; Lord Beaverbrook Hotel)*, two private dining rooms with an antiquated decor and a slightly aristocratic atmosphere. The chef specializes in steak and seafood.

In summertime when the weather is mild, it would be hard to imagine a better spot for a drink, light snack or meal than **The Dip** *($$-$$$; Sheraton Inn)*, a terrace restaurant with a bistro menu. Besides the attentive and courteous service, The Dip offers an absolutely unbeatable view of the St. John River. If the season or the weather proves prohibitive, you can always take shelter at **Bruno's** *($$$)*, the indoor restaurant at the Sheraton Inn (see p 83). The cuisine is just as good, the service, impeccable and the ambiance, cosy.

■ **Tour B: Saint John River Valley**

Grand Falls (Grand-Sault)

As you can probably guess **The Little Pizza House** *($; 238 Broadway)* specializes in pizzas and other Italian dishes. The daily specials served at noon during the week are a good deal. There are several other restaurants of the same type on Broadway and close to the access roads of the TransCanada.

The Grand Falls region is a big potato producer, so much so that the house specialty of the **La Renaissance** *($$; Motel Léo)* restaurant is the "stuffed potato": half a baked potato stuffed with ham, chicken, cheese, etc. Whatever the variation, the "stuffed potato" is quite filling and makes an economical meal. The rest of the menu includes typical home-style cooking. The decor is simple and the service is courteous.

La Violette *($$; Motel Près du Lac)* is also a family restaurant, but with a more elaborate menu than its competitor's at the Motel Léo. The layout of the dining room is more open and elegant. They menu includes meat, chicken, seafood... basically, a bit of everything!

Woodstock

Both a bar and a restaurant serving home-style cooking, the **J.R.** *($-$$, Main Street, 500 m after the community college)* is somewhat of an institution in Woodstock. This spot is quite popular on weekends when young college students and locals come here for drinks, dinner or dancing.

Heino's restaurant *($$; 8 km south of Woodstock)* in the John Gyles Motor Inn is famous throughout the region for its excellent German family cuisine. Of course several varieties of sausage figure on the menu, as well as the great classics of that country's cuisine.

Gagetown

The menu of the **Steamers Stop Inn** *($$-$$$; Front Street)* is rich in traditional regional specialties, with a particular attention paid to the choice of fresh ingredients in the preparation of the meals. Diners can enjoy a lovely view of the river from the back veranda.

■ Tour C: Bay of Fundy Shore

St. Andrews By-The-Sea

Imagine America in the fifties and you've got the decor of the **Chef Café** *($; 180 Water Street, ☎ 529-8888)*, a popular but rinky-dink restaurant that clashes with the inherent chic that is St. Andrews. The menu includes simple dishes like fish and chips and lobster rolls, as well as several inexpensive breakfasts. For a more sophisticated menu, pick a spot at the back of the restaurant, in the cosier dining room known as the Captain's Table.

The Gables *($$; 143 Water Street, ☎ 529-3440)* has adopted a simple but proven formula: serve a variety of dishes at reasonable prices along with a selection of beer and alcohol in the laid-back atmosphere of a pub with a terrace. Evenings seem to stretch long into the night for the young clientele that flock here.

For many visitors, fresh lobster at a reasonable price is in itself enough of a reason to visit the Maritimes. When passing through St. Andrews, these seafood fanatics converge on **The Lighthouse Restaurant** *($$-$$$, Patrick Street, ☎ 529-3082)*. This pretty spot looking out over Passamaquoddy Bay is on the last street at the eastern edge of St. Andrews.

The **Passamaquoddy Veranda** *($$$; Algonquin Hotel, ☎ 529-8823)* offers an outstanding dining experience, as much for the elegance of its decor as for the exceptional quality of its international and regional cuisine. A meal at the Veranda is not within everyone's budget, but fortunately there is a much less expensive lunch menu and a Sunday brunch, which starts at $18.50.

Saint John

If you like satisfying your hunger in eclectic and colourful places, you will certainly feel at home at **Wild Willie's** *($; 112 Prince William Street)*, a long narrow restaurant with an updated 1950s decor. Light meals and a good selection of vegetarian dishes make up the menu.

There is nothing wrong with wanting a good cup of coffee, even in Saint John. And **Mother Nature's Bistro** *($; 20 Charlotte Street)* seems to sympathize. As well as the great coffee, there is cappuccino and espresso, along with cakes, bagels, great salads and a few light dishes.

For fans of Mexican cuisine, cold margaritas and Carta Blanca all at reasonable prices, the **Mexicali Rosa's** *($-$$; 88 Prince William Street)* restaurant chain is a sure bet. The Saint John branch is well located and very popular.

Grannan's Seafood Restaurant and Oyster Bar *($$; Market Square,* ☎ *634-1555)* is on its way to becoming an institution in Saint John. The restaurant, whose decor is a hodgepodge of eccentric maritime-related relics and photos, a real fishmonger's paradise, opens onto an outdoor terrace, perfect for those warm summer evenings.

Without question one of the trendiest spots in Saint John, the **Incredible Edibles Café** *($$; 42 Princess Street)* serves excellent continental cuisine and superb desserts. Feasters can sit out in the garden or in the delightful interior dining room.

Dufferin Hall *($$$; 357 Duffferin Row,* ☎ *635-5698)* is an inn on Saint John's west side. Guests can stay here for the night, but it is actually the excellent restaurant, without a doubt one of the best in the region, that has established the inn's reputation. The German couple who own the place prepare refined and original continental cuisine accompanied by a choice selection of wines and liqueurs.

The **Turn of the Tide** *($$$; Hilton Hotel)* offers a varied menu, typical of a hotel of this calibre, with a vast choice of meat, game, and of course the prerequisite fresh seafood and fish. The menu is a bit pricey, but the food is sure to please, and the view of the port makes it all the more worthwhile. The decor is classic, airy and tasteful.

St. Martins

To complement a romantic trip to the peaceful town of St. Martins, treat yourselves to the delicious pleasure of a candlelight dinner at the famous **St. Martins Country Inn** *($$$;* ☎ *633-4534)*. The menu is made up of local and international specialties served in intimate dining rooms to the crackle of a warm fire.

Moncton

A stroll along Main Street is all it takes to experience Moncton's North American atmosphere, but a Latin spirit does lurk nearby at **Joe Moka** *($; 187 Robinson Street,* ☎ *852-3070)* which serves a wide selection of coffee, pastries and sandwiches. Patrons come to this charming little café to chat with friends or simply to bury themselves in a good book or the newspaper. In the summer the tables are set outside making this the best possible place to people-watch from.

Either you'll love it or you'll hate it, but one thing is for sure: you won't remain neutral when it comes to **Fat Tuesday's Eatery & Pub** *($; 720 Main Street)*, especially on weekend nights when the place is overrun by a young and noisy crowd with partying on their minds and often a drink too many under their belts. The basic formula is quite simple: serve inexpensive simple food and most of all lots of beer. The menu: burgers, sandwiches, fries, etc.

Crackers *($-$$; 700 Main Street, ☎ 858-8440)* is a charming fashionable little restaurant that serves pasta, sandwiches and other simple dishes as well as sinfully delicious desserts. The comfortable decor is inviting and has made this place a favourite with Moncton's younger crowd.

The **Café Bleue** ($-$$; 376 St. George Street, ☎ 855-8096) is a veritable institution of the Acadian community, frequented by young people, artists and students. Muffins, croissants and light meals are served at this cute little café whose picture windows look out onto the street.

Visitors can enjoy a taste of life *à la française* at great spots like the **Café de Paris** *($-$$; 37 Botsford Street, ☎ 855-8096)*, a charming café-restaurant that serves simple but meticulously-prepared cuisine and divine desserts. On warm summer evenings, a fine glass of red wine on the tiny terrace is a pure delight. The service is friendly yet discreet.

In business for more than half a century, **Cy's Seafood** *($$; 170 Main Street, ☎ 857-0032)* has adopted one of the Maritimes' treasures, the lobster, as its house specialty. The menu lists other types of seafood as well, all prepared simply and deliciously.

With its typical French bistro atmosphere and refined cuisine **Gaston's** *($$-$$$; 644 Main Street, ☎ 858-8998)* has built itself an enviable reputation in Moncton. It is a favourite with business people at lunch time, while in the evenings couples and groups of friends come here to enjoy a good meal. Long reputed for its seafood, Gaston's is becoming more and more well-known for its excellent international cuisine.

Sackville

The **Marshlands Inn** ($$$; 59 Bridge Street, ☎ 536-0170) offers fine dining to satisfy the most discerning of palates. The menu is quite extensive and features mostly continental specialties as well as several regional dishes. The atmosphere is quite formal, but also very friendly.

■ Tour D: The Acadian Coast

Shediac

When the owners of the **Café Péché Mignon** *($; 15 Queen Street, ☎ 532-6555)* opened for business in the summer of 1994, they did so believing there was space for a little French café, in Shediac. They couldn't have been more right! Besides excellent desserts and coffees, the menu includes a good choice of simple dishes like excellent quiche and some Acadian specialties. The atmosphere is particularly friendly and reflects the bohemian spirit of the owner, who is a painter.

The **Café Bistro 654** *($-$$; 654 Main Street)* is an inexpensive family restaurant featuring specialties from the German host's home country, including, of course, lots of sausage.

The **Four Seas Restaurant** *($$; 762 Main Street, ☎ 532-2585)*, in the motel of the same name, is another family restaurant. This one offers a more varied menu, including seafood. Patrons surely don't come for the relatively boring decor, but rather for the reasonable prices and the quality of the food.

About 5 km outside of Shediac, towards Cap-Pelé, a small road leads to the famous **Paturel** *($$-$$$; Cape Bimet Road,* ☎ *532-4774)*, a simple restaurant with a view of the ocean, which serves fresh seafood at prices that are reasonable, all things considered. Portions are generous, especially the Seafood Platter, which includes samples the abundant variety of seafood of the region. As if to add to the atmosphere, the restaurant lies right next to Paturel Seafood Ltd., a seafood processing plant.

No surprises at the **Fisherman's Paradise** *($$-$$$; Main Street,* ☎ *532-6811)*, which as its name suggests is devoted to the treasures of the sea, and where a special place is reserved on the menu for the king of seafood: the lobster. With its exquisite interior decor made up of numerous model ships, this place is among the most chic in Shediac.

Undeniably one of the best restaurants in the region, **Chez Françoise** *($$$; 93 Main Street,* ☎ *532-4233)* offers refined French cuisine and an excellent selection of wine. And to add to your dining pleasure, the dining room is decorated with elegance and style. If you plan on treating yourself to one good meal during your stay in New Brunswick, you won't go wrong choosing Chez Françoise. This place is chic but not stuffy.

Bouctouche

L'Ordre du Bon Temps *($-$$; at the entrance to the Pays de la Sagouine,* ☎ *743-1400)* the restaurant at the *Pays de la Sagouine* offers visitors the chance to sample traditional Acadian specialties like *fricot de poulet, poutine râpée* or *poutine à trou, pâté à la râpure* or *pâté aux palourdes*. The menu probably has the most extensive selection of Acadian dishes in all of Acadia, so take advantage of it.

Acadian hospitality is at its best at **Tire-Bouchon** *($$-$$$; Old Presbytery,* ☎ *743-5568)* the excellent dining room in the Old Presbytery, where chef, Marcelle Albert introduces diners to the most refined regional specialties. The name, which means "corkscrew", is quite fitting considering the fine bottles stocked in the wine cellar.

Tracadie Sheila

The **Maison de la Fondue** *($$; 3613 Luce Street,* ☎ *393-1110)* offers a fine menu with an emphasis on seafood, meat and of course, fondues - Swiss, Chinese, Spanish and seafood.

Shippagan

Very elegant and endowed with a splendid view of the port, the **Jardin de la Mer** *($$-$$$; next to the Aquarium,* ☎ *336-8454)* is, as one might expect, an excellent fish and seafood restaurant. Lunchtime, when the lobster rolls and other small meals are available at relatively reasonable prices, is a good time to stop in for a bite. Evenings, gourmets benefit from a wide choice. Those with a big appetite can attempt to discover all the wonders of the sea in one meal with the *Sea in Your Plate*.

Caraquet

For dining in a friendly family atmosphere check out the **Caraquette** *($-$$; 151 St. Pierre Blvd West,* ☎ *727-6009)*. The reasonably priced menu is varied and includes steaks, pasta, chicken and sandwiches, as well as lots of fish and seafood. Most dishes cost less than $10.

The **Hôtel Paulin dining room** *($$; 143 St. Pierre Blvd West,* ☎ *727-9981)* offers what has become something of a rarity in the region, a *table d'hôte* or set menu, instead of the usual *à la carte* service. Regional and French specialties make up the menu.

Airy and modern, but at the same time friendly and inviting, the **Auberge de la Baie dining room** *($$; 139 St. Pierre Blvd,* ☎ *727-3485)* offers a good variety of dishes, including seafood and steaks. The service is very attentive.

Grande-Anse

If you miss inexpensive simple family-style cooking go to **Chez Abel** *($; 260 Acadie Street)*, a small restaurant with daily specials for less than $6.

La Poissonnière *($$; 484 Acadie Street,* ☎ *733-2000)* is a tremendous seafood and fish restaurant in the heart of the community of Grande-Anse. Everything is prepared with precision and served with care, taking full advantage of the sea's treasures.

Paquetville

If your tummy starts to grumble as you pass through the little town of Paquetville, silence it with a stop at **La Crêpe Bretonne** *($-$$; 1085 rue Du Parc,* ☎ *764-4344)*, a small restaurant whose specialties are crepes and seafood. These two are sometimes combined in scallops and béchamel crepes, lobster and béchamel crepes, crab and béchamel crepes, etc. A good place for an inexpensive lunch or a good evening meal.

 Entertainment

■ **Tour A: Fredericton**

Every weeknight, live music can be heard at **The Exchange** *(365 Queen Street)*, a smoky little bar in downtown Fredericton, which also has an outdoor terrace. The clientele is generally young.

Always hopping, even on a Sunday night, **The Upper Deck Sport's Bar** *(2nd floor, next to The Exchange)* is one of the most popular spots with young Frederictonians. The place features pool tables and regular live music.

The students may come and go, but the **Social Club** at the University of New Brunswick *(Student Union Building)* remains a sure bet year after year. It is packed just about every night in winter, while in the summer, most of the action is limited to weekends.

■ **Tour B: The St. John River Valley**

Grand Falls (Grand-Sault)

Suzanne's *(Court Street near Broadway)*, a dance bar in the centre of Grand Falls, is clearly the hot spot where Madawaskans are concerned, since the place is crammed with a young and rowdy crowd each weekend. Concerts are occasionally given in the basement.

Fans of heavier music may opt for the **Broadway** *(248 Broadway)*, located a few hundred metres away.

■ **Tour C: The Fundy Shore**

St. Andrews By-The-Sea

The **Library Bar** *(Algonquin Hotel)* exudes the elegance and relaxing ambiance one would expect in the piano bar of a hotel of such standing. Fine liqueurs are served. Ironically the rowdiest place to get a drink in town is also at the Algonquin. The **Dock Side Pub** *(in the basement of the hotel)* is a popular meeting place with the younger employees of the hotels and restaurants of St. Andrews.

Saint John

The Irish influence is known to be very strong in Saint John. It is therefore no surprise to find **O'Leary's** *(46 Princess Street)*, an excellent Irish pub. The clientele is generally young, and musicians are often presented.

Sherlock's *(next to Market Square)* is set up in a beautiful building with elegant wood-panelling. The young clientele comes for beer and dancing on weekends.

The **Brigandine Lounge** *(Hilton Hotel)* is charming, with an unimpeded view of the port and its busy piers across the St. John River. Guests of this rather chic hotel make up most of the clientele of this quiet bar, which has an interesting selection of liqueurs. Evenings are usually enhanced by a piano-player.

Moncton

The sumptuous **Capitol Theatre** *(811 Main Street, ☎ 856-4377)* is the main performing arts centre in Moncton. Since its reopening in 1993, after renovations restored the panache of days gone by, the theatre has presented a variety of quality productions.

There is no way to miss when looking for a bar in Moncton since they are all located on Main Street. For fans of decibels and dancing, **Ziggy's** *(730 Main Street)* is a sure thing on the weekend. The clientele is young.

Bar-hopping and pub-crawling does not appeal to everyone. Luckily there is an alternative, **Caesar's Piano Bar** *(Hotel Beausejour, 750 Main Street)*, which serves excellent liqueurs in a relaxing soothing atmosphere that is actually conducive to conversation.

The **student bar** at the University of Moncton presents concerts in the summer, providing visitors an excellent opportunity to experience the culture and music of modern-day Acadians.

■ **Tour D: The Acadian Coast**

Caraquet

The **Brasserie au 49** *(49 St. Pierre Blvd)* is the all-round favourite for a beer and some socializing with the people of Caraquet. There is an outdoor terrace and a pool table.

 Shopping

■ **Tour A: Fredericton**

No visit to Fredericton would be complete without a stop at **Gallery 78** *(796 Queen Street)*, which exhibits and sells works by some of the most well-known

New Brunswick artists. It is also a wonderful way to visit a sumptuous Victorian house overlooking the St. John River. With its high ceilings, large rooms, hardwood floors and stately staircase, you'll be wishing it was for sale too!

The **Arts Council of New Brunswick** *(103 Church Street)* (Conseil d'Artisanat du Nouveau-Brunswick) boutique exhibits and sells a superb collection of high quality products created by the province's artists and crafts-people. It is one of the best craft boutiques in New Brunswick.

Cultures *(383 Masochist Lane)* is an innovative shop selling crafts and products made in developing nations. There are several beautiful objects. The boutique is located at what is probably one of the most difficult corners to find in Fredericton: a small alley ending at York Street, between King and Queen Streets.

Without a doubt one of the best bookstores in Fredericton, **West Minister Books** *(465 King Street)* offers an excellent selection of English-language novels and essays. The staff are particularly helpful and more than willing to point out the works of authors from this region and from the Maritimes in general.

■ **Tour B: The St. John River Valley**

Woodstock

The **duty-free shop in Woodstock** *(on Route 95 near the U.S. border, ☎ 328-8880)* offers all the goods normally found in such shops: wine and spirits, cigarettes, perfumes, jewellery, watches, figurines, etc. The quantity of untaxable items for sale in limitless.

Kings Landing

The **Kings Landing Shop** *(☎ 363-5805)* sells not only a good selection of souvenirs of the site, but also a wide selection of books on the history of the region and the Maritime provinces.

Gagetown

The charming contemporary **Acadia Gallery of Canadian Art** *(☎ 488-1119)*, located in the centre of Gagetown, exhibits a particularly interesting selection of works by artists using a variety of media. Since the gallery also serves as a workshop, it is often possible to meet some of the artists inspired by this enchanting site along the St. John River.

■ **Tour C: The Fundy Shore**

St. Stephen

The oldest candy maker in Canada (1873), **Ganong Chocolatier** *(73 Milltown Boulevard, ☎ 465-5611)* is also the first producer of chocolate bars. Today, the shop sells about 75 different varieties of chocolate; just try to choose...

St. Andrews By-The-Sea

North of Sixty Art *(238 Water Street, ☎ 529-4148)* is an Inuit art gallery that can be visited like a museum. Works exhibited include uniquely diverse and beautiful sculptures. Among the dozens of boutiques along Water Street, this one is probably the most interesting.

The **Boutique La Baleine** *(173 Water Street, ☎ 529-3926, ⇄ 529-3088)* is known mostly for the quality of its crafts; however, it also sells several other products, including books, trinkets and some clothing. There is another Boutique La Baleine inside the Algonquin Hotel.

Cottage Craft *(200 Water Street,* ☎ *529-3190)* is worth visiting for its interesting selection of tweed clothing and items knitted with 100% pure wool as well as the array of coloured yarn for sale.

Saint John

The Great New Brunswick Bookstore *(114 Prince William Street,* ☎ *633-0587)* is located on the pretty and unavoidable Prince William Street, at the corner of Princess Street. It offers a good selection of books and claims to be the biggest specialist in works published in New Brunswick.

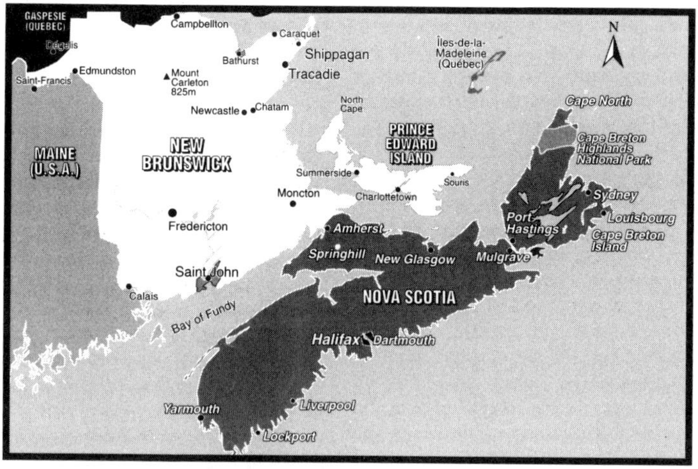

NOVA SCOTIA

The magnificent province of Nova Scotia looks like a long peninsula, connected to the continent by nothing more than the narrow strip of land known as the Chignecto Isthmus. In "Canada's Ocean Playground", the sea is never far away. In fact, no part of the territory of Nova Scotia is more than 49 km from the water, be it the Atlantic Ocean, the Northumberland Strait or the Bay of Fundy. The proximity of the coast has shaped the character and lives of Nova Scotians as much as it has the splendid maritime landscape. The coastline, stretching hundreds of kilometres, is punctuated with harbours and bays, their shores dotted with fishing villages and towns. What is most striking about Nova Scotia is the way its architectural heritage blends so harmoniously with the natural setting. From the tiniest fishing village to Halifax, the capital, there are few places where the architecture of the houses and buildings, often dating back to the 19th century, does not fit in beautifully with the surrounding landscape.

There are countless reasons to visit Nova Scotia and many splendid sights to discover here. Everyone has heard of the legendary beauty of Cape Breton Island, whose mountainous landscape, with its magnificent cliffs overhanging the deep blue sea, is among the most spectacular in Eastern Canada. But Cape Breton is only one of many scenic regions in Nova Scotia. For example, tucked away along the Lighthouse Route, which runs from Halifax to Yarmouth, is a multitude of picturesque villages steeped in history, such as Peggy's Cove, Mahone Bay and

Lunenberg. Farther along, near the Bay of Fundy, visitors can explore the former Acadia, whose rich farmlands formed the heart of the Acadian territory from 1605 to 1755. Equally delightful is Halifax, the beautiful, vibrant capital of Nova Scotia and the largest city in the Maritimes.

For a period of time, the magnificent land of Nova Scotia was the focus of the rivalry between the French and British empires. Originally inhabited by Micmac Amerindians, it was the site of the first European colony in America to be founded north of Florida. In 1605, one year after a failed attempt to settle Île Sainte-Croix, a French expedition led by De Monts founded Port-Royal at the mouth of the river now known as the Annapolis. The founding of this permanent settlement marked the birth of Acadia. Port-Royal continued to grow over the following decades, and the Acadians even founded new settlements on the shores of the Bay of Fundy. The many wars between the French and the British proved fatal for Acadia, however. In 1713, with the signing of the Treaty of Utrecht, France ceded Acadia to Great Britain, and the territory was renamed Nova Scotia. British citizens of French origin, the Acadians declared themselves neutral in the conflict between France and Great Britain. British authorities, however, were not reassured. In 1755, when war was imminent, the British decided to take a drastic step and deport the Acadians. In the following decades, various immigrants settled in Nova Scotia, including Planters seeking new land to farm, Loyalists, after the American Revolution, and citizens of the British Isles, especially Scots. Visitors will discover many fascinating sites bearing witness to Nova Scotia's turbulent history, such as the Fortress of Louisbourg on Cape Breton Island, Citadel

Hill in Halifax, the Grand-Pré National Historic Site, commemorating the deportation of the Acadians, or the *Abitation de Port-Royal*, a replica of the first permanent French settlement in North America (1605).

 Finding Your Way Around

We have divided Nova Scotia into 6 sections and outline a tour of each below: **Tour A: Halifax ★★★**; **Tour B: The Cape Route ★**, leads from Amherst to the outskirts of Windsor; **Tour C: Old Acadia ★★**, from Windsor to Yarmouth; **Tour D: The Lighthouse Route ★★**, from the outskirts of Yarmouth to Peggy's Cove; **Tour E: Cape Breton Island ★★★**, skirts round Cape Breton Island and finally **Tour F: The Northumberland Strait ★**, which leads from Antigonish to the border of New Brunswick.

■ **By Car**

Nova Scotia has a good road network. When following the tours outlined in this guide, visitors will usually have a choice between a picturesque route and an expressway. Keep in mind that the foggy conditions common along the coast call for prudent driving.

Visitors can reserve a car by contacting the provincial reservation service at ☎ 1-800-565-0000.

Halifax

Entering Halifax and reaching the downtown area is generally very easy by car, since the way is always clearly indicated. If in doubt, remember that Halifax lies on the southwest side of the harbour (Dartmouth is on the other

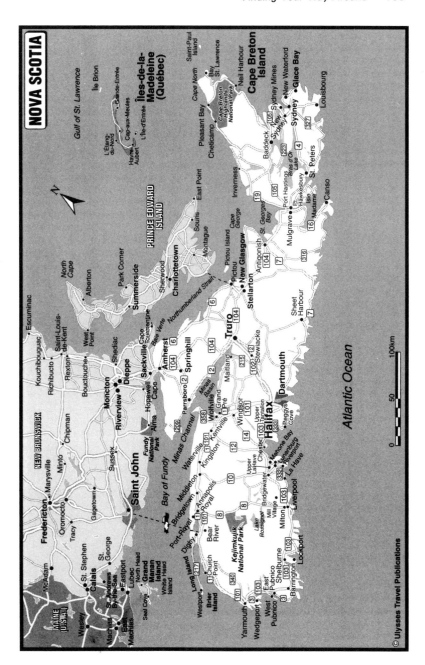

side), and the downtown area faces right onto the port. Visitors will have little trouble finding their bearings downtown, since Citadel Hill and the port serve as landmarks. The most important downtown artery is Barrington Street.

Cape Breton Island

From Halifax, take Highway 7 to Antigonish, then take the TransCanada to Canso Strait, which separates Nova Scotia from Cape Breton Island.

Visitors can also reach Cape Breton Island by driving along the shoreline. From Halifax, take Highway 7, but instead of heading inland near Stillwater, continue along Route 211, and then the 316. When you reach Highway 16, take it to Highway 4.

Either of these routes will take you to Cape Breton Island. Once there, you can go either to Sydney, Louisbourg or near Baddeck, which marks the beginning of the Cabot Trail.

■ By Airplane

Halifax International Airport is served by planes from Europe as well as elsewhere in Canada. Air Canada, Canadian Airlines, Air France, British Airways, KLM, American Airlines and Delta Airlines offer flights from various capital cities to Halifax. For more information, please refer to the "Practical Information" chapter, see p 23.

There is a shuttle service from the airport to the city.

☎ 429-9271

■ By Ferry

Nova Scotia is linked to Prince Edward Island, Newfoundland and Maine by ferry.

The ferry linking Caribou (Nova Scotia) to Wood Islands (Prince Edward Island) provides daily service from May to December.
Northumberland Ferry
Box 634
Charlottetown, P.E.I.
C1A 7L3
☎ (902) 566-3838 or 1-800-565-0201, from Nova Scotia and Prince Edward Island

From Port-aux-Basques (Newfoundland) to North Sydney (Nova Scotia):
Two departures daily year-round
Marine Atlantic
Box 250
North Sydney
B2A 3M3
☎ (902) 794-5700

From Portland (Maine) to Yarmouth (Nova Scotia):
Daily departures from May to October
Prince of Fundy Cruise
Box 4216, Station A
Portland, Maine
04101
☎ 1-800-341-7540 from Canada and the United States

From Bar Harbor (Maine) to Yarmouth (Nova Scotia)
Three departures weekly mid-May to mid-September
Marine Atlantic
Box 250
North Sydney, Nova Scotia
B2A 3M3
☎ (902) 794-5700

■ By Train

There is a train that runs from Montréal across New Brunswick to Nova Scotia. This is a comfortable means of transportation, but relatively slow; the trip from Montréal to Halifax takes 20 hours. The train is equipped with a dining car and sleeping berths.

Via Rail Canada (Halifax)
☎ 429-8421

■ By Bus

A number of buses crisscross Nova Scotia. There are links between Montréal and Nova Scotia (departure aboard Voyageur with a transfer to SMT Bus Lines in New Brunswick and Acadian Lines in Nova Scotia).

Visitors can reach a variety of destinations within Nova Scotia, since there are buses running from Halifax to Yarmouth, Amherst and Sydney *(Acadian Lines,* ☎ *454-9321)* and along the southern coast of the province, from Yarmouth to Halifax *(MacKenzie Bus Lines,* ☎ *543-2491)* and from Halifax to Sherbrooke *(Zinck's Bus Co.,* ☎ *468-4342)*.

Cape Breton Island

From Halifax, visitors can take the bus as far as Sydney. It is worth noting, however, that no bus goes all the way around the island (aside from private tour buses). There is no way to get around easily, except in Sydney, so it is best either to rent a car or rely on your own resources (hitchhiking, cycling).

Acadian Lines (Halifax to Sydney) ☎ 454-9321 or 454-8279; Transit Cap Breton (around Sydney) ☎ 539-8124

■ By Bicycle

Seasoned cyclists might consider a tour of the province, which promises some extremely pleasant excursions. Some regions, however, are quite difficult, with many steep hills. This is particularly true of Cape Breton Island. Not recommended for the casual cyclist.

? Practical Information

The provincial government operates a reservation service for hotels, bed & breakfasts, campsites and car rentals.

Information on festivals, ferry service and weather forecasts is also available. Dial ☎ 1-800- 565-0000.

Area code: 902

■ Tour A: Halifax

By mail:
Tourism Halifax
Box 1749
Halifax
B3J 3A5
☎ 421-8736
⇄ 421-2842

On site:
Historic Properties
Lower Water Street
Open all year

■ Tour B: The Cape Route

By mail:
Central Nova Tourist Association
Box 1761
Truro
B2N 5Z5
☎ and ⇄ 893-8782

On site:
Highway 104
At the New Brunswick border
Open all year

■ Tour C: Old Acadia

By mail:
Yarmouth County Tourist Association
Box 477
Yarmouth
B5A 4B4
☎ 742-5355
⇄ 742-6644

On site:
Annapolis Royal
Annapolis Tidal Project
Route 1
Open from mid-May to mid-Oct

Digby
Shore Road
Towards the ferry landing
Open from mid-May to mid-Oct

Yarmouth
228 Main Street
Open from early May to end of Oct

■ Tour D: The Lighthouse Route

On site:
Blockhouse Hill Road
Lunenberg
☎ 634-8100

■ Tour E: Cape Breton Island

By mail:
Cape Breton Tourist Association
20 Keltic Drive
Sydney River
☎ 539-9876
⇄ 539-8340

On site:
On the way onto the island, along
the Canso Causeway
Port Hastings
Open from mid-May to mid-Oct

There are also booths in Louisbourg,
Baddeck and Margaree Forks.

■ Tour F: The Northumberland Strait

By mail:
Antigonish-Eastern Shore Tourist
Association
Musquodoboit Harbour
BOJ 2L0
☎ and ⇄ 889-2362

On site:
At the intersection of Highway 106 and
Route 6
Pictou
Open from mid-May to mid-Oct

 Exploring

■ Tour A: Halifax ★★★

A city with a rich architectural heritage,
built at the foot of a fortified hill overlooking one of the longest natural
harbours in the world, Halifax is a
delightful place to visit. The city's
location, which is outstanding from
both a navigational and a strategic
point of view, has been the deciding
factor in its growth. In 1749 the British
began developing the site, which had
long been frequented by Micmac
Amerindians. That year, 2,500 British
soldiers and colonists led by Governor
Edward Cornwallis settled here with
the aim of securing Britain's claim to
the territory of Nova Scotia. At the
time, France and its North American

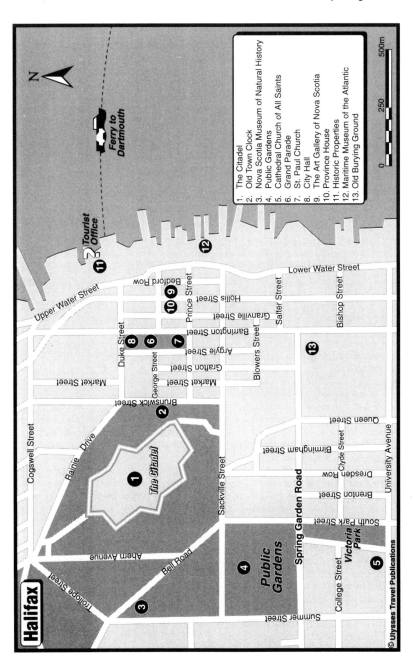

Halifax

N

Ferry to Dartmouth

Tourist Office

1. The Citadel
2. Old Town Clock
3. Nova Scotia Museum of Natural History
4. Public Gardens
5. Cathedral Church of All Saints
6. Grand Parade
7. St. Paul Church
8. City Hall
9. The Art Gallery of Nova Scotia
10. Province House
11. Historic Properties
12. Maritime Museum of the Atlantic
13. Old Burying Ground

0   250   500m

The Citadel

Public Gardens

Victoria Park

Spring Garden Road

© Ulysses Travel Publications

Cogswell Street
Trollope Street
Rainie Drive
Ahern Avenue
Bell Road
Summer Street
College Street
South Park Street
Brenton Street
Dresden Row
Birmingham Street
Queen Street
University Avenue
Clyde Street
Sackville Street
Market Street
Brunswick Street
George Street
Grafton Street
Market Street
Argyle Street
Barrington Street
Blowers Street
Granville Street
Hollis Street
Prince Street
Bedford Row
Upper Water Street
Lower Water Street
Salter Street
Bishop Street
Duke Street

colonies were the enemy. Over the following decades, Halifax served as a stronghold for British troops during the American Revolution and the War of 1812 against the United States. A military past is evident in the city's present-day urban landscape, its most striking legacy being, of course, the Citadel, whose silhouette looms over the downtown area. Not only a military city, Halifax has always been a commercial centre as well. Its access to the Atlantic, its excellent port and, starting in the late 19th century, its connection to the Canadian rail network have all favoured trade. Historic Properties, made up of warehouses built on the pier, is the oldest architectural grouping of its kind in the country, bearing witness to the city's long-established commercial tradition. Halifax is now the largest urban centre in the Maritime provinces, with a population of over 330,000 (including the inhabitants of its twin city, Dartmouth). It has a more varied, even cosmopolitan, appearance than the rest of the Maritimes, and boasts several superb museums and a whole slew of other attractions. Visitors are sure to enjoy strolling around Halifax and scouting out its restaurants, bustling streets and wide assortment of shops.

The Citadel and Its Surrounding Area

The **Halifax Citadel National Historic Site** ★★★ **(1)** *(adults $2; mid-Jun to early Sep, 9 AM to 6 PM; Citadel Hill; ☎ 426-5080)* is the most striking legacy of the military history of Halifax, a city that has played an important strategic role in the defense of the East Coast ever since it was founded in 1749. The fourth British fort to occupy this site, this imposing star-shaped structure overlooking the city was built between 1828 and 1856. It was the heart of an impressive network of defenses intended to protect the port in the event of an attack, which incidentally never took place. Visitors can explore the Citadel alone or take part in an interesting guided tour, which traces the history of the various fortifications that have marked the city's landscape since 1749, and explains their strategic value. All of the rooms used to accommodate soldiers and store arms and munitions are open to the public, and visitors can move about through the corridors leading from one room or level to another. It is also possible to walk along the ramparts, which offer an incomparable view of the city and its port. In summer, students dressed and armed like soldiers of the 78th Highlanders and the Royal Artillery perform manœuvers within these walls. The site also includes a **military museum** *(☎ 427-5979)*, which houses an extensive collection of British and Nova Scotian arms and uniforms. A fascinating, 15-minute audio-visual presentation on the history of Halifax may be viewed as well.

Right in front of the Citadel, towards the port, stands one of the most famous symbols of Halifax, the **Old Town Clock** ★ **(2)** *(Citadel Hill, opposite the main entrance of the Citadel)*, with its four dials. The clock was presented to the city in 1803 by Prince Edward, son of George III of Britain, who served as commander in chief of the Halifax garrison from 1794 to 1800. It serves as a reminder that the prince was a great believer in punctuality.

Northwest of the Citadel, visitors will find the **Nova Scotia Museum of Natural History** ★★ **(3)** *(adults $3; Jun to mid-Oct, Mon, Tue, Thu and Fri 9:30 AM to 5:30 PM, Wed 9:30 AM to 8 PM, Sun 1 PM to 5:30 PM; mid-Oct to end of May, Tue, Thu, Fri and Sat 9:30 AM to 5 PM, Wed 9:30 AM to*

8 PM, Sun 1 PM to 5 PM; 1747 Summer Street; ☎ *424-7353),* whose mission is to collect, preserve and study the objects and specimens most representative of Nova Scotia's geology, plant and animal life and archaeology. The museum features exhibits on subjects such as botany, fossils, insects, reptiles and marine life. One of the most noteworthy items on display is a whale skeleton. Visitors can also view a film on the birds living along the province's coast. The archaeology exhibit is particularly interesting, presenting the lifestyle and material possessions of the various peoples who have inhabited the province's territory over the centuries. The exhibit is organized in chronological order, starting with the Paleolithic age, then moving on to the Micmacs, the Acadians and finally the British.

Stretching southwest of the Citadel are the lovely, verdant **Public Gardens ★★ (4)** *(main entrance on South Park Street),* a Victorian garden covering an area of 7 ha, which dates back to 1753. Originally a private garden, it was purchased by the Nova Scotia Horticultural Society in 1836. The present lay-out, completed in 1875, is the work of Richard Power. A fine example of British know-how, the Public Gardens are adorned with stately trees concealing fountains, statues, charming flowerbeds, a pavilion and little lakes where ducks and swans can be seen swimming about. This is an absolutely perfect place to take a stroll, far from the occasionally turbulent atmosphere of downtown Halifax. During summer, concerts are held here on Sunday afternoons, and the Friends of Public Gardens organization offers guided tours of the garden *(☎ 422-9407).*

South of the Public Gardens, near Victoria Park, stands the **Cathedral Church of All Saints ★ (5)** *(free admission; mid-Jun to mid-Sep, 1:30 PM to 4:30 PM; 1720 Tower;* ☎ *424-6002),* whose remarkable stained-glass windows and exquisite woodwork will take visitors' breath away. The structure was completed in 1910, two centuries after the first Anglican service was held in Canada. It is located in a pretty part of the city, where the streets are flanked by stately trees. Some of Halifax's most prominent educational establishments can be found nearby.

Downtown Halifax and the Port

As early as a decade after Halifax was founded, **Grand Parade (6)** *(between Harrington and Argyle Streets)* had become a trading and gathering place for residents of the city. It is now a garden in the heart of the downtown area, flanked by tall buildings on all sides. At the south end of Grand Parade, visitors will find **St. Paul Church ★ (7)** *(free admission; Jun to Sep, Mon to Sat 9 30 AM to 4:30 PM; Oct to May, Mon to Fri 9 AM to 4:30 PM; Grand Parade),* the oldest Protestant church in Canada, built in 1750 on the model of St. Peter's Church in London, England. Despite the wearing effects of time and the addition of several extensions, the original structure has been preserved. Inside, visitors can examine a piece of metal from the *Mont Blanc,* one of the ships that caused a terrible explosion in Halifax in 1917. On the north side of Grand Parade stands **City Hall (8)** *(free admission),* an elegant Victorian style building dating back more than a century. In summer, Mayor Moira Ducharme invites both residents and visitors here to meet her and have tea *(Jul and Aug, Mon to Fri 3:30 PM to 4:30 PM).*

In the Dominion Building, a fine example of the city's rich architectural heritage, erected at the end of the last century, visitors will find the **Art Gallery of Nova Scotia** ★★★**(9)** *(adults $2.50; Jun to early Sep, Tue, Wed and Fri 10 AM to 5 PM, Thu 10 AM to 9 PM, Sat and Sun 12 PM to 5 PM; early Sep to May, Tue to Fri 10 AM to 5 PM, Sat and Sun 12 PM to 5 PM; 1741 Hollis, opposite Province House;* ☎ *424-2836)*, four flours of modern exhibition space containing the most remarkable art collection in Nova Scotia. The permanent collection, consisting of nearly 3,000 pieces, is devoted to both popular and contemporary art. Although many works are by painters and sculptors from Nova Scotia and the Maritime Provinces in general, artists from other Canadian provinces, the United States and Europe are also represented. The Art Gallery presents the occasional touring exhibition as well. Lastly, there is a wonderful boutique selling local crafts.

Seat of the government of Nova Scotia, **Province House** ★ **(9)** *(free admission; Jul and Aug, Mon to Fri 9 AM to 5 PM, Sat and Sun 10 AM to 4 PM; Sep to Jun, Mon to Fri 9 AM to 4 PM; Hollis Street;* ☎ *424-4661)*, an elegant Georgian style edifice dating from 1819, is the oldest provincial legislature building in Canada. Visitors can take a guided tour through the Red Chamber, the library and the legislative assembly chamber.

The buildings and old warehouses along the Halifax pier, the oldest of their kind in Canada, have been renovated and now form an attractive and harmonious architectural grouping known as **Historic Properties** ★★ **(11)** *(bordered by Duke and Lower Water Streets)*. Numerous shops, restaurants and cafés have set up business here, along with an excellent provincial tourist information office. This is a very popular, pleasant place, whose narrow streets lead to a promenade along the pier. The *Bluenose II* is often moored here during the summer. Built in Lunenberg in 1963, the *Bluenose II* is a replica of the most beloved ship in Canadian history, the *Bluenose*, which sailed the seas from 1921 to 1946 and is depicted on the Canadian ten-cent piece. When it is moored here, the *Bluenose II* offers two-hour cruises in the Halifax harbour. A tour of Halifax's impressive port aboard this or any other ship offering similar excursions is a marvellous way to get to know the city *(for more information, contact the tourist information office, Historic Properties;* ☎ *424-4247)*.

Looking right out onto the harbour, the **Maritime Museum of the Atlantic** ★★ **(12)** *(adults $3; Jun to Sep, Mon 9:30 AM to 5:30 PM, Tue 9:30 AM to 8 PM, Wed to Sat 9:30 AM to 5:30 PM, Sun 1 PM to 5:30 PM; Oct to May, Tue 9:30 AM to 8 PM, Wed to Sat 9:30 AM to 5:30 PM, Sun 1 PM to 5:30 PM; 1675 Lower Water Street, near the port;* ☎ *424-7490)* presents a wonderful exhibition offering a comprehensive overview of the city's naval history. On the ground floor, there is a reconstruction of *William Robertson and Son*, a store that furnished shipowners, shipbuilders and captains with materials for a century. On the same floor, visitors will find an assortment of historical artifacts related to Halifax's military arsenal and a varied collection of small craft, particularly lifeboats. The second floor features an absolutely extraordinary assortment of boat models, from sailboats to steamships. Visitors can also tour the *Acadia*, which is moored at the pier behind the museum. This ship first sailed out of Newcastle-on-Tyne, England back in

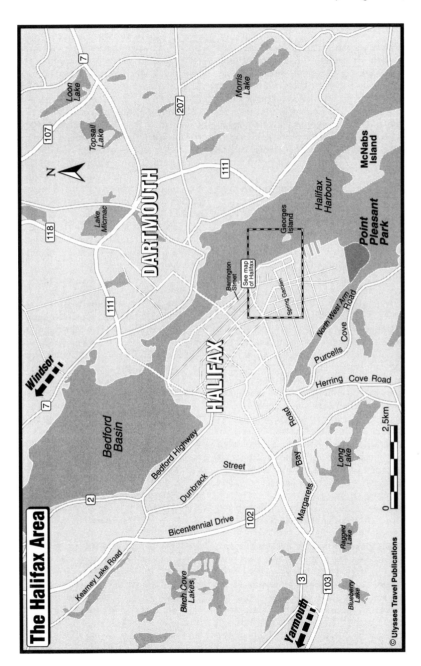

The Halifax Area

7

Loon Lake

107

Topsail Lake

207

Morris Lake

118

Lake Micmac

111

DARTMOUTH

111

N

Windsor

7

Bedford Basin

2

Bedford Highway

Dunbrack Street

Bicentennial Drive

Kearney Lake Road

102

Birch Cove Lakes

HALIFAX

Barrington Street

See map of Halifax

Spring Garden

Georges Island

Halifax Harbour

McNabs Island

Point Pleasant Park

North West Arm Road

Purcells Cove Road

Herring Cove Road

Margarets Bay Road

Long Lake

Ragged Lake

Blueberry Lake

3

103

Yarmouth

0   2,5km

© Ulysses Travel Publications

1913 and spent most of the following 57 years gathering information for charts of the Atlantic coast and the shores of Hudson Bay. The **HMCS Sackville** is a convoy ship that was used in World War II and has now been converted into a museum dedicated to the sailors who served in that war. At the interpretive centre, located in an adjacent building, visitors can view a 15-minute film on the Battle of the Atlantic.

Farther south, on Barrington Street, at the corner of Spring Garden Road, lies the **Old Burying Ground ★ (13)** *(free admission; Jun to Sep, 9 AM to 5 PM; Barrington Street and Spring Garden Road)*, Halifax's first cemetery, which is now considered a national historic site. Some of the old tombstones are veritable works of art. The oldest, marking the grave of John Connor, was erected in 1754. A map containing information on the cemetery is available at St. Paul Church *(Grand Parade)*.

While visiting Halifax, make sure to stroll along **Spring Garden Road ★**, the busiest and most pleasant commercial street in the Maritimes. Lined with all sorts of interesting shops, restaurants and cafés, it looks like the local Latin Quarter. Parallel to Spring Garden Road, but farther north, **Blowers Street** is another attractive artery, flanked by somewhat less conventional shops and businesses.

On the Outskirts of Halifax

Point Pleasant Park ★ *(free admission; Jul to Sep, 10 AM to 6 PM; early Sep to Jun, 10 AM until dark; at the end of Young Avenue)* covers an area of 75 ha on Halifax's south point. Here, visitors will find kilometres of hiking trails along the coast, offering lovely views through the forest. Due to its location at the

entrance of the harbour, Point Pleasant was of great strategic importance to the city for many years. The first Martello tower in North America, now the **Prince of Wales Tower National Historic Site ★** *(free admission; Jul and Aug, Mon to Fri 9 AM to 5 PM, Sat and Sun 10 AM to 4 PM; Sep to Jun, Mon to Fri 9 AM to 4 PM; Point Pleasant Park; ☎ 424-4661)*, was erected here in 1796-97. Drawing inspiration from a supposedly impregnable tower on Corsica's Martello Point, the British erected this type of structure in many places along their country's and colonies' shores. The Prince of Wales Tower was part of Halifax's extensive network of defenses. It now houses a museum, where visitors can learn about its history.

McNabs Island, measuring 4.8 km by 1.2 km and located right at the entrance of the harbour, was also part of the city's defenses. The British erected Fort McNab here between 1888 and 1892, equipping it with what were then the most powerful batteries in all of the city's fortifications. Visitors can examine the vestiges of the structure at the **Fort McNab Historic Site ★** *(☎ 426-5080)*, while enjoying a stroll around this peaceful, pretty island, which features a number of hiking trails. The ferry to McNabs Island leaves from Cable Wharf. For the schedule, contact the tourist information office *(Historic Properties, ☎ 424-4247)*.

Dartmouth

From the pier in front of Historic Properties in Halifax, visitors can take a **ferry** *(adults about $1)* to Dartmouth, on the opposite shore, which offers a splendid view of both the port and McNabs Island. The town of Dartmouth boasts an attractive waterfront, beautiful residences, a variety of shops and restaurants and several tourist attractions, including the **Historic Quaker House** ★ *(free admission; 57-59 Ochterlaney Street)*. This is the only remaining example among some 22 similar houses built around 1785 by Quaker whalers who came to Dartmouth from New England. Guides in period dress tell visitors about the Quaker lifestyle.

■ **Tour B: The Cape Route** ★

This route runs from Amherst to the outskirts of Windsor, skirting round Minas Basin, which is the part of Nova Scotia that extends farthest into the Bay of Fundy. The landscape all along this cape-studded coast is transformed twice a day by the most powerful tides in the world. The tour leads through several peaceful villages and the odd town. One of these, located inland, is Springhill, which has a long mining history.

Amherst

Gateway to Nova Scotia, Amherst is home to several hotels and a large provincial tourist information centre. This site, on the Chignecto Isthmus, first attracted Acadians, who founded a settlement named Beaubassin here in 1672. Controlled by the British since 1713, Beaubassin was abandoned in 1750 by order of the French army, which erected Fort Beauséjour (New Brunswick) several kilometres to the north, on French territory, the following year. The British responded by building Fort Lawrence on the former site of Beaubassin. This fort was abandoned in 1755, after the British captured Fort Beauséjour, an event that heralded the deportation of the Acadians. In 1764, one year after the signing of the Treaty of Paris, under which France ceded all of its North American possessions to Great Britain, colonists from the British

Isles began flooding into the region, where they founded Amherst. This community flourished in the 1880s, when it was integrated into the Canadian rail network. It is now a quiet town with about 10,000 inhabitants. The centre of Amherst boasts several magnificent public buildings made of stone. Visitors will also find the **Cumberland County Museum** *(adults $1; Jun to early Sep, Mon to Sat 9 AM to 5 PM, Sun 2 PM to 5 PM; Jun to early Dec, Tue to Sat 10 AM to 4 PM; Dec to early Mar, Tue to Sat 10 AM to 4 PM; Mar to early Jun, Tue to Sat 10 AM to 4 PM; 150 Church Street; ☎ 667-2561)*, which exhibits an assortment of objects related to local history.

From Amherst, visitors can take Route 242 along the banks of Cumberland Basin and Chignecto Bay. Those who so desire can stop at the **Joggins Fossil Centre** *(adults $3.50 for the centre, $10 for a guided tour of the Fossil Cliff; early Jul to end of Sep; Main Street; ☎ 251-2727)*, which features the world's largest collection of fossils. Visitors can also take a guided tour of a site containing a large number of fossils.

Route 2 and Highway 104 both lead from Amherst to Springhill.

Springhill

Springhill was founded in 1790 by Loyalist colonists who intended to support themselves by farming. The area did not actually develop, however, until 1871, when the Springhill Mining Company's coal mine opened. For nearly a century after, Springhill was one of the largest producers of coal in Nova Scotia. This difficult and dangerous task was not carried out without accidents or loss of life. In 1891, 125 men and boys perished in an accident in one of the galleries, and then two catastrophes, one in 1956, the other in 1958, claimed the lives of 39 and 75 men respectively. After that, several mines remained in operation, but large-scale coal mining came to an end in Springhill. To cap off this string of bad luck, the city was also the victim of two devastating fires (1957 and 1975).

To find out everything there is to know about popular singer Anne Murray, a Springhill native, head to the **Anne Murray Centre** *(adults $5; end of May to early Oct, 9 AM to 5 PM; Main Street; ☎ 597-8614)*. Fans of the singer will be delighted by the exhaustive collection of objects that either belonged to her at one time or summon up key moments in her life and career. Audiovisual aids frequently complement the presentation. Few details have been neglected; the exhibit starts off with a family tree tracing Murray's family origins back two centuries.

The **Springhill Miners' Museum ★★** *(adults $3.50; end of May to early Oct, 9 AM to 5 PM; on Route 2, take Black River Road; ☎ 597-3449)* offers an excellent opportunity to discover what life was like for Springhill's miners. A visit here starts out with a stop at the museum, which explains the evolution of coal mining techniques and tells the often dramatic history of Springhill's mining industry. Visitors are then invited to tour an old gallery.

Continue along Route 2 to Parrsboro

Parrsboro

At the edge of Minas Basin, marking the farthest end of the Bay of Fundy, Parrsboro is a small community graced with several pretty buildings dating back to the last century. The region's often dramatic shoreline, which has been sculpted by the tides, is a treasure-trove for geologists. It is therefore no surprise that Parrsboro was chosen as the location for the **Fundy Geological Museum ★** *(adults $5; early Jun to mid-Oct, Mon to Sat 9:30 AM to 5:30 PM, Sun 1 PM to 5:30 PM; Two Island Road, near the centre of Parrsboro; ☎ 254-3814)*, a provincial museum devoted to the geological history of Nova Scotia and other regions. The exhibits, which include various types of fossils, rocks and stones, are lively and interesting, and have been created with the lay person in mind. There is also a fun video, designed to teach children about geography.

Continue on Route 2 then Highway 104 to Truro.

Truro

Served by the railway since 1858, and now located at the heart of the province's road network, Truro is the region's chief industrial and commercial centre. The town, which has a population of about 12,000, features several historic buildings and numerous shops, restaurants and accommodations. The downtown area lies on either side of the Salmon River, which empties into the Minas Basin farther on. A rather strange natural phenomenon caused by the powerful tides in the Bay of Fundy can be observed here: the **tidal bore ★**, a wave that flows upriver twice a day. In the centre of town, visitors can relax or go for a walk in **Victoria Park ★** *(entrance on Brunswick Street)*, a 400 ha natural park with a stream running through it. There are several waterfalls along the stream.

From Truro, continue along Route 2, then take the 215 towards Maitland.

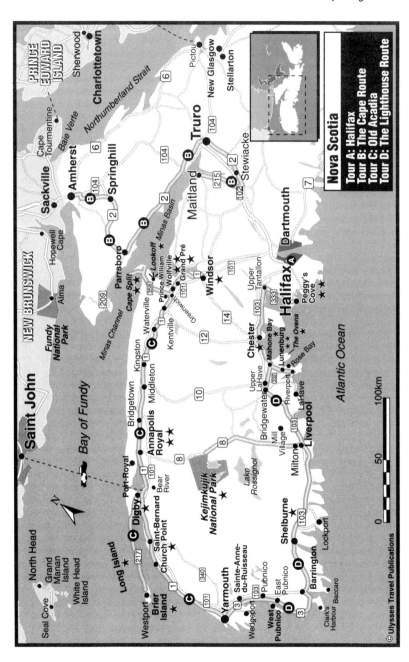

Visitors who don't wish to go to Maitland can reach Windsor quickly by taking Highway 102 and then Highway 101.

Maitland

A major shipbuilding centre in the 19th century, Maitland is now a tiny hamlet with a few lovely residences. It was here that a prosperous local entrepreneur named William D. Lawrence built what proved to be the largest wooden ship in the history of Canada. The *William D. Lawrence*, a magnificent vessel with three 80-m masts, nearly ruined its creator. Completed in 1874, the boat nevertheless ended up enjoying a very successful career, sailing across oceans all around the world.

Today, visitors can tour the **Lawrence House** ★ *(free admission; early Jun to early Sep, 9 AM to 5 PM; Route 215, ☎ 261-2628)*, the entrepreneur's principal residence, built in 1870 at the top of a valley looking out over the bay. Most of the furniture adorning this beautiful house belonged to Lawrence. In one of the rooms, visitors will find a 2-m model of the *William D. Lawrence*.

Continue along the 215 to reach Windsor.

■ Tour C: Old Acadia ★★

The odyssey of the Acadian people began here. In 1605, one year after arriving in North America, Pierre du Gua, Sieur de Monts, accompanied by Samuel de Champlain and several dozen men founded the first permanent European settlement north of Florida, Port-Royal, at the mouth of the Annapolis River. Acadia's development would centre around Port-Royal until 1755, the year the Acadians were deported. In this region, with its mag-

nificent scenery and charming towns and villages, visitors will find a number of historic sites that summon up images of old Acadia.

Windsor ★

The site now occupied by Windsor, at the confluence of the Avon and Sainte-Croix Rivers, was frequented by Micmac Amerindians for many years before being colonized. They referred to it as Pisiquid, meaning "meeting place." Acadians began settling here in 1685 and succeeded in cultivating the land by creating a network of dykes. Although this part of Acadia was ceded to Great Britain under the terms of the Treaty of Utrecht in 1713, the British presence was not felt in the area until Charles Lawrence erected Fort Edward here in 1750. By building the fort, Lawrence was attempting to strengthen Britain's authority over the territory and protect the British from the Acadians. In 1755, about 1000 of the region's Acadians were rounded up here before being deported. During the 19th century, Windsor was an important centre for shipbuilding and the exportation of wood and gypsum. Despite major fires in 1897 and 1924, the town has managed to preserve some lovely residences. It is the starting point of the Evangeline Route.

The **Fort Edward National Historic Site** ★ *(free admission; early Jun to early Sep, 10 AM to 6 PM; in the centre of Windsor; ☎ 542-3631)* consists only of a blockhouse, the oldest fortification of its kind in Canada. This structure is all that remains of Fort Edward, erected in 1750. An interpretive centre provides information on the history of the fort. The site also offers a gorgeous view of the Avon River.

In the 1670s, a small group of Acadians moved from the region of Port-Royal, the first Acadian settlement, founded in 1605, to the fertile land along Minas Basin. These industrious farmers managed to free up excellent grazing grounds alongside the basin by developing a complex system of dykes and aboideaus. The area became relatively prosperous, and its population grew steadily over the following decades.

Not even the signing of the Treaty of Utrecht in 1713, under which France ceded Acadia to Great Britain, could hinder the region's development. Relations between the Acadian colonists and British authorities remained somewhat ambiguous, however. When France and Great Britain were preparing for a final battle for control of North America, the Acadians declared themselves neutral, refusing to swear allegiance to the British crown. The British accepted this compromise at first. However, as the tension mounted between the two colonial powers, the British began to find the Acadians' neutrality more and more irritating.

Various events, such as the surprise attack on the British garrison at Grand-Pré by troops from Québec—with the help, it was suspected, of Acadian collaborators—increased British doubts about the Acadians' sincerity. In 1755, the governor of Nova Scotia, Charles Lawrence, decided to take an extraordinary step, ordering the expulsion of all Acadians. With 5,000 inhabitants, the region along Minas Basin was the most populated part of Acadia, and Grand-Pré the largest community. That year, British troops hastily rounded up the Acadians, confiscated their land and livestock and burned their houses and churches.

The Acadians were put on boats, often separated from their families, and deported. Of the approximately 14,000 colonists living in Acadia at the time, about half were sent away. Some of the ships went down at sea, while others deposited their passengers at ports in North America, Europe and elsewhere. After years of wandering, some of these Acadians, the ancestors of today's Cajuns, found refuge in Louisiana. Those who escaped deportation had to hide, fleeing through the woods to the northeast coast of present-day New Brunswick, all the way to Québec or elsewhere. One thing is for sure: the deportation order issued by Charles Lawrence succeeded in wiping Acadia from the map. In the following years, the land was offered to Planters from New England, who were joined by Loyalists at the end of the American Revolution, in 1783.

Erected in 1835, **Haliburton House ★** *(early Jun to mid-Oct, Mon to Sat 9:30 AM to 5:30 PM, Sun 1 PM to 5:30 PM; Clifton Avenue;* ☎ *798-2815)*, also known as **Clifton House**, was the residence of Thomas Chandler Haliburton (1796-1865), judge, politician, businessman, humorist and successful author. This plain-looking wooden house is adorned with magnificent Victorian furniture. It stands on a large, attractively landscaped piece of property, which covers 10 ha. Haliburton made a name for himself in Canada and elsewhere by writing novels featuring the character Sam Slick, an American merchant who comes to Nova Scotia to sell clocks. Through this colourful character, Haliburton offered a harsh but humorous critique of his fellow Nova Scotians' lack of enterprise. A number of the expressions Haliburton created for his character such as "Truth is stranger than fiction" are commonly used today in both French and English.

Shand House *(early Jun to mid-Oct, Mon to Sat 9:30 AM to 5:30 PM, Sun 1 PM to 5:30 PM; Avon Street;* ☎ *798-8213)*, a fine example of Victorian architecture, was built between 1890 and 1891. The furniture inside belonged to the family of Clifford Shand, the house's original owner.

From Windsor, Route 1 leads to Grand-Pré, then passes through the communities of the Annapolis valley.

Grand-Pré ★

The **Grand-Pré National Historic Site ★★** *(free admission; open all year, church open mid-May to mid-Oct, 9 AM to 6 PM; Route 1 or Route 101, Exit 10;* ☎ *542-3631)* commemorates the tragic deportation of the Acadians. Here, visitors will find a replica of the Acadian church that occupied this site before the Deportation, Église Saint-Charles, which houses a museum. The walls are hung with six large and extremely moving paintings by Robert Picard, depicting life in colonial Acadia and the Deportation. The stained-glass windows, designed by Halifax artist T.E. Smith-Lamothe, show the Acadians being deported at Grand-Pré. Visitors will also find a bust of American author Henry Wadsworth Longfellow and a statue of Evangeline. In 1847, Longfellow wrote a long poem entitled "Evangeline: A Tale of Acadie," which told the story of two lovers separated by the Deportation. The site also includes a smithy and a placard explaining the principal behind the dykes and aboideaus developed by the Acadians before they were expelled from the region.

Wolfville ★★

Wolfville is a charming little university town. Its lovely streets are lined with stately elms concealing sumptuous Victorian residences. The city has about 3,500 permanent residents, while the university, **Acadia University**, founded in 1838, welcomes about 4,000 students a year. With its Victorian atmosphere, excellent cafés and restaurants and magnificent inns, this beautiful town is a perfect place to stay during a tour of the region. Wolfville was founded in 1760, several years after the deportation of the Acadians, by Planters from New England, who were attracted by the excellent farmlands available here. The community was known as Upper Horton and then Mud Creek before being christened Wolfville in honour of local judge Eilsha DeWolf in 1830. Twice a day, from the shores of the small, natural harbour, visitors can observe the effects of the high tides in the Bay of

Fundy. Aboideaus constructed by the Acadians in the 17th century can be seen nearby.

While touring the pretty university campus, take the time to stop in at the **Acadia University Art Gallery** *(free admission; early Jun to mid-Sep, 12 PM to 5 PM; mid-Sep to end of May, Tue 11 AM to 8 PM, Wed to Fri 11 AM to 5 PM, Sat and Sun 12 PM to 4 PM; Beveridge Art Centre, at the corner of Main Street and Highland Avenue; ☎ 542-2202 ext. 1373)*, which often presents interesting exhibitions of contemporary art, as well as works from other periods.

The **Randall House Historical Museum** *(free admission; mid-June to mid-Sep, 10 AM to 5 PM, Sun 2 PM to 5 PM; 161 Main Street; ☎ 684-3876)* displays objects, furniture, paintings and photographs from the region dating from 1760 to the present day.

Continue along Route 1 to Greenwich, then take Route 358 to Port Williams. Once there, turn right and keep going until you reach Starrs Point.

Starrs Point

This prosperous rural region is home to the **Prescott House Museum ★** *(free admission; early Jun to mid-Oct, Mon to Sat 9:30 AM to 5:30 PM, Sun 1 PM to 5:30 PM; near Route 358; ☎ 542-3984)*, a remarkable Georgian style residence erected around 1814. Its first owner was Charles Ramage Prescott, a local businessman and eminent horticulturist, who introduced a variety of new plant species into the province. The interior, decorated with period furniture, is magnificent. Most delightful of all, however, is the little garden, where visitors can stroll about.

Continue along Route 358 towards Cape Split.

The Route to Cape Split ★★

After passing through some of the region's magnificent rolling landscape and picturesque little villages, take a few moments to stop at the **Lookoff ★** *(Route 368)*, which offers an extraordinary view of Minas Basin and the Annapolis valley. Then go to the end of Route 358, where a trail (13 km return) leads to the rocky points of **Cape Split ★★**.

At Cape Split, get back onto Route 1, heading to the right. This road runs along the Annapolis valley to Annapolis Royal, passing through a number of lovely communities founded in the late 18th century along the way. Before reaching Annapolis Royal, turn right.

Port-Royal

In 1604, one year after the king of France granted him a monopoly on the fur trade in Acadia, Pierre du Gua, Sieur de Monts, accompanied by Samuel de Champlain and 80 men, launched the first European attempt to colonize North America north of Florida. In the spring of 1605, after a difficult winter on Île Sainte-Croix, De Monts and his men settled at the mouth of the waterway known today as the Annapolis River, where they founded Port-Royal. From 1605 to 1613, the settlement of Port-Royal occupied the area now known as the Port-Royal National Historic Site. After efforts to colonize this region were abandoned, the capital of Acadia was moved first to La Have (on the Atlantic coast) for several years, and then to the present site of Annapolis Royal.

The **Port-Royal National Historic Site** ★★ *(mid-May to mid-Oct, 9 AM to 6 PM; from Route 1, take the road leading to Granville Ferry; ☎ 532-2898)* is an excellent reconstruction of the small wooden fortification known as "*Abitation*" as it appeared in 1605. It was here that fruitful, cordial relations were established between the French and the Micmacs. This site also witnessed the first performance of the Neptune Theatre and the founding of the first social club in North America, known as *L'Ordre du Bon Temps*. Today, visitors can see the various facilities that enabled the French to survive in North America. Staff in period costume take visitors back to those long-lost days. One of the guides is of Micmac origin and can explain the nature of the relationship between the French and the Micmacs, who were always allies. Acadian visitors can ask to see a map of the region, which shows where each Acadian family resided in the mid-17th century.

The **Annapolis Tidal Project** *(free admission; Route 1, ☎ 532-5454)* is an experimental project where visitors can discover how the powerful tides in the Bay of Fundy can be used to produce electricity. There is a tourist information office here as well.

Annapolis Royal ★★

It was here that Port-Royal, the capital of Acadia, was established in 1635. Because of its advantageous location, the settlement was able to control maritime traffic. In 1710, the British took over the site and renamed the town Annapolis Royal in honour of Queen Anne. Until Halifax was founded in 1749, Annapolis Royal was the capital of the British colony of Nova Scotia. Today, Annapolis Royal is a peaceful village with a rich architectural heritage, graced with residences dating back to the early 18th century. Wandering along its streets is a real pleasure. It is also possible to stay in some of the lovely houses here.

At the **Fort Anne National Historic Site** ★★ *(free admission; mid-May to mid-Oct, 9 AM to 6 PM, until 5 PM the rest of the year; St.George Street; ☎ 532-2397)*, visitors will find an old fort, in the heart of which lie the former officers' quarters, now converted into a historical museum. The exhibition provides a detailed description of all the different stages in the history of the fort, which was French before being taken over by the British. Visitors can enjoy a pleasant stroll around the verdant grounds, which offer a lovely view of the surrounding area.

While in the area, make sure to take a walk in the **Annapolis Royal Historic Gardens** ★★ *(adults $3.50; end of May to mid-Oct, 8 AM until dark; ☎ 532-7018)*, which have been carefully laid out according to British and Acadian horticultural traditions.

Digby ★

A charming town with a picturesque fishing port, Digby lies alongside Annapolis Basin and the Digby Strait, which opens onto the Bay of Fundy. It is known for its scallop fishing fleet, the world's largest. Its port is therefore a very lively place, where visitors will be tempted to linger, fascinated by the coming and going of the boats. Since Digby features a wide range of restaurants and accommodations, it is an excellent place to stay during a tour of the region. Visitors can also head over to Saint John, New Brunswick aboard the ferryboat *MV Princess of Acadia*, which sets out from the port.

From Digby, Route 217 leads to Brier Island.

Long Island and Brier Island ★

Veritable havens of peace, Long Island and Brier Island attract thousands of visitors each year because the waters off their shores are frequented by sea mammals, especially whales, who come to the Bay of Fundy to feed during summertime. Whale-watching cruises set out from Westport (Brier Island) and Tiverton (Long Island) every day during summer.

From Brier Island, visitors have no other option but to head back towards Digby.

Saint-Bernard

Heading out of the very Anglo-Saxon Annapolis Royal valley, visitors will be surprised by the sudden change in the architecture. Case in point, an imposing Catholic church stands in the centre of the little Acadian village of Saint-Bernard. The **Église Saint-Bernard** is a symbol not only of the fervour of the local Catholics, but also of the courage and perseverance of the Acadian people. It was built over a period of 32 years, from 1910 to 1942, by villagers who volunteered their time and effort. From Saint-Bernard to the outskirts of Yarmouth, the coast is studded with more than a dozen Acadian villages. These communities were founded after the Deportation by Acadians who, upon finding their former land around Grand-Pré and Port-Royal occupied by Planters, began settling along this barren coast in 1767.

Pointe-De-l'Église ★

Farther along the coast, the road passes through another little Acadian village, Pointe-de-l'Église (Church Point), which is home to the splendid **Église Sainte-Marie ★**. Built between 1903 and 1905, it is the largest and tallest wooden church in North America. The interior has a very harmonious appearance. Right next-door stands **Université Sainte-Anne**, Nova Scotia's only French-language university, which plays an important cultural role in the province's Acadian community. The university houses a museum containing objects related to the history of the local Acadians. A visit to Pointe-de-l'Église and its surroundings would not be complete without taking the time to eat a *pâté de râpure*, a local dish available at the university snack-bar, among other places.

Yarmouth

Yarmouth was founded in 1761 by colonists from Massachusetts. Life here has always revolved around the town's bustling seaport, which is the largest in western Nova Scotia. Now a major port of entry for visitors from the United States, Yarmouth has a large selection of hotels and restaurants, as well as an excellent **tourist information office** *(288 Main Street)*. Two ferries link Yarmouth to the state of Maine: the *Bluenose (☎ 742-6800)*, which shuttles back and forth between Yarmouth and Bar Harbor all year round, and the *MS Scotia Prince (☎ 1-800-341-7540)*, which offers service between Yarmouth and Portland from the beginning of May to the end of October.

A good way to learn about Maritime history and the town's heritage is to view the extraordinarily rich collection on display at the **Yarmouth Country Museum ★** *($2)*, a small regional museum set up inside a former Presbyterian church. This vast jumble of objects includes miniature replicas of ships, furniture, old paintings, dishes, etc. The museum's most important piece, however, is an octagonal lamp formerly used in the Cape Fourchu lighthouse.

Equally remarkable is the **Firefighters Museum** ★ *($1; Jun, Mon to Sat 9 AM to 5 PM; Jul and Aug, Mon to Sat 9 AM to 9 PM, Sun 10 AM to 5 PM; Sep, 9 AM to 5 PM; Oct to May, Mon to Fri 10 AM to 12 PM and 2 PM to 4 PM; 451 Main Street; ☎ 742-5525)*, which displays two full floors of fire engines. The oldest vehicle, which the firefighters had to pull, dates back to the early 19th century.

Cape Fourchu ★ *(turn left after the hospital and continue for 15 kilometres)* is undeniably less spectacular than Peggy's Cove, but much more peaceful. Its lighthouse, erected in 1839, stands on a rocky promontory. Visitors who arrive at the right time will be able to see Yarmouth's impressive fishing fleet pass by just off shore.

From Yarmouth, head east on Route 3 to begin the Lighthouse Route.

■ Tour D: The Lighthouse Route ★★

This route, which runs along the southwest coast of Nova Scotia, boasts some of the most picturesque scenes in the province. Here, a string of charming villages blends harmoniously into the beautiful, unspoiled natural setting. While exploring the area, visitors will pass through hamlets and fishing ports with wooden houses dating back to the 19th century, when the region enjoyed an era of prosperity due to the local construction of fishing schooners. The tips of rocky capes all along the coast are crowned by silhouettes of lighthouses, the most famous being the one at Peggy's Cove.

A few kilometres east of Yarmouth, the road leads through several little Acadian fishing villages, including **Wedgeport, Sainte-Anne du Ruisseau, West Pubnico** *(Route 335)* and **East Pubnico**. Acadians have been living in this part of Nova Scotia continuously since 1653.

Continue heading east on Route 3.

Barrington

Barrington was founded in 1761 by about a dozen Quaker families from Cape Cod, in the United States. Four years later, the community began building a **Meetinghouse** *(free admission; early Jun to end of Sep, Mon to Sat 9:30 AM to 5:30 PM, Sun 1 PM to 5:30 PM; Route 3)*, to be used for religious services or any other type of gathering. This was the first nonconformist place of worship in Canada. Barrington features another interesting historic site as well, the **Wooden Mill** *(free admission; early Jun to end of Sep, Mon to Sat 9:30 AM to 5:30 PM, Sun 1 PM to 5 PM; Route 3, ☎ 637-2185)*, a mill built in 1884 and originally powered by a waterfall. The Wooden Mill is an interpretive centre where visitors can learn how mills revolutionized the process of weaving wool.

Shelburne ★

Shelburne was founded in 1783, the final year of the American Revolution, when about thirty ships carrying thousands of Loyalists arrived in Nova Scotia. By the following year, the town already had over 10,000 inhabitants, making it one of the most densely populated communities in North America. Today, Shelburne is a peaceful village. **Dock Street** ★, which runs alongside the natural harbour, is flanked by lovely old buildings, which form a harmonious architectural ensemble.

This historic section features several points of interest, including the **Ross Thomson House** *(free admission; early Jun to mid-Oct, 9:30 AM to 5:30 PM; Charlotte Line;* ☎ *875-3141)*, whose general store dates back to the late 19th century. It is furnished in a manner typical of that type of business in those years. In the same neighbourhood, visitors can stop in at the **Dory Shop** *(free admission; mid-Jun to mid-Sep, 9:30 AM to 5:30 PM; Dock Street;* ☎ *875-3219)*, a workshop where fishing vessels were built in the last century. Also noteworthy is the **Shelburne County Museum** *(free admission; mid-May to late Oct; Dock Street;* ☎ *875-3219)*, whose collection deals with the arrival of the Loyalists and the history of shipbuilding in this area, among other subjects.

The lovely beaches nestled along the coast between Shelburne and Liverpool are safe for swimming. Near Port Joli, visitors can also stop at **Kejimkujik Seaside Adjunct National Park** ★ (see p 136), and hike a few kilometres along one of the trails there.

Liverpool

In the late 19th and early 20th centuries, the port of Liverpool was commonly frequented by privateers recruited by Great Britain. Privateers differed from pirates in that they were working in the name of a government, which gave them an official status of some sort, thereby protecting them. After pillaging villages or attacking enemy ships, they had to hand over a part of the booty to their protector.

The **Perkins House** ★ *(adults $1; Jun to mid-Oct, Mon to Sat 9:30 AM to 5:30 PM, Sun 1 PM to 5:30 PM; 105 Main Street;* ☎ *354-4058)* was the home of writer Simeon Perkins, famous for his journal describing life in the colony between 1766 and 1812. The Perkins House, now open to the public, is an example of the Connecticut style and dates back to 1876.

From Liverpool, visitors can set off on an excursion to **Kejimkujik National Park** ★ (see p 136) by taking Route 8.

Those who don't wish to go to Kejimkujik National Park can take Route 3 east to Exit 17, near Mill Village, to get back onto Route 331.

La Have

Christened La Have by Champlain and de Monts, who stayed here for a while in 1604, this little cape was chosen by Isaac de Razilly to be the site of the capital of Acadia from 1632 to 1636. Visitors will now find a monument marking the location of the former Fort Sainte-Marie-de-Grâce, built to protect the little colony. Right nearby, the **Fort Sainte-Marie-de-Grâce Museum** *(free admission; Jun to Aug, 10 AM to 6 PM; Sep, Sat and Sun 1 PM to 5 PM; Route 331)* presents an exhibition on local history and the early days of the colony.

Bridgewater

Located on either side of the La Have River, Bridgewater is a bustling little town with several restaurants and hotels. Visitors can stop at the **DesBrisay Museum** *(free admission; mid-May to end of Sep, Mon to Sat 9 AM to 5 PM, Sun 1 PM to 5 PM; Oct to mid-May, Tue 1 PM to 5 PM, Wed 1 PM to 9 PM, Thu to Sun 1 PM to 5 PM; Jubilee Road;* ☎ *543-4033)*, which houses a collection of objects related to local history and regularly hosts touring exhibitions in a modern space. To learn all there is to know about how the mill revolutionized the wool weaving industry, head to the **Wile Carding Mill** ★ *(free admission; early Jun to end of Sep, Mon to Sat 9:30 AM to 5:30 PM, Sun 1 PM to 5:30 PM; Route 325, at the corner of Pearl Street and Victoria Road;* ☎ *543-4033)*. Guides in period dress offer interesting tours of the mill and explain the various steps involved in weaving wool.

At Upper La Have, take Route 332 towards Riverport and Rose Bay.

Rose Bay

In 1861, gold diggers came to try their luck at **The Ovens Natural Park** ★ *($3; mid-May to mid-Oct, 9 AM to sunset; Route 332;* ☎ *766-4621)*. Little by little, these prospectors abandoned the area, only to be replaced by other inquisitive individuals, who were more attracted by the beauty of the setting than anything else. For many years, the sea has been sculpting the rock of the cliffs here, hollowing out caves, which the water surges into with great force. Paths have been cleared alongside the precipices, affording some magnificent views. Boating excursions make it possible to view the cliffs from the water as well.

Get back on Route 3 near Lunenberg

Lunenburg ★★

Lunenburg is definitely one of the most picturesque fishing ports in the Maritimes. Founded in 1753, it was the second British settlement in Nova Scotia, Halifax being the first. Its original population consisted mainly of "foreign Protestants" from Germany, Montbelliard and Switzerland. German was commonly spoken in Lunenburg up until the end of the last century, and various culinary traditions have survived to the present day. The village occupies a magnificent site on the steep shores of a peninsula with a natural harbour on either side. A number of the colourful houses and buildings here date back to the late 18th and early 19th centuries. In fact, because of the architecture, parts of Lunenburg are somewhat reminiscent of the Old World. A very busy fishing port, Lunenburg also has a long tradition of shipbuilding. The celebrated *Bluenose*, a remarkable schooner never once defeated in 18 years of racing, was built here in 1921. Lunenburg is an extremely pleasant place to visit in the summertime. Its streets are lined with shops selling quality products. The art galleries are particularly interesting. The atmosphere here is also enlivened by all sorts of activities, including the **Nova Scotia Fisheries Exhibition and Fisherman Reunion**, a celebration of the world of fishing, which has been held each year at the end of August since 1916.

The **Fisheries Museum of the Atlantic** ★★ *(adults $5; mid-May to mid-Oct, 9:30 AM to 5:30 PM; on the waterfront;* ☎ *634-4794)*, set up inside an old fish-processing plant, commemorates the heritage of the fishermen of the Atlantic provinces. Visitors will find an exhaustive, three-floor introduction to the world of fishing, including an aquarium, an exhibit on the 400-year history of fishing in the Grand Banks of Newfoundland, a workshop where an artisan can be observed building a small fishing boat, an exhibit on whaling and another on the history of the *Bluenose*, etc. Three ships are tied to the pier behind the building, including the *Theresa E. Connor*, a schooner built in Lunenburg in 1938 and used for fishing on the Banks for a quarter of a century.

Expect to spend at least three hours for full tour of the museum.

Make sure to take the opportunity to visit the little fishing hamlet of **Blue Rock** ★, located a short distance from Lunenburg. Peaceful and picturesque, this handful of houses lies on a rocky cape overlooking the ocean.

Continue heading east on Route 3.

Mahone Bay ★

Mahone Bay is easily recognizable by its three churches, each more than a century old, built side by side facing the bay. Like Lunenburg, it was first settled by "Protestant foreigners" in 1754, and like a number of other communities on the Atlantic coast, its port served as a refuge for privateers. Until 1812, these individuals pillaged enemy ships and villages, while paying British authorities to protect them. Later, until the end of the 19th century, Mahone Bay enjoyed a period of great prosperity due to fishing and shipbuilding. The lovely old houses lining the streets of the village bear witness to this golden era. Mahone Bay has a pretty sailing harbour and several good inns and bed & breakfasts. Visitors can also go to the **Settlers Museum** *(free admission; mid-May to early Sep, Tue to Sat 10 AM to 5 PM, Sun 1 PM to 5 PM; 578 Main Street;* ☎ *624-6263)*, which features a collection of antique furniture, dishes and other old objects from the area. The house itself dates back to 1850.

Continue along Route 3.

Chester ★

Chester was founded in the 1760s by families from New England. It has been a popular vacation spot since the begin-ning of the last century. Many well-heeled residents of Halifax have secondary homes here, and visitors will find a number of quality hotels and restaurants, an 18-hole golf course, three sailing harbours, several craft shops and a theatre, the **Chester Playhouse**. Perched atop a promontory overlooking Monroe Bay, Chester cuts a fine figure with its lovely residences and magnificent trees.

From Chester, Route 12 leads to the **Ross Farm Museum** ★ *(adults $2; early Jun to mid-Oct, 9:30 AM to 5:30 PM; New Ross;* ☎ *689-2210)*, a 23 ha farm inhabited by five successive generations of the Ross family from 1916 onwards. Guides in period dress liven up the museum, which has about 10 buildings typical of those found on large farms in the 19th century.

At Upper Tantallon, take Route 333.

Peggy's Cove ★★

The picturesque appearance of the tiny coastal village of Peggy's Cove has charmed many a painter and photographer. The little port, protected from turbulent waters, is lined with warehouses standing on piles. Farther along, visitors can stroll across the blocks of granite that serve as a base for the famous lighthouse of Peggy's Cove, which houses a post office during summertime. It is best to be careful when walking here, especially when the water is rough. On the way out of Peggy's Cove, visitors can stop at the **William F. deGarthe Memorial Provincial Park** ★ to see a sculpture of 32 fishermen, along with their wives and children, carved into a rock face 30 m long. William de Garthe, who spent five years creating this sculpture, was fascinated by the beauty of Peggy's Cove, where he lived from 1955 until his death in 1983, and by the lifestyle and courage of the local fishermen.

■ Tour E: Cape Breton Island ★★★

Northeast of Nova Scotia, lie the charming villages, untouched forests and rugged cliffs of Cape Breton Island. The the meeting of land and sea will take your breath away. The island was discovered in 1497 by John Cabot, and colonized quite early by the French, who settled here in the 17th century. They called the island Île Royale. In 1713, Acadia was ceded to Great Britain under the Treaty of Utrecht. France compensated for this loss by accelerating development on Île Royale, most importantly by building the Fortress of Louisbourg in 1719. Acadian villages also sprang up along the north shore of Île Royale. The island did not remain under French rule, however, and finally ended up in the hands of the English in 1758. Louisbourg was destroyed two years later, in 1760. Since rebuilt, the fortress ranks among the most impressive historic sites in Eastern Canada.

In addition to its historic sites, Cape Breton boasts marvellous stretches of wilderness, to the delight of countless nature lovers each year. One of these is Cape Breton Highlands National Park, with its hiking trails and spectacular vantage points. The Cabot Trail is the best way to enjoy and appreciate the beauty of Cape Breton Island. This steep winding road makes a complete circle around the island, passing through dense forests and charming villages along the way. No visit to Nova Scotia would be complete without seeing Cape Breton Island.

From Halifax to Cape Breton Island

The quickest way to get to Cape Breton Island is via Highway 102, and then the TransCanada to Port Hastings. The island is also accessible by taking Highway 7 which follows the Atlantic Ocean.

The route passes through peaceful rural communities and a few fishing ports, among them Musquodoboit Harbour with its superb stretches of sand at **Martinique Beach.**

Sherbrooke

A handful of quaint little houses make up this tiny hamlet of 397 people, but it is the fishing in the St. Mary's River, flowing nearby, that attract most travellers. Take time also to visit the **Sherbrooke Village** *($4; early Jun to mid-Oct, 9:30 AM to 5:30 PM; ☎ 522-2400, ⇄ 522-2974)*, a reconstruction of a 1860-1880 village. Guides in period costume lead tours of the thirty buildings.

Continue on Route 211, then Route 316 until it intersects with Highway 16. Continue towards Canso.

Canso

The post of Canso was established on this site as of 1605 because of the protection from strong ocean currents afforded it by Grassy Island, and because of its location at the entrace to Chedabucto Bay. The town is a departure point for visits to the **Grassy Island National Historic Site** *(free admission; early Jun to mid-Sep, 10 AM to 6 PM, boat departs at 11 AM, second departure Jul and Aug at 2 PM; Box 159, Baddeck, B0E 1B0, ☎ 295-2069)*. An integral part of the fishery during the 18th century, the region of Canso was coveted by many and the object of dispute between the English and the French. At the Canso **Visitor Reception Centre** a short film on the colonization

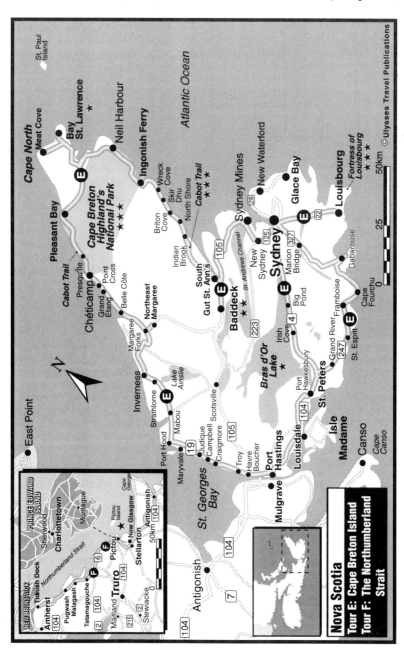

© Ulysses Travel Publications

Nova Scotia
Tour E: Cape Breton Island
Tour F: The Northumberland Strait

of Grassy Island and its eventual destruction in 1744, can be viewed. Visitors can then take a boat to the island, where an interpretive trail leads to eight attractions.

Regain the TransCanada by Highway 16.

Port Hastings

The small town of Port Hastings is the gateway to Cape Breton Island. Although not a particularly pretty town, it is a major crossroads for travellers, with highways leading to both Baddeck and Sydney. Port Hastings does offer many practical facilities, including restaurants, service stations and most importantly, a tourist information office (see p 108).

Head towards Sydney via Highway 4. At Louisdale, you can take Route 320 to get to Isle Madame.

Isle Madame

This tranquil peninsula covers an area of 42.5 km² and has some nice picnic areas. Isle Madame was settled by the Acadians and a francophone presence still remains today.

Go back to Highway 4 and continue towards Sydney.

St. Peters

St. Peters is situated on the narrow strip of land that separates the Atlantic Ocean from Bras d'Or Lake. Colonists settled here in 1630 and built a fort called Fort Saint-Pierre. About twenty years later, Nicolas Denys took over the fort and turned it into a trading and fishing post. To learn more about this French pioneer, visit the **Nicolas Denys Museum** *($0.50; Jun to Sep, open everyday 9 AM to 5 PM).*

The trading post developed gradually, but business really began to take off when 140 years ago, a canal was dug between Bras d'Or Lake and the ocean to provide a passage for boats. Each year, many ships (maximum tonnage 4.88 t) can be seen passing through the canal from the park on either side. An outdoor display shows how the locks work.

Bras d'Or Lake ★

Bras d'Or Lake is an inland sea with 960 km of shoreline. It thus occupies a good part of the island, dividing it into two areas, the Cape Breton Lowlands and Highlands. This vast expanse of salt water attracts many animal species, including the magnificent bald eagle which can be seen on occasion. For those who like to fish, trout and salmon abound in the lake and its many channels (St. Andrews Channel, St. Patrick Channel).

Native peoples have long been attracted to the shores of this lake with its abundance of fish. It was the Micmac Amerindians who established themselves permanently here. Their presence remains constant to this day on the four reserves that have been created—the Whycocomagh, Eskasoni, Wagmatcook and Chapel Island. Besides the reserves, there are several villages around the lake, including St. Peters. The **Bras d'Or Scenic Drive ★** *(follow the signs marked with a bald eagle)* goes all the way around the lake.

From St. Peters to Sydney

The fastest way to Sydney is along Highway 4.

The road to Sydney passes through small towns along the shores of Bras d'Or Lake. It also goes through the Chapel Island Micmac Reserve.

Another option: from St. Peters, take Route 247 along the ocean. At Marion Bridge take Route 327 which goes to Sydney.

This road winds along the coast and passes through several charming fishing villages, including l'Archevêque. Unfortunately, the road is in poor condition.

Sydney

With a population of 25,000, Sydney is the largest town in the area. J.F.W. DesBarres, a Loyalist from the United States, founded the town in 1785. A few years later, Scottish immigrants settled here. Sydney grew quickly at the beginning of the century, when coal-mining industries were established here. Coal-mining is still Sydney's primary industry. The town has all the services necessary to accommodate visitors and is a good place to stop for a rest before going on to Louisbourg. Otherwise, Sydney offers few attractions.

Cossit House *(Jun to mid-Oct, 9:30 AM to 5:30 PM; 75 Charlotte Street, ☎ 539-7973)* is the oldest house in town. Restored and decorated with period furniture, it looks just as it did long ago. Guides dressed in period costume lead tours through the house and are available to answer any questions.

Nearby, also on Charlotte Street, is the **Jost House** *(Jul and Aug, Mon to Sat 10 AM to 4 PM; Sep to Jun, Tue to Fri 10 AM to 4 PM, Sun 1 PM to 4 PM; 54 Charlotte Street, ☎ 539-0366)*, which was the home of a rich merchant.

To find out more about Sydney's history, visit **St. Patrick's Church** *(87 Esplanade)*. Built in 1828, this Catholic church is the oldest in Cape Breton. It features an exhibit on the town's past.

Take Highway 22 to Louisbourg.

Louisbourg

Visitors are drawn to Louisbourg because of the nearby Fortress of Louisbourg, the area's main attraction. Many of the local businesses, including hotels, motels and restaurants, are geared towards tourists. It takes a full day to see the fortress, while the town itself offers few attractions.

The **Fortress of Louisbourg** ★★★ *(adults $6.50, children $3.25, family $16; Jun and Sep 9:30 AM to 5 PM, Jul and Aug 9 AM to 6 PM; ☎ 733-2280)* was built at a strategic point at the water's edge, from where enemy ships could be seen and attacks could be countered. The fortress is ideally-located since it was built outside of the town itself and is removed from all the modern development. It has therefore been easier to recreate the atmosphere of the fledgling French colony back in 1744. Cars are not permitted close to the fortress, and a bus provides transportation to the site.

During the 18th century, France and England fought over territory in America. The French lost Acadia, which then became Nova Scotia. It was during this turbulent period in 1719, that French authorities decided to build a fortified city on Île Royale and began construction of the Fortress of Louisbourg. As the most complex system of fortifications in New France, this undertaking presented some major challenges.

Besides being a military stronghold, Louisbourg was also a fishing port and a commercial centre. Within a short time, its population had grown to 2,000 inhabitants. Everything was designed to enable colonists and soldiers to adjust to their new environment and barracks, houses and garrisons were all erected. Nevertheless conditions were rough, and colonists sometimes had difficulty adapting. Despite the hardships, the colony grew and local business flourished.

The French presence on Île Royale was a thorn in the side of the English colonies stationed further south. In 1744, when war was declared in Europe between France and England, the Louisbourg garrison took advantage of its position to attack the English villages in the area and thus take over an English outpost. The situation incensed the English in New England, and provoked William Shirley, governor of Massachusetts, to send his troops to attack the offending French bastion in 1745. Four thousand New England soldiers ventured an attack on the Fortress of Louisbourg, which was said to be impenetrable. Despite this reputation, the French troops were under-equipped and poorly organized. They had never even imagined such an attack possible, and could not defend themselves. After a six week-long siege, the Louisbourg authorities surrendered to the British troops.

A few years later, in 1748, Louisbourg was returned to France when the two nations signed a peace treaty. Life carried on in the fortress, and within a year, Louisbourg was as active as ever before. This renewed prosperity was short-lived, however, since in 1758 the fortress was conquered once and for all by the British troops, thus ending the French presence in the area.

Hardly 10 years after this conquest, the fortress was left to ruin, and only much later was it rebuilt. Today, almost one quarter of the fortress has been restored, and during the summer, people dressed in period costume bring it to life again, recreating the Louisbourg of long ago. There are soldiers, a baker baking bread and a fisherman with his family. The scene is most convincing, and a stroll down the streets of this old French fortress is a fascinating experience.

To get to Glace Bay, go back to Sydney, and from there take Highway 4.

Glace Bay

Glace Bay lies on the Atlantic coast. The area is rich in coal which forms the base of Glace Bay's industry. The name of this town is of French origin and refers to the pieces of ice *(glace)* that can be seen drifting along the coast. This small town, which has a population of about 20,000, features two interesting attractions.

Guglielmo Marconi (1874-1937) became famous for proving that it was possible to send messages using a wireless telegraph. At the age of 22, Marconi had already developed a wireless station from which a message could be sent over a short distance. In 1902, he sent the first trans-Atlantic message from his transmitting station at Table Head. At the **Marconi National Historic Site ★** *(free admission; Jun to mid-Sep, 10 AM to 6 PM)* visitors can learn about Marconi's discoveries and see his work table, as well as the radio station from which the first message was sent.

Alexander Graham Bell was born in 1847 in Edinburgh, Scotland. He settled in Canada, in Brantford, Ontario with his parents in 1870. From very early on, the brilliant inventor was interested, like his father, in teaching sign language to the deaf. Bell's research led him to teach at the University of Boston, where he trained teachers to work with the deaf. He created an artificial ear that could record sounds, and this led to his invention of the telephone in 1876. Bell became rich and famous, and spent a number of years with his wife Mabel, herself deaf, at his summer home in Baddeck (Nova Scotia), where he continued to do research in various fields.

The Glace Bay area's mining industry dates back many years. As long ago as 1790, French soldiers from Louisbourg were already coming to Port Morien for coal. The industry really took off at the beginning of the 20th century, when mines were dug here, most importantly at New Waterford. Today, Glace Bay produces more coal than any other town in Eastern Canada.

To learn more about this industry, visit the **Miner's Museum** ★★ *(adults $2.75; Jun to early Sep, 10 AM to 6 PM, Tue until 7 PM; rest of the year Mon to Fri 9 AM to 4 PM; 42 Birkley Street, ☎ 849-4522)*, which has exhibits showing the various tools and techniques used in coal mining. There is also a recreation of a typical mining town from the beginning of the century.

Finally, the most fascinating part of the museum is a guided tour of a coal mine.

Go back to Sydney via Highway 4. To reach Baddeck, take Route 125, then take the TransCanada (Highway 105).

Baddeck ★★

Baddeck is a charming village, perfect for taking a stroll or enjoying a bite to eat on a terrace. Whether you decide to stay for a few days to enjoy the comfortable hotels and calm atmosphere, or simply stop for a few hours before heading off on the Cabot Trail, Baddeck offers many attractions that make it worth the detour. One fascinating sight is the summer home of the inventor Alexander Graham Bell.

The **Alexander Graham Bell National Historic Site** ★★ *(adults $2; Jul and Aug, 9 AM to 8 PM; Sep, 9 AM to 6 PM; rest of the year, 9 AM to 5 PM; town's east exit, Chebucto Street ☎ 295-1512)*. Many of Bell's inventions are on display, as are the instruments he used in his research. Bell's life story is also told. Visitors will learn, for example that after teaching sign language for many years, he created an artificial ear that recorded sounds. This experiment led to his invention of the telephone.

From Baddeck, the Cabot Trail is the only road that goes around this part of the island. Take this route north towards Ingonish.

The Cabot Trail ★★★

The Cabot Trail follows steep precipitous cliffs that plunge out over the Atlantic Ocean, and passes through some picturesque little villages. Leaving Baddeck, the road follows the shore before climbing up to the plateau on the north end of the island. The many lookouts along this road offer magnificent panoramic views. It's worth taking the time to stop and appreciate the wild beauty of the landscape, where a restless sea with steep hills and a dense forest are home to a variety of animal species.

The first village after Baddeck is tiny **South Gut St. Ann's**, home to the **Gaelic College**, an institution devoted to the survival of Gaelic culture in North America. Courses are offered in Gaelic language, singing and bagpipe playing.

The road continues along the coast to **Ingonish Ferry**, where it starts climbing the vast plateau occupying the north end of the island at an elevation of 366 m. The natural scenery grows increasingly spectacular. **Cape Breton Highlands National Park** ★★★ (see p 136) begins near here. The park spreads over 950 km² and features many hiking trails through the forest.

At Cape North, the road heads back south, but you can contiunue further north by taking the small road to Meat Cove.

This road leads first to a charming fishing village called **Bay St. Lawrence** ★. Built at the water's edge, the village has little wooden houses and a picturesque port, where cormorants can be seen gliding above the waves. The road climbs along the **cliffs** ★★ and winds its way to **Meat Cove**, a perfect place to stop for a picnic and enjoy the **superb view** ★ over the ocean waves.

To get back on the Cabot Trail, you will have to retrace your steps.

The road continues west. From Cape North to Pleasant Bay, visitors can gaze at the canyon formed by the sides of the hills. The **view** ★★ is stunning.

The plateau ends near Petit Étang. The road heads back down and follows the Gulf of St. Lawrence to the Acadian region of Cape Breton. The landscape is surprising, as forests and steep cliffs give way to a barren plateau studded with Acadian villages. Among these is Chéticamp, a quiet village with simple little houses and a fishing port. It is a departure point for seal and whale-watching excursions. More villages with French names follow, including Grand Étang, Saint-Joseph du Moine, Cap-Lemoine and Belle Côte.

The west part of the Cabot Trail ends at Margaree Harbour. You can continue your journey by cutting across the plateau to return to Baddeck. The highlight along this route is the **Margaree Salmon Museum** *(adults $0.50, mid-Jun to mid-Aug, 9 AM to 5 PM; ☎ 248-2848)* in **Northeast Margaree**. The museum displays the various implements used for salmon fishing.

To leave Cape Breton Island from Baddeck, take the TransCanada (Highway 105). You can also continue along the west coast of the island.

Ceildish Trail

The road along the west coast of the island leads to the Ceildish Trail. This region was settled by Scots, and vestiges of Gaelic culture still remain. Here, the warm waters wash up against a few of the island's beautiful beaches, especially near Mabou. There are a number of modest little villages along the Gulf of St. Lawrence. A few kilometres past Mabou is the **Glenora Distillery**, which recently began producing a single malt whisky.

This road leads to Port Hastings, where you can get back on the TransCanada again.

■ **Tour F: The Northumberland Strait** ★

A few historic villages and towns lie tucked along the coast of the Northumberland Strait between Cape Breton and the New Brunswick border. The first Scottish settlers arrived here at the end of the 18th century. There are also several lovely beaches, washed by the warmest waters in the province. In fact, because of the Gulf Stream, the Northumberland Strait has the warmest waters north of the Carolinas in the United States.

Antigonish

Antigonish is a small town, home to the lovely buildings of **St. Francis Xavier University**, founded in 1853. Like Pictou, Antigonish welcomes many Scottish colonists from the 1770s onwards. The Highland Games, a huge celebration of traditional Scottish music, dance and sports, have been held here since 1861. Since Antigonish lies at the intersection of several major thoroughfares, it does have a few places to spend the night, as well as a number of restaurants and shops.

Melmerby Beach

Near New Glasgow, Route 289 leads to **Melmerby Beach Provincial Park**, which has some picnic areas and a lovely beach.

Pictou ★

Pictou has a symbolic importance in Nova Scotia's history. This is where the *Hector*, a ship carrying the first Scottish settlers to Nova Scotia, dropped anchor. Many Scots later followed, seduced by the climate and geography reminiscent of home. They colonized other parts of the coast and Cape Breton Island. Pictou's lively downtown streets are lined by handsome buildings dating back to those early years of colonization. A ferry service runs between Caribou, just beside Pictou, to Wood Islands, on Prince Edward Island. Not far away, **Caribou Provincial Park** has a beautiful beach that is perfect for swimming.

Hector Heritage Quay ★ *($3.50; Jun to mid-Oct 10 AM to 8 PM; downtown, at the port,* ☎ *485-8028)* is an interpretive centre devoted to the history of the *Hector*, the schooner that carried the first Scottish settlers to Pictou in 1773. The exhibition is very thorough. Behind the building, visitors can watch artisans reconstructing an exact replica of the *Hector*.

The **McCulloch House** ★ *(free admission; early Jun to mid-Oct, Mon to Sat 9:30 AM to 5:30 PM, Sun 1:30 PM to 5:30 PM; Old Haliburton Road,* ☎ *485-4563)* is a modest house that was built in 1806 for Reverend Thomas McCulloch, one of the most influential people in the Pictou area at the time. The house is furnished with original pieces.

Housed in the old railway station, the **Northumberland Fisheries Museum** ★ *(free admission; end of Jun to early Sep; Front Street)* contains a collection of items related to the history of fishing in this region, and features an authentic fishing hut.

Tatamagouche

Less than two kilometres east of this little community, lies **Tatamagouche Provincial Park** where the warm waters of the Northumberland Strait are great for swimming.

Malagash

Malagash is home to one of Nova Scotia's two vineyards. Make sure to stop at **Jost Vineyards** *(free admission; mid-May to mid-Oct; Route 2, ☎ 257-2636)* for some wine-tasting. The Jost family, originally from the Rhine Valley in Germany, came to Canada in 1970.

Pugwash

Pugwash is a popular vacation spot. **Gulf Shore Provincial Park**, located about five kilometres north of the village, has a long beach ideal for swimming

Tidnish Dock

Tidnish Dock Provincial Park has a small beach which is good for swimming.

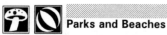 **Parks and Beaches**

There are two magnificent national parks in Nova Scotia: Cape Breton Highlands National Park, on the northern part of Cape Breton Island, and Kejimkujik National Park, in the very heart of the province. Visitors will also find more than a hundred provincial parks, that are smaller in size but offer access to picnic areas, campsites and beaches.

■ Parks

Kejimkujik and Cape Breton Highlands are the two largest parks in the province. Veritable sanctuaries, they welcome large numbers of visitors, who come here to indulge in a variety of outdoor activities and enjoy the beautiful, unspoiled natural setting.

Kejimkujik National Park ★★ *($5 per day; mid-Jun to mid-Oct; P.O. Box 236, Maitland Bridge, BOT 1BO; ☎ 682-2772)* covers 381 km² in the heart of Nova Scotia. Crisscrossed by peaceful rivers teeming with fish, this territory was once inhabited by Micmac tribes, who established their hunting and fishing camp here. It is still considered a prime location for canoeing. The park also features camping sites, a pleasant beach (Merrymakedge) and various trails leading into the forest.

A part of the park, **Kejimkujik Seaside Adjunct National Park ★**, stretches 22 km along the shoreline, near Port Mouton. The landscape here is more rugged than in the rest of the park. Although the area is bordered by steep cliffs sculpted by glaciers, there are a few coves nestled here and there, with sandy beaches tucked inside. Trails have been cleared to enable visitors to explore the park and observe the local plant and animal life; seals can sometimes be spotted along the shore.

Created in 1936, **Cape Breton Highlands National Park ★★★** protects 950 km2 of wilderness inhabited by moose and bald eagles. A wide range of activities are offered throughout this the oldest park in Eastern Canada, with just about everything an outdoor-enthusiast could desire: magnificent views, a forest inhabited by fascinating animal life, 27 hiking trails, beaches, campsites and even a golf course.

■ Beaches

Sandy beaches that are ideal for swimming can be found in various parts of Nova Scotia. Two regions have pleasant beaches: the north coast of the province, along the Northumberland Strait, where the shore is washed by delightfully warm waters, and the

Atlantic coastline. A number of provincial parks have been established in order to protect these areas, and we have selected some of those with the loveliest beaches.

A particularly noteworthy spot on the north coast of the island, along the Northumberland Strait, is **Lavilette Beach**, a ribbon of white sand stretching 1.5 km and located within the park of the same name. Visitors can also head to **Blomidon Park**, which boasts a superb red sand beach.

There are some beautiful beaches along the Sunrise Trail, including those in **Amherst Shore** *(Route 366, west of Northport)*, **Gulf Shore** *(5 km north of Pugwash)*, **Heather** *(Port Howe)*, **Caribou** *(near Pictou)* and **Pomquit Beach** *(on the road north of Pomquet)* Provincial Parks.

On Cape Breton Island, there are also lovely beaches near Mabou and in **Trout Brook Park**, **Inverness** and **Ingonish**.

On the south coast of Nova Scotia, visitors will find a number of gorgeous sandy beaches washed by the Atlantic Ocean at **Martinique Beach Provincial Park** *(11 km south of Musquodoboit)*, whose beach stretches 3 km, **Clam Harbour Beach Provincial Park** *(Lake Charlotte)* and **Taylor Head Provincial Park** *(east of Spry Bay)*.

There are some large beaches on the southwest coast as well, the most noteworthy being **Sand Hills Beach** and **Queensland Beach**.

 Outdoor Activities

 Bicycling

Many visitors decide to tour Nova Scotia by bicycle, either bringing their own or renting one in Halifax or Sydney. Here are a few places that offer rentals:

Halifax

Atlantic Canada Bicycle Rally
Box 1555
B3J 2Y3
☎ 469-1253

Cape Breton

Open Horizons Cycling
Auberge Gisèle Country Inn
Box 132
Baddeck
B0E 1B0
☎ 295-2849

Sea Spray Cycle Center
R.R. 2
Dingwall
B0C 1G0
☎ 383-2732 or 1-800-265-7779

 Hiking

Visitors to Nova Scotia can enjoy the use of many trails leading into the heart of superb natural settings or offering lovely views of the coast. The government publishes a book on these trails entitled *Hiking Trails of Nova Scotia*, which is available by contacting:

Nova Scotia Government Bookstore
Box 367
1700 Granville Street
Halifax
B3J 2T3
☎ 424-7580

Visitors can also obtain a copy of a pamphlet entitled *Walking in Nova Scotia* by calling ☎ 1-800-448-3400.

Kejimkujik National Park has 14 trails ideal for the entire family. These lead through the woods, offering an opportunity to observe the local plant and animal life. Moree difficult trails are located in the part of the park that runs along the shore.

Visitors can explore **Cape Breton Highlands National Park** by hiking along one of its 27 trails. There is something for everyone here, from short trails that take about twenty minutes to long excursions leading to the top of steep hills. The tourist information centre distributes a pamphlet entitled *Walking in the Highlands*.

Those interested in joining an organized hiking expedition can contact:

Highland Hiking Expeditions
R.R. 2
Dingwall
B0C 1G0
☎ 383-2933

Several provincial parks feature lovely hiking trails. **Delaps Cove** has three trails covering a total of 15 km and leading to the Bay of Fundy and into the surrounding forests, while **Blomidon Park** has 16 km of maintained trails. The beautiful trails in **Taylor Head Park** are also worth mentioning.

Some parks include nature trails near salt-water marshes, revealing various facets of the animal life inhabiting these areas. The trail in **Sand Hill Park** is particularly pleasant.

To see some lovely waterfalls while you're walking about, head to **Victoria Park** in Truro.

 Bird-watching

Cormorants, bald eagles, Atlantic puffins, kingfishers and great blue herons are just a few of the bird species that can be observed in Nova Scotia. These animals can be found in many of the province's parks; in order to spot them, visitors need only arm themselves with a pair of binoculars and bit of patience. Various species can be spotted in the following areas:

Migrating geese stop in Nova Scotia, and are often spotted at McElmon's Pond.

Bald eagles come to Caddel Rapids Lookoff for fish during winter.

The salt-water marshes in Martinique Beach Park (south of Musquodoboit) attract large numbers of shorebirds, making the area a treasure trove for amateur ornithologists.

Cape Breton is another excellent location for bird-watching. From cormorants and kingfishers to impressive bald eagles, a variety of species can be spotted near the coast, around Bras d'Or Lake and in Cape Breton Highlands National Park.

 Whale-watching

Every year, whales come to the Gulf of St. Lawrence and the waters south of the island, in the Atlantic Ocean. During this period, visitors can take part in one of the whale-watching expeditions organized by various local companies (approx. 3 h).

Lunenburg Whale Watching Tours
Box 475
Lunenburg
☎ 525-7175

Brier Island Whale & Seabird Cruises *(two departures daily)*
Westport
☎ 839-2995

Pirate's Cove *(adults $33; two departures daily 9 AM and 1 PM)*
Tiverton
☎ 839-2242

Cape Breton

Atlantic Whale Watch *(adults $20, children $10; departures at 10 AM, 1:30 PM and 4:30 PM)*
Ingonish Beach
☎ 285-2320

Whale Watch *(adults $25, children $12; departures at 10:15 AM, 1:30 PM and 4:30 PM)*
Bay St. Lawrence
☎ 383-2981

Aspy Bay Tour *(departures at 9:30 AM, 1 PM and 4:30 PM)*
Box 87
Dingwall
☎ 383-2847

Pleasant Bay *(adults $24, children $10; Jul and Aug, departures at 9 AM, 1 PM and 6 PM)*
☎ 224-1315

Seaside Whale & Nature Watch *(adults $25, children $10; three departures daily)*
Laurie's Motor Inn
Chéticamp
☎ 224-3376 or 1-800-95-WHALE

Whale Cruisers *(adults $25, children $10; Jul and Aug, departures at 9 AM, 1 PM and 6 PM)*
Grand Étang
☎ 224-3376

 Canoeing

The best place to go canoeing in Nova Scotia is undoubtedly **Kejimkujik National Park**, which is crisscrossed by scores of rivers that are easily accessible with these vessels. From amateurs interested in short excursions to more experienced canoeists, everyone can enjoy this thrilling activity here. Canoes may be rented at Jakes Landing *($3 an hour, $15 a day)*.

Before setting out on an excursion, it is important to have all necessary maps and information. Visitors can purchase maps of all seven of the rivers that can be canoed in Nova Scotia, including Musquodoboit and St. Mary's. This information is available at:

Canoe Nova Scotia
5516 Spring Garden Road
Box 3010
South Halifax
B3J 3G6
☎ 425-5450

Land Registration and Information Service
Box 310
Amherst
B4H 3Z5
☎ 667-7231

The Trail Shop
6260 Quinpool Road
Halifax
B3J 1A3
☎ 423-8736

A number of outfits organize canoe and kayak trips in various parts of Nova Scotia

Adventure Outdoor Recreation Service
Box 7, Site 9, R.R. 3
Middleton
B0S 1P0
☎ 825-2589

Spring Haven Canoe Outfitting
Box 156, R.R. 3
Tusket
B0W 3M0
☎ 648-0146

Kayak Cape Breton
R.R. 2
West Bay
B0E 3K0
☎ 535-3060

Coastal Adventure (sea-kayaking)
Box 77
Tangier
B0J 3H0
☎ 772-2774

 Fishing

This sport can be enjoyed in many of the province's parks, since several, including **Porters Lake Park** (west of the Porter Lake Route) and **Kejimkujik National Park**, have lovely rivers full of fish. Others, such as **Sherbrooke Park** (on the banks of St. Mary's River) are known for their salmon. Bras d'Or Lake, on Cape Breton Island, is another choice spot for fishing. Don't forget to obtain a fishing license, available from the Department of Natural Resources.

Fishing in the parks requires a special permit, which can be obtained at the welcome centre of the park in question. A special permit is also required for salmon fishing. For more information on regulations, contact:

Department of Natural Resources
Box 68
Truro
B2N 5B8

For inquiries regarding salmon fishing:

Department of Fisheries and Oceans
Box 550
Halifax
☎ 426-5952

 Deep-Sea Fishing

Various outfits organize deep-sea fishing expeditions. Participants are provided with all necessary equipment and instruction.

Whale Island *(adults $25, children $12)*
Ingonish
☎ 285-2338 or 1-800-565-3808
⇄ 285-2338

Deep-Sea Fishing Chéticamp *(adults $25, children $12)*
P.O. Box 221
Chéticamp
B0E 1H0
☎ 224-3606

 Golf

Nova Scotia boasts a number of superb golf courses. We can't possibly list them all, but here are a few of the more noteworthy ones:

There are lovely 18-hole courses near Chester and Digby.

In Cape Breton Highlands National Park, visitors will find the magnificent Highland Links *(Ingonish, ☎ 285-2600)*, which ranks among Nova Scotia's most spectacular golf courses.

 Cross-Country Skiing

Both national parks, **Kejimkujik** and **Cape Breton Highlands**, include cross-country trails, stretching 43 km and 55 km respectively. Heated shelters have been set up along the way.

 Downhill Skiing

Although Nova Scotia has very few mountains, visitors can still find a handful of small ski resorts here. **Keltic Cape Smokey** *(☎ 285-2778)*, at Ingonish Bay, has the highest vertical drop (305 m). There is another resort in Antigonish, **Ski Wentworth** *(☎ 548-2089)*.

 Snowmobiling

Nova Scotia is crisscrossed by scores of snowmobile trails. Clubs have been set up all over the province in order to meet the needs of snowmobilers.

For more information, contact:

Snowmobile Association of Nova Scotia
Box 30010
South Halifax
B3J 3G6
☎ 425-5450

 Accommodation

■ **Tour A: Halifax**

Several hundred metres from the train station and about fifteen minutes by foot from the city's main attractions, the **Halifax Heritage House Hostel** *($12.75 for members, $15.75 for non-members; 1253 Barrington Street, B3J 1Y3, ☎ 422-3863)* is part of the International Youth Hostel Federation. A pretty, historic building, it can accommodate about 50 people and is equipped with a kitchenette.

A number of other institutions offer inexpensive accommodation. During summer, rooms are available in the residence halls at **Dalhousie University** *($29 for a single room, $43 for a double room; front desk Howe Hall, 6136 University Avenue, B3H 4J5, ☎ 494-2108, 494-3831 or 494-8840)*, **St. Mary's University** *($25 for a single room. $45 for a double room; 923 Robie Street, B3H 3C3, ☎ 420-5591)* and the **Technical University of Nova Scotia** *($25 for a single room, $40 for a double room; 527 Morris Street, ⇄ 420-2628)*. Students are usually offered a discount. Rooms are also available at the **YMCA** *($28 for a single room, $38 for a double room; 1565 South Park Street, ⇄ 425-0155)* and the **YWCA** *($32 for a single room, $47 for a double room; 1239 Barrington Street, ⇄ 423-7761)*. The latter accepts women only.

The **Lord Nelson Hotel** *($49; 174 rooms, tv; 1515 South Park Street. B3J 2T3, ☎ 423-6331 or 1-800-565-2020, ⇄ 423-7148)* appears to have seen better days, but still offers many advantages. Located in an extremely lively section of Halifax, it stands opposite the magnificent Public Gardens, just steps away from Spring Garden Road, the city's busiest commercial artery, and a short distance from several colleges and universities. The smallest rooms rank among the least expensive in Halifax. Although modestly furnished and a bit outdated in appearance, they nevertheless offer an acceptable level of comfort. The Lord Nelson's impressive entrance hall, with its coffered ceiling, is a vestige of the *belle époque*. This is a good option for travellers on a limited budget.

The **Waverley Inn** (*$55; 32 rooms, tv, ℜ; 1266 Barrington Street, B3J 1Y5, tel 423-9346, ⇄ 425-0167)* boasts a rich tradition of hospitality dating back more than a century. This sumptuous house, built in 1865-66, was the personal residence of wealthy Halifax merchant Edward W. Chipman until 1870, when a reversal of fortune plunged him into bankruptcy. A few years later, sisters Sarah and Jane Romans purchased the house for the sum of $14,200. In October 1876, the Waverley Inn threw open its doors and was considered the most prestigious hotel in the city for several decades to follow. It has welcomed many famous individuals, including English author Oscar Wilde, who stayed here in 1882. Despite the passing of time, the Waverley Inn has managed to preserve most of its original grandeur. Of course, it is no longer as luxurious, since its rooms, decorated in a rather heavy style, are now outmoded according to modern standards of comfort. However, this inn is sure to interest visitors seeking a truly authentic Victorian atmosphere. The price of the room includes breakfast and an evening snack. The Waverley Inn is located near the train station, about fifteen minutes' walk from the city's major attractions.

Comfortable but somewhat lacking in charm, the **Citadel Inn Halifax** (*$79; 270 rooms, tv, ℜ, ≈; 1960 Brunswick Street, B3J 2G7, ☎ 422-1391 or 1-800-565-7162, ⇄ 429-6672)* is attractively located just a stone's throw away from the Citadel. Guests have access to an indoor pool and a gym, as well as a dining room and a bar. Breakfast is included in the price of the room. Furthermore, the parking is free, which is a real bonus in Halifax.

Halliburton House Inn (*$90; 30 rooms, tv, ℜ; 5184 Morris Street, B3J 1B3; ☎ 420-0658, ⇄ 423-2324)* lies tucked away on a quiet residential street near the train station, just a short distance from Halifax's main attractions. A pleasant, elegant place, it offers an interesting alternative to the large downtown hotels. In terms of comfort, Halliburton House Inn has all angles covered. The pleasant rooms are well-decorated and adorned with period furniture, giving them a lot of character. There are also several lovely common rooms, including a small living room to the left of the entrance, a library and an elegant dining room where guests can enjoy excellent cuisine (breakfast is included in the price of the room). The inn's three buildings look out on a peaceful, pretty garden full of flowers, where guests can sit at a table beneath a parasol. Halliburton House Inn, erected in 1809, was originally the home of Sir Brenton Halliburton, chief justice of the Supreme Court of Nova Scotia.

An elegant building located just steps away from Historic Properties, the **Delta Barrington** (*$89; 201 rooms, tv, ℜ, ≈; 1875 Barrington Street, B3J 3L6, ☎ 429-7410 or in Canada 1-800-268-1133 or in the United States 1-800-877-1133, ⇄ 420-6524)* looks out on a lively neighbourhood full of shops, restaurants and outdoor terraces. The rooms are a bit old-fashioned but nevertheless decently furnished and comfortable.

The **Prince George Hotel** *($100; 200 rooms, tv, ℜ, ≈; 1725 Market Street, B3J 3N9, ☎ 425-1086 or 1-800-565-1567, ⇄ 429-6048)* offers excellent accommodation in rooms that are quite attractively furnished and luxurious. Located right near the World Trade and Convention Centre, this place is particularly popular among businesspeople, and features a conference room that can accommodate up to 200 people. The hotel terrace offers a splendid view of the city.

A member of the Canadian Pacific hotel chain, the **Chateau Halifax** *($105; 300 rooms, tv, ℜ, ≈; 1990 Barrington Street, B3J 1P2, ☎ 425-6700 or 1-800-441-1414, ⇄ 425-6214)* offers superior accommodation in spacious, sober and very comfortably furnished rooms. The friendly, pleasant hotel bar, Sam Slick's Lounge, is a perfect spot to enjoy a drink with friends or hold an informal meeting. The Chateau features an indoor pool and numerous sports facilities. It allows access to a shopping centre containing stores and restaurants, and lies just minutes away from the city's main sights and the World Trade and Convention Centre.

Halifax is home to a good number of luxury hotels. None of these, however, boasts a more spectacular or enchanting site than the **Sheraton Halifax** *($165; 353 rooms, tv, ℜ, ≈; 1919 Upper Water Street, B3J 3J5, ☎ 421-1700 or 1-800-325-3535, ⇄ 422-5805)*, located right on the pier, next to Historic Properties. Furthermore, particular care was taken to ensure that the building would blend harmoniously with its surroundings, which make up the oldest part of the city. The rooms are spacious, well-decorated and inviting. There are two restaurants in the hotel, one of which, the Harbourfront, offers a magnificent view of the port and becomes a bar in the evening. The Sheraton is also equipped with conference rooms, an indoor pool and several other athletic facilities.

■ **Tour B: The Cape Route**

Amherst

If you are driving in from New Brunswick, this is the first town you will pass through. It is a good place to stay overnight, since there are several motels here, most situated alongside the big access roads. The inexpensive **Victorian Motel** *($38; 20 rooms, pb, tv; 150 East Victoria Street, B4H 1Y3, ☎ 667-7211)*, located downtown, is a good option for travellers on a limited budget. Rooms are clean and quiet, if not exactly charming. The rooms at the **Journey's End Motel** *($52; 60 rooms, pb, tv; 143 South Albion Street, B4H 2X2, ☎ 667-0404 or 1-800-668-4200)*, located near the downtown area, shopping malls and fast food restaurants, offer a standard level of comfort, perfect for businesspeople or travellers stopping for the night.

Springhill

Although Springhill has little to offer in terms of accommodation, visitors can stay at the **Rollways Motel** *($36; 12 rooms, pb, tv; 9 Church Street, B0M 1X0, ☎ 597-3713)*, whose rooms are decent, but no more than that.

Truro

Located at the heart of Nova Scotia's road network, Truro has several hotels and motels belonging to big North

American chains known for providing decent rooms at reasonable rates. One of these is the **Howard Johnson** *($50; 40 rooms, C, R, tv, pb; 165 Willow Street, B2N 4Z9, ☎ 893-9413, ⇄ 897-9937)*, which offers comfortable rooms, some equipped with a kitchenette. In the same category, is the **Journey's End Motel** *($63; 81 rooms, tv; 12 Meadow Drive, B2N 5V4, ☎ 893-0330 or 1-800-668-4200)*, whose modern rooms are well-suited to the needs of businesspeople.

■ **Tour C: Old Acadia**

Windsor

Not far from the centre of town, visitors will find the **Hampshire Court Motel** *($50; tv; 1080 King Street, B0N 2T0, ☎ 798-3133)*, a rather charming place set in the midst of a pretty, peaceful garden. The rooms are pleasant and well-kept. Small cottages are also available for rent.

Wolfville

The charming village of Wolfville boasts several high-quality, luxurious establishments, most of which are located along Main Street. One of these, **Victoria's Historic Inn** *($60; 18 rooms, tv, pb; 416 Main Street, B0P 1X0, ☎ 542-5744)*, harks back to another era. A lovely residence dating from 1893, it has been renovated in order to make the rooms more comfortable and improve the decor. Furthermore, all of the rooms include a private bath. The inn is adjoined by a motel with several rooms.

The superb **Tattingstone Inn** *($80; 10 rooms, ≈, △, R, pb; 434 Main Street, B0P 1X0, ☎ 542-7696, ⇄ 542-4427)* offers tastefully decorated rooms, some containing 18th-century furniture. The accent here is on comfort and elegance. Guests can stay in one of two buildings; the main residence has the most luxurious rooms.

At the elegant **Blomidon Inn** *($80; 26 rooms, R, pb, tv; 127 Main Street, B0P 1X0, ☎ 542-2291 or 1-800-565-2291, ⇄ 542-7461)*, visitors can stay in a sumptuous manor built in 1877. At the time, costly materials were used to embellish the residence, which still features marble fireplaces and a superb staircase made of carved wood. This place has all the ingredients of a top-quality establishment: a splendid dining room where guests can enjoy refined cuisine; impeccable, friendly service and richly decorated sitting rooms. This majestic building stands in the centre of a large property bordered by stately elms. The Blomindon Inn is a veritable symbol of Nova Scotian hospitality. All of the rooms are adorned with antique furniture and include a private bath.

Annapolis Royal

Several bed & breakfasts and excellent inns offer visitors the pleasure of staying in the heart of Annapolis Royal, one of the oldest towns in North America. One of these is the **Garrison House Inn** *($48; 7 rooms, C, pb and cb; 350 George Street, B0S 1A0, ☎ 532-5750, ⇄ 532-5501)*, a charming 19th-century house attractively located in the centre of town. Its seven rooms are pretty and well-kept; a few of them have no private bath, however.

Digby

Digby is a sizeable vacation spot with a number of impressive hotel complexes. Visitors can, however, find clean, inexpensive rooms here. Two options are the **Siesta Motel** *($44; 15 rooms, pb, tv; 81 Montague Row, B0V 1A0, ☎ 245-2568, ⇄ 245-2025)* and the nearby **Seawind Motel** *($55; 7 rooms, tv, pb; 90 Montague Row, B0V 1A0, ☎ 245-2573).* Both have the advantage of being located alongside Digby's natural harbour, just a few minutes' walk from most of the local restaurants.

The impressive **Pines Resort Hotel** *($130; 87 rooms, ≈, ℂ, tv, pb; Shore Road, B0V 1A0, ☎ 245-2511 or 1-800-667-4637, ⇄ 245-6133)* stands on a hill overlooking the bay, in a lovely natural setting. Every part of this hotel was conceived to ensure an excellent stay, from the superb interior design and pretty, comfortable rooms to the excellent restaurant and inviting bar. Guests also have access to a wide range of athletic facilities, including tennis courts, a swimming pool and a gym; there is also a golf course nearby.

Westport

On Brier Island, visitors can stay at the **Brier Island Lodge** *($60; pb and cb, ℂ, tv; P.O. Box 1197, B0V 1H0, ☎ 839-2300, ⇄ 839-2006)*, which stands on the edge of a cliff, offering a stunning view of St. Mary's Bay and Westport. This is a delightfully peaceful place set in the heart of the countryside. The rooms meet modern standards of comfort.

Mavilette Beach Park

Driving along the coast between Digby and Yarmouth, visitors will pass through several Acadian communities. The **Cape View Motel and Cottages** *($45; 20 rooms, tv, pb, ℂ; Salmon River, B0W 2Y0, ☎ 645-2258)* lies near one of these villages, alongside a beach. This is not a very luxurious place, but the rooms are well-kept and decently furnished. The region itself is conducive to relaxation, and visitors can enjoy pleasant strolls along the beach.

Yarmouth

The **Midtown Motel** *($46; 21 rooms, tv; 13 Parade Street, B5A 3A5, ☎ 742-5333)* is a handsome, two-story building with large porches where guests can sit and relax. It is located in a peaceful, pleasant residential area in the heart of town, not far from the museum. The rooms are decent.

At the entrance to town, on the way in from Digby, the **Best Western Mermaid Motel** *($79; 45 rooms, tv, 545 Main Street, B5A 1J6, ☎ 742-7821)* offers comfortable accommodation. Its restaurant, Captain Kelly's, located five houses north, is a good place to eat in Yarmouth.

The **Rood Colony Harbour Inn** *($81; 65 rooms, tv, ℜ; 6 Forest Street, B5A 3K7, ☎ 742-9194 or 1-800-565-7633)* lies directly opposite the boarding point for the ferry to Maine. Since it is located on the side of a hill, there is a lovely view from the back. The rooms are spacious and well-designed. The bar is a pleasant place for a drink.

■ Tour D: The Lighthouse Route

Shelburne

Toddle Inn Bed & Breakfast *($40; 4 rooms, ℜ; at the corner of Water and King Streets, B0T 1W0, ☎ 875-3229)* is a pretty residence with a dining room on the ground floor. This place has a lot of charm.

For inexpensive accommodation, opt for the peaceful **Cape Cod Colony Motel** *($46; 23 rooms, tv; 235 Water Street, B0T 1W0, ☎ 875-3411)*, which has clean, modern rooms and lies just a short walk from Dock Street.

Located in the very heart of Shelburne's historic section, looking out on the harbour, the lovely **Cooper's Inn** *($56; 5 rooms, ℜ; 875 Dock Street, BOT 1W0, ☎ 875-4656)* is one of the oldest residences in town, erected around 1785 by wealthy Loyalist merchant George Gracie. Despite several modifications, including the addition of private baths to each room, the building's original character has been largely preserved. Guests will especially appreciate the period decor and the old furniture in the rooms.

Summerville Beach

The extremely appealing **Quarterdeck Cabins** *($65; 15 rooms, ℜ, tv; Route 3, Exit 20 off of Highway 103, BOT 1T0, ☎ 683-2998, ⇄ 683-2998)* consists of fifteen rooms, some in cabins and others in a motel-style building looking out onto a long and lovely sandy beach. The cabins all have two or three rooms, making them ideal for families or groups of friends. It is easy to feel at home in these rustic-looking rooms, where you'll be rocked to sleep by the sound of waves crashing on the rocky beach. A very convivial, relaxing atmosphere prevails at the Quarterdeck, which also features a good restaurant.

White Point

The **White Point Beach Resort** *($85; 47 rooms, tv, ℜ, ≈; Route 3. Exit 20A or 21 off of Highway 103, BOT 1G0, ☎ 354-2711 or 1-800-565-5068)* offers luxurious modern accommodation in small cottages or in a large building facing directly onto a beach that stretches a kilometre and a half. The complex is attractive, and has been carefully and tastefully laid out in order to

make the most of the beautiful surroundings. In addition to swimming at the beach or in the pool, visitors can play golf or tennis or go fishing. The bar, which offers a magnificent view of the ocean, is especially pleasant.

Liverpool

Lanes Privateer Inn *($53; 27 rooms, ℜ, tv; 27 Bristol Avenue, BOT 1K0, ☎ 354-3456, ⇄ 354-7220)* offers clean, modestly decorated rooms at reasonable rates. It is well-located alongside the Mersey River, on the shore opposite the centre of town. After the local bed & breakfasts, this is one of the least expensive places in the area.

Bridgewater

Bridgewater has several modern motels, including the **Auberge Wandlyn Inn** *($57; 74 rooms, ℜ, tv, ≈; 50 North Street, B4V 2W6, ☎ 543-7131 or 1-800-561-0000, ⇄ 543-7170)*, whose rooms have little charm but are clean and well laid-out. The Wandlyn Inn, like other establishments in Bridgewater, has the advantage of being a half-hour drive from Lunenburg, where the choice of accommodations is sometimes limited during the summer.

Lunenburg

A superb Victorian house dating from 1888, **Boscawen Inn** *($50; 7 rooms, ℜ; 150 Cumberland, B0J 2C0, ☎ 634-3325)* lies in the heart of Lunenburg, on the side of the hill overlooking the port. The location is spectacular, and the pleasant terrace offers an unimpeded view of the town's historic section. Guests can also relax in one of three sitting rooms, which, like all the other rooms in the house, are adorned with period furniture.

A visit to Lunenburg offers an opportunity to discover the old-fashioned charm of the town's numerous 19th-century residences, many of which have been converted into pleasant inns. One good, relatively inexpensive option is the **Compass Rose Inn** *($55; 4 rooms, ℜ; 15 King Street, BOJ 2CO, ☎ 1-800-565-8509)*, a lovely Victorian house built around 1825. The decor remains quite typical of that era, when tastes leaned towards heavily furnished rooms. Breakfast is included in the price of the room. In the evening, guests can enjoy a delicious meal in the dining room.

The **Bluenose Lodge** *($65; 9 rooms, ℜ, tv; at the corner of Falkland and Dufferin Avenues, BOJ 2CO, ☎ 634-8851)* is a splendid Victorian house located a few minutes' walk from the centre of Lunenburg. Furnished with antiques, the rooms have a lot of character, and all include a private shower. Guests can enjoy an excellent meal in the dining room on the ground floor. This place is highly prized by individuals who relish an authentic Victorian atmosphere and fine food. Excellent service is a priority here.

The **Brigantine Inn** *($65; 17 rooms, ℜ, tv; 82 Montague Street, BOJ 2CO, ☎ 634-3300)* is extremely well-located in front of the port. Most of the spotless, attractively decorated rooms feature large windows and a balcony with a splendid view. Breakfast is included in the price of the room.

Mahone Bay

The village of Mahone Bay is sure to please visitors with a taste for large 19th-century houses. Some of these residences are now high-quality bed & breakfasts. One of the best is the **Sou'Wester Inn** *($65; 4 rooms;*

788 Main Street, BOJ 2EO, ☎ 624-9296), a magnificent Victorian residence originally owned by a ship-builder. The entire house is furnished in the style of the era in which it was built. Guests are invited to relax on the terrace overlooking the bay.

Chester

Chester has always been a favourite with wealthy families. However, the relatively low prices of the rooms at the **Windjammer Motel** *($45; ℜ, tv, ≈; Route 3, BOJ 1JO; ☎ 275-3567)* help make the local tourist industry a bit more democratic. The rooms, fairly standard for this type of accommodation, have been renovated. The Windjammer lies at the entrance to town on Route 3, on the way in from Mahone Bay.

A charming residence built at the end of the 19th century, the **Mecklenburg Inn** *($59; 4 rooms; 78 Queen Street, BOJ 1JO, ☎ 275-4638)* has adorable rooms, a terrace and a charming sitting room where guests will enjoy relaxing. Breakfast is included in the price of the room, and the dining room is open in the evening.

Visitors who opt for the **Captain House Inn** *($65; 9 rooms, ℜ; 129 Central Street, BOJ 1JO, ☎ 275-3501, ⇄ 275-3502)* will stay in a superb house dating back to the early 19th century. The top-notch rooms have been furnished and decorated with a great deal of taste. In addition to this elegant setting, guests enjoy an outstanding view of the bay. Breakfast is included in the price of the room.

Hubbards

Built high up on the shores of Hubbards' Cove, the **Dauphinee Inn** *($69;*

6 rooms, ℜ, tv; 167 Shore Club Road, BOJ 1TO, ☎ 857-1780, ⇄ 857-9555) is an extremely peaceful place, which offers an opportunity to relax in an enchanting setting. Each room has a wide balcony where guests can sit comfortably and gaze at the boats sailing in and out of the bay. Equipped with a whirlpool, the suites, located on the top floor, are particularly beautiful. In the evening, guests can savour excellent cuisine in the dining room or on the terrace, which is very pleasant at sunset.

■ Tour E: Cape Breton Island

Sydney

Downtown Sydney consists mainly of a few streets alongside the river, and it is here that most of the town's hotels are located. One of these is the **Delta Sydney** (*$69; 152 rooms, ≈, ℜ, tv, ⊘, ◉; 300 Esplanade, B1P 6J4, ☎ 562-7500 or 1-800-268-1133, ⇄ 562-3023*), whose façade looks out on the Sydney River. The rooms are a bit lacking in charm, but thoroughly functional. As a bonus, the hotel features a lovely swimming pool with a slide, a sure hit with the children.

Right next-door stands the **Cambridge Suites Hotel** (*$98; 150 rooms, ≈, C, ℜ, △, ⊘; 380 Esplanade, B1P 1B1, ☎ 562-6500 or 1-800-565-9466, ⇄ 564-6011*), which is about as comfortable as the Delta, although more care has been taken with the decor. The rooms are actually small apartments equipped with a kitchenette.

For charming accommodation in a peaceful environment that is nevertheless close to the downtown area, head to the **Rockinghorse Inn** (*$75; 8 rooms, tv; 259 Kings Road, B1S 1A7, ☎ 539-2696*). This renovated Victorian residence has eight charming rooms, each with its own private bath. Staying here makes it easy to forget that Sydney is an industrial town.

Louisbourg

There are quite a few bed & breakfasts in Louisbourg; a list is available at the tourist information office. In any case, they are easy to spot, since most are identified by a sign.

Another option is the **Motel Louisbourg** (*$45; 45 rooms, tv; 1225 Main Street, BOA 1MO, ☎ 733-2844*), which is not at all picturesque, stretched along the road like every other motel in North America. The rooms are nonetheless decent for the price.

Baddeck

The **Telegraph House** (*$55; 43 rooms, tv, ℜ; 205 Chebucto Street, BOE 1BO, ☎ 295-9988*) is a fine-looking Victorian house set in the heart of town. Its 43 rooms, which have a slightly old-fashioned charm about them, are pleasant and comfortable.

Visitors can enjoy a particularly relaxing atmosphere at one of a handful of charming inns along the waterfront, including **Duffus House** (*$60; 9 rooms, tv; Water Street, BOE 1BO, ☎ 295-2172*), one of the oldest residences in town. Built in the 19th century, it is attractively furnished with antiques and boasts a lovely garden. Each room has its own private bath.

The **Silver Dart Lodge** (*$60; 82 rooms, ≈, tv; Route 205, BOE 1BO, ☎ 295-2340 or 1-800-565-VIEW, ⇄ 295-2484*) and **McNeil House** (*$125; 6 rooms*) share a magnificent park covering some 38 ha and looking out onto beautiful Bras d'Or Lake. Given the exquisitely peaceful setting, this is a perfect place to relax. The Silver Dart has pretty, comfortable rooms and several cottages, some with a fireplace, while the McNeil offers luxurious rooms, some of which also feature a fireplace.

At the cozy **Inverary Inn** *($60; 150 rooms, tv, ℜ; Shore Road, BOE 1B0, ☎ 295-3500 or 1-800-565-5660, ⇄ 295-3527)*, guests can stay either in the main building or in charming little wooden cottages. The decor and the vast grounds give this place a rustic feel well-suited to the Nova Scotian countryside.

Also on the shores of Bras d'Or Lake, offering rooms with a lovely view, the **Auberge Gisèle** *($65; 19 rooms, ≈, △; Route 205, BOE 1B0, ☎ 295-2849, ⇄ 295-2033)* is a good place to keep in mind. Upon arriving, visitors will be enchanted by the pine-bordered lane leading up to this lovely residence, whose rooms are all attractively decorated. There are a few more rooms in a nearby annex.

Ingonish Beach

There are several camping sites in Cape Breton Highlands National Park. Average rates are about $11 for a tent and $17 for a trailer. No reservations.

The **Keltic Lodge** *($175; 98 rooms, ≈, C, tv; Middle Head Peninsula, BOC 1L0, ☎ 285-2880 or 1-800-565-0444, ⇄ 285-2859)* boasts a spectacular location alongside a cliff overlooking the sea. Slightly removed from the access roads, in the heart of a veritable oasis of peace, the Keltic Lodge offers top-notch accommodation just a short distance from the Cabot Trail. The buildings are handsome and the rooms, some of which are in cottages, are both charming and comfortable. The dining room features a gourmet menu.

Dingwall

An excellent place to relax, admire the sea, walk along the beach or set off to explore the Cabot Trail, the **Markland** *($85; C, ℜ, tv; 3 km from Dingwall, BOC 1G0, ☎ 383-2246 or 1-800-565-0000)* offers comfortable accommodation in wooden cottages with a cozy, rustic-looking interior. Each cottage has several rooms equipped with a terrace. The large, grassy piece of land opposite the cottages leads to an untouched beach. The Markland is an ideal spot for couples or families who enjoy a peaceful, secluded setting and wide open spaces. The fine food served in the dining room hits the spot after a long day in the fresh air.

Chéticamp

There are several places to stay in the centre of the Acadian community of Chéticamp. One of these is **Laurie's** *($68; 61 rooms, C, tv; Main Street, BOE 1H0, ☎ 224-2400)*, a motel stretching alongside the Gulf of St. Lawrence. Although the decor is not very original, the rooms are clean and comfortable. If you're famished or just want to enjoy a satisfying meal, don't hesitate to stop in at the motel's dining room, which has a very decent menu. The seafood is especially good.

The **Auberge Doucet** *($60; 8 rooms, tv; on the way out of Chéticamp, BOE 1H0, ☎ 224-3438)*, which stands on a hill at the edge of town, rents out large, comfortable rooms. Although the lay-out of the front garden is somewhat disappointing, the inn boasts a lovely setting and a beautiful view of the Gulf of St. Lawrence.

Margaree Valley

The **Normaway Inn** *($159 1/2p; 28 rooms, ℭ, tv; Margaree Valley, BOE 2CO, ☎ 248-2987 or 1-800-565-9463, ⇄ 248-2600)* has been welcoming vacationers for over 60 years now. The place has a great deal of charm, due to its magnificent garden, which stretches across several hundred hectares, creating a pastoral atmosphere. Appropriately, the main building looks somewhat like a farmhouse. The rooms are located inside this building and in a number of cottages. Some of them include a fireplace and a whirlpool bath. Guests also have access to a cozy living room.

■ **Tour F: The Northumberland Strait**

Antigonish

Well-located in the heart of town, the **Antigonish Wandlyn** *($73; 35 rooms; tv, ℜ; 158 Main Street, ☎ 863-4001 or 1-800-561-0000 from Canada or 1-800-561-0006 from the U.S., ⇄ 863-2672)* offers comfortable accommodation in spacious modern rooms. In terms of the decor, a lot of care has been taken to make the place feel cozy and inviting. The Library Lounge is reminiscent of an English pub.

Pictou

Attractively located on a beach several kilometres from town, the **Pictou Lodge** *($99; 29 rooms, ℜ, tv; Breashore Road, BOK 1HO, ☎ 485-3222, ⇄ 485-4948)* is a comfortable place with a cozy decor, perfect for a short stay in the area.

Located in the heart of Pictou, the **Walker Inn** *($66; 10 rooms, ℜ, tv; 34 Coleraine Street, BOK 1HO, ☎ 425-1433)* is a pretty brick building dating

back to 1865. This place has a great deal of charm. The rooms have been renovated in order to furnish each with a private bath. Breakfast is included in the price of the room.

Tatamagouche

The pretty **Train Station Inn** *($40; 4 rooms, tv; Station Road, BOK 1VO, ☎ 657-3222)* is a former railway station dating back more than a century. Its four rooms, each with a private bath, are adorned with period furniture. Guests have access to a terrace on the second floor.

 Restaurants

■ **Tour A: Halifax**

What a pleasure it is to enjoy an excellent cup of coffee while poring over a book! That's the concept behind the **Trident Booksellers & Café** *($; 1570 Argyle Street, ☎ 423-7100)*, an extremely friendly, airy place located a few steps away from Blowers Street. The menu is limited to an extensive choice of coffees, hot chocolates, teas and, during summertime, cold drinks. A small assortment of pastries tops off the offerings. Newspapers are always available for customers, and books (often second-hand), are sold at modest prices.

A pleasant café with a menu made up of sandwiches, quiche and other light dishes, the **Green Bean Coffeehouse** *($; 5220 Blower Street, ☎ 425-2779)* is a very casual place frequented mainly by young people and university students. The owner, who is Lebanese, serves delightfully full-flavoured espresso.

A good place to stop for a snack or continental breakfast during a stroll along Spring Garden Road, **Grabbajabba** *($; Spring Garden Road, near Birmingham Street)* is a small café that serves excellent capuccino, espresso and other types of coffee. The menu also includes a small assortment of breads, buns, muffins and sandwiches priced at less than $5.

Vegetarians and other fans of vegetarian cuisine will be in their element at the **Satisfaction Feast** *($, 1581 Grafton Street, ☎ 422-3540)*, where the aromas wafting through the air will make your mouth water with expectation. You won't be disappointed, since the chef seems to have unlimited imagination when it comes to preparing meals that are balanced, appetizing and inexpensive. Breakfast is served here. No smoking permitted.

A good place to see and be seen, the **Peddler's Pub** *($; Granville Street, Barrington Place)* serves light, inexpensive meals throughout the day. The food is fairly typical pub fare. Seating is also available on a pleasant terrace.

An unpretentious restaurant boasting a prime location on Blowers Street, **Hungry Hungarian** *($; 5215 Blowers Street, ☎ 423-4264)* is just one example of the cultural diversity of Halifax, the only city in the Maritimes with a significant number of residents who are neither anglophone nor Acadian. A very simply decorated restaurant with slightly wobbly tables and chairs, it offers a menu made up of Hungarian and Eastern European dishes. Guests can enjoy one of a wide selection of imported beers with their meal.

Lyn D's Carribean Deli and Café *($$; 1524 Queen Street)* offers visitors an often all too rare opportunity to discover the flavours (and spices!) of the Caribbean. Many of the dishes, such as Jerk Pork and Jerk Chicken, have been taken from the Jamaican repertoire. The ambiance is relaxed, the music, appropriate and the lay-out, simple but attractive.

Just a few steps away from Historic Properties, **Sweet Basil** *($$; 1866 Upper Water Street, ☎ 425-2133)* is a very good restaurant that serves bistro-style cuisine. The chef outdoes himself concocting delicious dishes prepared and presented in an original manner. Top billing goes to pasta, which is served with fresh, quality ingredients. Both the cuisine and the decor evoke a subtle blend of Latin and modern styles. There is seating outside on the little terrace at the back. This place offers a good quality/price ratio. No smoking allowed.

To satisfy your hunger while enjoying a lovely view of the port, head to **Salty's** *($$; Historic Properties, ☎ 423-6818)* restaurant located right on the pier. The menu is appropriate for the setting, featuring a good selection of seafood. Other dishes are available as well, including steak. Salty's is also a very popular pub.

A well-known Canadian institution, the restaurant **Mother Tucker's** *($$; 1668 Lower Water Street, ☎ 422-4436)* has a branch in Halifax, right near Historic Properties. Mother Tucker's is known mainly for its excellent roast beef, but the menu also lists steak and, on rare occasions, lobster. Brunch is served on Sunday.

A Halifax classic, the **Upper Deck Restaurant** *($$-$$$; Privateer's Warehouse, Historic Properties, ☎ 422-1289)* occupies the top floor of the Privateer's Warehouse. Everything in the restaurant, starting with the nautical decor, reminds guests that the house specialty is seafood. The menu does, however, include steak, chicken and other kinds of meat as well.

Much more than a simple French restaurant, **La Maison Gallant** *($$-$$$; 1541 Birmingham Street, ☎ 492-4339)* offers a whirlwind tour of the flavours of French-speaking America and Europe. The rather eclectic menu includes the great classics of Cajun cuisine (both appetizers and main dishes), family-style and popular cuisine from Acadia and Québec and a variety of French specialties, particularly from Provence. The food is served either in the relaxing atmosphere of the dining room, which has a classic decor, or, when the weather is fair, on the peaceful terrace.

The dining room of the elegant **Halliburton House Inn** *($$$; 5184 Morris Street, ☎ 420-0658)* is a perfect place to enjoy a long, intimate dinner for two or linger over a meal among friends. Furnished in a tasteful, elegant manner, the place has a lot of style and emanates an atmosphere of opulence. Aside from a few exceptions, like the alligator appetizer, the menu is made up of classics, including an excellent *steak au poivre* flambéd with brandy, lamb *à la provençale*, Atlantic salmon and *coquilles Saint-Jacques*.

Set up inside one of the oldest buildings in town, an old school that has now been renovated, the **Five Fishermen** *($$$; 1740 Argyle Street, ☎ 422-4421)* is a great favourite with fish and seafood lovers. Lobster, king of the shellfish, obviously gets top billing on the menu. Other dishes include Atlantic salmon and trout, as well as a variety of steaks. It is worth noting that the kitchen closes later than most others in town, around 11 PM on Sunday and at midnight during the rest of the week. The wine list, furthermore, is very extensive.

■ **Tour C: Old Acadia**

Wolfville

If you're craving a good cup of coffee, head over to the **Coffee Merchant** *($; at the corner of Main and Elm)*, which serves good capuccino and espresso. This is a pleasant place, where it is tempting to linger, reading the newspaper of gazing out the window at the comings and goings of the people on the street. The menu is fairly limited, but nevertheless lists a few sandwiches and muffins.

Frequented by students from the nearby campus, **Al's Deli** *($; 314 Main Street)* is a perfect spot to grab a quick bite to eat. The food, which is served in a nondescript room, consists of various meat and sausage dishes, as well as chicken and lobster rolls. This place is both unpretentious and inexpensive.

The **Blomidon Inn** *($$-$$$; 127 Main Street, ☎ 542-2291)* has two dining rooms—a small, very cozy one in the library and a larger one richly decorated with mahogany chairs. The latter is embellished by a picture window that looks out onto a beautiful landscape. The menu is equally exceptional, featuring such delicious dishes as poached salmon and scallops and salmon Florentine.

Annapolis Royal

After visiting Fort Anne, it is pleasant to sit down and enjoy a refreshment or a light meal at the **Sunshine Café** *($, 274 St. George)*. Big windows make this place bright and cheerful. The coffee is good, and the menu consists of simple, inexpensive and well-prepared dishes.

Digby

For an inexpensive meal, visitors can head to the **Red Raven Pub** *($; 100 Water Street, ☎ 245-5533)*, which serves typical pub fare, such as hamburgers and fried chicken. The menu also includes Digby's famous scallops of course.

At the dining room of the **Pines Resort Hotel** *($$$; Shore Road, ☎ 245-2511)*, visitors will find classic cuisine served in a refined atmosphere. The menu features an excellent Bras d'Or salmon. This restaurant also boasts a well-stocked wine cellar.

■ Tour D: The Lighthouse Route

Shelburne

Claudia's Diner *($; 149 Water Street, ☎ 875-3110)* is a picturesque place with a decor that will take you back a quarter of a century. The food is fairly simple: hamburgers, fries and other similar offerings. Fish dishes are also available.

For family-style cuisine with a Maritime flavour, head to the **Loyalist Inn** *($; 160 Water Street, 975-2343)*, which, in spite of its nondescript dining room, features a good menu. The food is simple—seafood chowders, lobster rolls, poached fish and all sorts of other dishes, especially meat and chicken. This is a good place to enjoy a satisfying meal with the family.

Cooper's Restaurant *($$$; Cooper's Inn, Dock Street, ☎ 875-4656)* offers the elegance and ambiance of a historic house built in 1785 and the flavours of refined regional cuisine. This is also an inn with several magnificent rooms (see p 146).

Summerville Beach

The **Quarterdeck Restaurant** *($$; Route 3, Exit 20 off of Highway 103, ☎ 683-2998)*, located almost right on Summerville Beach, is an excellent spot for fish and seafood. The restaurant, whose large back terrace stands on piles, looks out on the ocean. It is particularly pleasant to sit outside for breakfast. In the evening, guests can eat either on the terrace or in the warm inviting dining room. The food is succulent and the service, friendly and attentive. The Quarterdeck also rents out rooms and cottages looking out onto the beach.

Lunenburg

As far as restaurants and cafés are concerned, there are many little gems tucked away in the streets of Lunenberg. One of these, the **Colonial Marchant** *($; 138 Montague Street)*, is both a craft shop and a friendly café. People come here to savour a relaxing, peaceful atmosphere in a room adorned with beautiful woodwork, while observing the bustling activity at the nearby port.

For a delicious, inexpensive light meal, a good choice is **La Bodega Deli & Café** *($; 116B Montague Street, ☎ 634-4027)*, whose original menu mingles local specialties with dishes from Eastern Europe, the Middle East, India and elsewhere. For example, guests can start off their meal with an appetizer of tabbouleh, followed by a Montréal-style smoked meat sandwich and topped off with a piece of cheesecake and an espresso. La Bodega is also a pleasant place for breakfast, where the great coffee can be enjoyed with a croissant, muffin, etc. This is a friendly spot with a view of the harbour.

The **Bluenose Lodge** *($$; 10 Falkland Avenue, at the corner of Dufferin Avenue, ☎ 634-8851)*, which has been set up inside of a large Victorian house, has a lovely dining room on the ground floor. The menu consists mainly of fish and seafood, The Atlantic salmon and haddock with spinach sauce are especially delicious. The service is both friendly and professional and the staff will readily chat with guests about the world of fishing and the history of Lunenburg.

Lunenburg boasts a magnificent location overlooking a natural harbour. The **Boscawen Inn** *($$; 150 Cumberland Street, ☎ 634-3325)*, a Victorian house standing on the side of a hill, is a good place to appreciate the natural beauty of the surroundings and the harmoniousness of the local architecture. The dining room menu consists mainly of excellent fish and seafood dishes.

During summer, every evening of the week except Monday, the **Lunenburg Dinner Theater** *($$; 116 Montague Street, ☎ 634-4814)* combines dining with entertainment by presenting a musical. The atmosphere is friendly, and guests are sure to have a good laugh.

Chester

A well-known local institution, the **Foc'sle** *($; 42 Queen Street, at the corner of Pleasant)* serves family-style cuisine that is hardly original, but nonetheless satisfying and inexpensive. Since this is one of the oldest taverns in Nova Scotia, people also come here to enjoy a night out.

■ Tour E: Cape Breton Island

Sydney

On Charlotte Street, there are a number of little snack-bars serving hamburgers and fries.

Don't be scared off by the Western look of **Joe's Warehouse** *($$; 424 Charlotte Street, ☎ 539-6686)*, which happens to be a local institution. Although the decor is not exactly sophisticated and the music sounds like what you'd hear in a shopping mall, the atmosphere is still very inviting. In any case, people come to Joe's for the generous portions of delicious prime rib. Seafood is also included on the menu.

The Delta Hotel's restaurant, **Des Barres** *($$; 300 Esplanade, ☎ 562-7500)*, has a very decent menu featuring a fair number of fish dishes. With its large picture windows looking out onto the water, the place also boasts a lovely view. Breakfast served.

Louisbourg

At the fortress, a restaurant has been set up in one of the buildings facing the water. The food is no more than decent, but at least visitors can eat lunch without leaving the site.

Another possibility is the **Grubstake** *($$; ☎ 733-2308)*, whose specialty is seafood. For those who prefer grill or poultry, the menu also lists steak and chicken dishes.

Baddeck

In the centre of the village, visitors will spot a lovely terrace with a few tables on it. This belongs to the charming **Highlandheeler Café** *($; Chebucto*

Street), which serves delicious soups, healthy sandwiches, quiche and all sorts of desserts—everything it takes to put together an excellent picnic. Those who prefer to take advantage of the terrace can eat on the premises.

If you are hungry for lobster, head over to **Baddeck Lobster Suppers** *($$; Ross Street,* ☎ *295-3307)*. The main dish includes a lobster and unlimited seafood chowder, mussels, salad and dessert.

The Silver Dart Lodge (see p 148) is pleasantly located on the shores of Bras d'Or Lake. Its restaurant, **McCurdy's** *($$; Silver Dart Lodge, Shore Road,* ☎ *295-2340)*, which looks out onto this magnificent body of water, offers its guests an unbeatable atmosphere. In addition to the view, people come here to sample the tasty seafood dishes and savour the Scottish cuisine.

Ingonish Beach

The **Purple Thistle Dining Room** *($$$;* ☎ *285-2880)* is the restaurant of the magnificent Keltic Lodge (see p 149). In a refined atmosphere, guests savour a variety of specialties, many of which are made with seafood. The hotel has another, simpler restaurant, the **Atlantic** *($$)*, which is a good place to go for lunch.

Cape North

You can't miss **Morrison's Pioneer Restaurant** *($;* ☎ *383-2051)*, a wooden building located right alongside the road. Despite its modest appearance, it is one of the better family-style restaurants in the area. The food is simple (seafood chowder, beef stew, etc.), but good.

Dingwall

The restaurant of the **Markland Hotel** *($$;* ☎ *383-2246)* has a pine-panelled dining room with a decor that is stylish without being extravagant. The menu is extremely interesting, however; simply reading it over will whet your appetite. The offerings include grilled salmon with Mousseline sauce and grilled filet of pork with plums in a red wine and onion sauce.

Chéticamp

At **Laurie's** *($-$$;* ☎ *224-2400)*, visitors might be surprised to discover that the menu lists both lobster and hamburgers. In fact, this restaurant has something for everyone, in terms of both taste and budget. Guests are offered such succulent dishes as the fisherman's platter, which includes lobster, crab and shrimp. The Acadian staff is as friendly as can be, amiably telling their guests to "enjoy *le repas*."

■ **Tour F: The Northumberland Strait**

Pictou

The **Stone House Café and Pizzeria** *($; 11 Water Street)* is a pleasant place to enjoy a light meal in the historic section of Pictou. When the weather permits, guests can sit on the terrace, which offers a view of the harbour.

Simply perusing the menu at the **Walker Inn** *($$; 34 Coleraine Street,* ☎ *425-1433)* is enough to whet your appetite. There are a few local dishes and the requisite seafood and fish, but most of the specialties are European. The owners are of Swiss origin.

Entertainment

■ **Tour A: Halifax**

Music

Large-scale rock concerts are held at the **Halifax Metro Centre** *(1284 Duke Street, ☎ 451-1221)*. For that matter, when artists of international renown come to the Maritimes, they usually choose to play in Halifax. To know what concerts are scheduled, dial the number indicated above.

Fans of classical music can attend concerts given by the **Symphony Nova Scotia** *(1646 Barrington Street, ☎ 421-7311)*.

Theatre

Halifax's most renowned theatre company, the **Neptune Theatre** *(5216 Sackville Street, ☎ 429-7070)* is devoted to presenting classic plays to the public.

Movie Theatres

The latest American movies are presented at **Famous Players Cinemas** *(5657 Spring Garden Road, ☎ 423-5866)*. Other theatres show popular films, but they are all located outside the downtown area. To see what's playing and when, check the listings in the local newspaper. For less recent movies, head to **Wormwood's Dog & Monkey Cinema** *(2015 Gottingen Street, ☎ 422-3700)*, a repertory theatre.

Dinner Theatres

A dinner theatre, as its name suggests, offers an opportunity to attend a play while eating. Expect light entertainment. There are two of these establishments in Halifax: the **Crafton Street Dinner Theatre** *(1741 Crafton Street, ☎ 425-1961)* and the **Historic Feast Company** *(Simon's Warehouse, Historic Properties, ☎ 420-1840)*.

Pubs

To enjoy traditional Maritime music in an extremely relaxed atmosphere, head to the **Lower Deck Pub** *(Privateer's Warehouse, Historic Properties, ☎ 425-1501)*, a pleasant, friendly place with live music in the evening.

■ **Tour D: The Lighthouse Route**

Chester

During July and August, the **Chester Playhouse** *(about $18; 22 Pleasant Street, ☎ 275-3933)* presents plays and concerts in the evening.

Shopping

■ **Tour A: Halifax**

Without a doubt, the most pleasant place to shop is **Historic Properties** *(bordered by Duke and Lower Water Streets)*, the historic neighbourhood alongside the Halifax wharves. Shops selling crafts and clothing take up a large portion of the space in this harmonious architectural grouping built in the 19th century.

Another enjoyable place to shop is **Granville Promenade** and **Barrington Place Shops** *(on Barrington Street, near Historic Properties)*, two complexes located right near one another. Both are renovated historic buildings. Shoppers can stop for a refreshment on one of the many terraces of the nearby cafés and pubs.

For a pleasant stroll in a lively part of town that looks like the local Latin Quarter, take **Spring Garden Road** *(between Barrington and South Park Streets)*, a large commercial artery lined with cafés, restaurants and numerous shops.

A Selection of Shops

The **Gallery Shop** *(Art Gallery of Nova Scotia, 1741 Hollis, ☎ 424-2836)* offers an excellent selection of local crafts, as well as works by painters, sculptors and other artists from Nova Scotia. Pieces by Micmac artists are also available.

The **Micmac Heritage Gallery** *(Barrington Place Shops, Granville Level, ☎ 422-9509)* is the most impressive gallery dedicated to Micmac arts and crafts in the Maritime Provinces. Articles on display include leather mittens and moccasins, woven baskets, jewelry and paintings.

The **Houston North Gallery** *(Sheraton Hotel, 1919 Upper Water Street)* presents a remarkable collection of Amerindian and Inuit sculptures and paintings.

The **Book Room** *(1664 Granville Street)* is a large store with a wide selection of books published in Canada and abroad. Right nearby, the **Government Bookstore** *(1700 Granville Street)* sells all of the books and publications put out by the government of Nova Scotia. Many of these deal with plant and animal life, geology, history—in short, all sorts of subjects that might interest travellers curious to know more about Nova Scotia.

The **Daily Grind News Stand and Coffee Shop** *(Spring Garden Road, near South Park Street)* has an ample selection of magazines and foreign newspapers. There are tables at the back of the store, where customers can sit down and have a cup of coffee.

■ **Tour D: The Lighthouse Route**

Lunenburg

Visitors interested in Amerindian and Inuit art should make sure to stop in at the **Houston North Gallery** *(110 Montague Street, ☎ 634-8869)*, which displays a remarkable assortment of sculptures and paintings.

■ **Tour E: Cape Breton Island**

Baddeck

In the centre of town, visitors will find the **Village Shops**, which include an attractive craft shop with articles by local artisans.

Cabot Trail

Visitors will find a number of stores selling local and Amerindian crafts along the Cabot Trail. Quilts, wooden sculptures and pottery are among the products available.

■ **Tour F: The Northumberland Strait**

Pictou

Grohmann Knives *(88 Water Street, ☎ 485-4224)* is a family business founded in the 1950s. Their high-quality knives are now sold in many countries around the world.

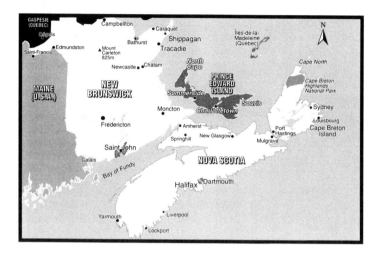

PRINCE EDWARD ISLAND

Think Prince Edward Island and many people envision a rare harmony of rural and maritime landscapes, the epitome of a gentle serene life. Set back from the peaceful roads and tucked away behind rolling valleys of farmland, lie picturesque little fishing villages, adorable white clapboard churches, or the pulsing glow of a lighthouse towering over the sea from isolated rocky outcrops. Most striking in these charming scenes is the brilliant palette of colours: the vibrant yellow and green of the fields falling over the cliffs of deep rust red into the lapis blue of the sea. Bathed to the north by the Gulf of St. Lawrence and to the south by the Strait of Northumberland, this island is above all known for its magnificent white sand dunes and beaches, often deserted and extending between sea and land as far as the eye can see.

It goes without saying that these ribbons of sand are among the most beautiful on the east coast of the continent. They offer great spots for swimming, long walks and discoveries. The beaches may be what initially attracts most visitors, but they quickly discover the many other treasures Prince Edward Island (P.E.I.) has to offer. For starters, the small capital city of Charlottetown, whose architecture and unique atmosphere give it an antique charm; from there the possibilities are virtually endless, the friendliest fresh lobster feasts you can imagine, the storybook world *Anne of Green Gables*, or the richness of the magnificent plants and wildlife of Prince Edward Island National Park.

Prince Edward Island is about 255 km long making it the smallest Canadian province. It was originally christened Île Saint-Jean by the explorer Jacques Cartier who sailed along its shores in 1534. Acadians began colonizing these Micmac Amerindian grounds in 1720, continuing until 1758 when the island fell into British hands, who rechristened it in honour of the son of King George III. As in other Maritime provinces, the shipbuilding years were a veritable golden age that ended in the second half of the 19th century. At the same time, discussions began between the North American British colonies about the possibility of creating a common political structure. It was in Charlottetown in 1864 that delegates of each of these colonies finally met, and three years later that the Dominion of Canada was born as a result of this conference. Today islanders are proud to remind you that their province was literally the birthplace of Canadian Confederation.

Finding Your Way Around

■ By Plane

Visitors arriving on the island by plane, come in to **Sherwood** airport, about 4 km north of downtown Charlottetown *(☎ 566-7992)*. Air Canada *(☎ 894-8825)*, and its partner Air Nova, as well as Canadian Airlines (☎ 892-5358), and its partner Air Atlantic are the major airline companies serving this airport. Four car rental agencies have offices in the airport.

■ By Ferry

There are two ferries from the mainland.

The busiest is the **Marine Atlantic** which links Cape Tourmentine (New Brunswick) to Borden in less than 45 min *(no reservation; car $18, passenger $7; ☎ 902-794-5700; for information in the off-season, ☎ 902-855-2030)*. There is a ferry every hour during the summer.

You can also reach P.E.I. by taking the **Northumberland Ferries** which link Caribou (Nova Scotia) to Wood Islands *(no reservation; car $26, passenger $8.50; ☎ 1-800-565-0201 from Nova Scotia, ☎ 902- 566-3838 from elsewhere)*. The trip takes 75 min. There are 15 ferries per day between 6 AM and 9:50 PM, in the summer.

P.E.I. is also accessible by ferry from the Îles-de-la-Madeleine (Québec) aboard the **Lucy Maud Montgomery** *(car $55, adults $28.75; one ferry per day, reserve if possible; ☎ (418) 986-3278)* which arrives in Souris, near the northeastern point of the island.

Practical Information

■ Area Code: 902

■ Tourist Information

Hotel Reservation Service

Everyday from 8 AM to midnight
☎ 1-800-265-6161

Tourist Information Office

Charlottetown
At the corner of Kent and Queen Streets
☎ 566-5548

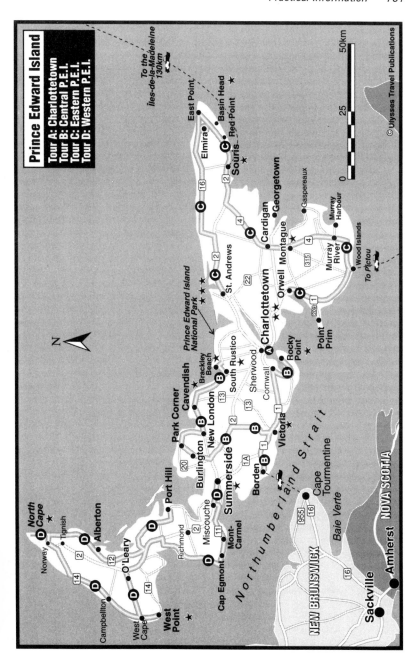

Prince Edward Island

Tour A: Charlottetown
Tour B: Central P.E.I.
Tour C: Eastern P.E.I.
Tour D: Western P.E.I.

© Ulysses Travel Publications

0   25   50km

To the
Îles-de-la-Madeleine
130km

East Point

Basin Head
Red Point
Souris

Elmira

16

2

4

Georgetown

Cardigan

Gaspereaux

Murray
Harbour

4

Orwell   Montague

315   Murray
River

Wood Islands

To Pictou

St. Andrews

2

22

1

209

Point
Prim

Charlottetown

Prince Edward Island
National Park

South Rustico

Sherwood

Rocky
Point

Cornwall

Brackley
Beach

13

Cavendish

Park Corner

New London

2

13

Victoria

1

N

Burlington

20

Summerside

1A

Borden

1

Port Hill

Miscouche

Richmond

2

Mont-
Carmel

11

North
Cape

Tignish

Alberton

Norway

O'Leary

12

Cap Egmont

Campbellton

14

14

West
Cape

West
Point

Northumberland Strait

Cape
Tourmentine

955

16

Baie Verte

NEW BRUNSWICK

16

Sackville

Amherst   NOVA SCOTIA

Emergency

Police: ☎ 368-2677
Royal Canadian Mounted Police
(RCMP): ☎ 566-7111
Hospital: ☎ 566-6111
Poison Control: ☎ 1-800-565-8161

 Exploring

■ **Tour A: Charlottetown**

Charming and quaint, Charlottetown has a unique atmosphere. Despite its size, Charlottetown is not just a small Maritime town like any other; it is also a provincial capital with all the prestige, elegance and institutions one would expect. Though everything here seems decidedly scaled down, the capital of Prince Edward Island has its parliament buildings and sumptuous Lieutenant-Governor's residence, a large complex devoted to the stage and visual arts, pretty parks and rows of trees concealing beautiful Victorian residences, a prestigious hotel and several fine restaurants. Adding to its charm is its picturesque location on the shores of a bay at the confluence of the Hillsborough, North and West Rivers. A meeting place of the Micmac, the site was known to explorers and French colonists in the 18th century. It was not until 1768, however, that the British settlers actually founded the city, named Charlottetown in honour of the wife of King George III of Great Britain. Less than a century later, Charlottetown made its way into history books as the cradle of Canadian Confederation. It was in this little town, in 1864, that the delegates of the North American British colonies met to discuss the creation of the Dominion of Canada.

The **Confederation Arts Centre** ★★ **(1)** *(adults $1; Jul to Aug, 9 AM to 8 PM; Sep to Jun, Mon to Sat 9 AM to 5 PM, Sun 2 PM to 5 PM; Grafton Street, corner Queen Street, ☎ 628-1864)* was constructed in 1964, one century after the decisive meeting of the Fathers of Confederation in Charlottetown. The complex was designed to increase public knowledge of Canadian culture today and its evolution over the last 130 years. The Arts Centre has many facets, including a museum with several impressive exhibits, an art gallery and a public library. There are also several beautiful auditoriums where visitors can take in a performance of *Anne of Green Gables*. Presented every summer for more than three decades, this musical is a fun way to spend an evening in Charlottetown and become immersed in the world of Prince Edward Island's most famous author, Lucy Maud Montgomery.

The **Province House National Historic Site** ★★ **(2)** *(free admission; Jul and Aug, 9 AM to 8 PM; Sep to Jun, Mon to Fri 9 AM to 5 PM; corner of Great George and Richmond Streets, ☎ 566-7626)* can honestly be considered the cradle of Canadian Confederation. It was here that the 23 delegates from United Canada (Ontario and Québec today), Nova Scotia, New Brunswick and Prince Edward Island assembled in 1864 to prepare the Confederation of 1867. Ironically, the host of this decisive conference, Prince Edward Island, did not join the Dominion of Canada until a few years later, in 1873. Visitors can see the rooms where the Canadian Confederation was worked out and watch a short film explaining

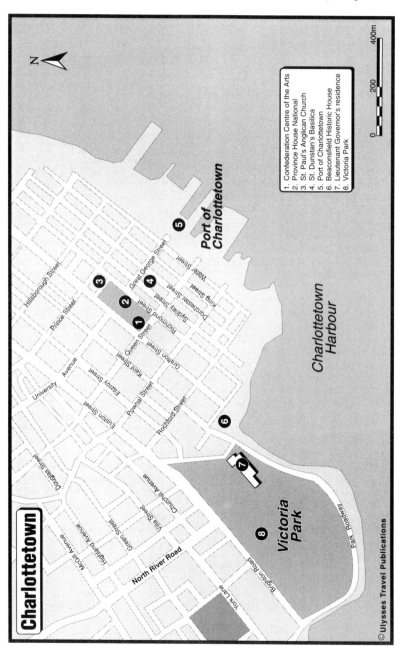

the significance of the event. Province House is now the seat of the Legislative Assembly of Prince Edward Island.

St. Paul's Anglican Church ★ (3) *(free admission; corner of Grafton and Prince Streets)* was erected in 1896 to replace several other Anglican churches built in the previous century. Its interior is splendid, especially the wooden vault and stained-glass windows.

St. Dunstan's Basilica ★ (4) *(free admission; corner of Great George and Sydney Streets)*, a beautiful example of the Gothic style, is the most impressive religious building on Prince Edward Island. Its construction began in 1914, on the same site occupied by three Catholic churches successively during the previous century.

Pretty Great George Street ends up at the small **port of Charlottetown (5)**, a pleasant area where visitors will find not only a park and marina, but also **Peake's Wharf ★** *(at the end of Great George Street)*, a collection of shops in charming renovated old buildings. Close by stands the classy **Prince Edward Hotel** (see p 179), as well as a few restaurants.

Beaconsfield Historic House ★ (6) *(adults $2.50; mid-Jun to early Sep, Tue to Sun 10 AM to 5 PM; Sep to end of Oct, Tue to Fri and Sun 1 PM to 5 PM; early Nov to mid-Jun, Tue to Fri 1 PM to 5 PM; 2 Kent Street, ☎ 368-6600)* was built in 1877 for wealthy shipbuilder James Peake and his wife Edith Haviland Beaconsfield. It is one of the most luxurious residences in the province, with 25 rooms and 9 fireplaces. After James Peake declared personal bankruptcy in 1882, his creditors, the Cunall family, moved in. The

family had no descendants, so Beaconsfield House served as a training school from 1916 on, and was converted into a museum in 1973.

On the other side of Kent Street, shielded behind a stately row of trees, stands the splendid **Lieutenant-Governor's residence (7)** *(corner of Kent Street and Pond Road)*. It has been the official residence of the British crown's representative on Prince Edward Island since 1835. Magnificent, beautifully designed **Victoria Park ★ (8)**, which spreads out before the residence, is a lovely place for a stroll.

■ **Tour B: Central P.E.I.**

This section covers the central region of the island, including the regions known as "Anne's Land" and "Charlotte's Shore". It extends from the southern coast along the Strait of Northumberland, east of Charlottetown to the northern shores on the Gulf of St. Lawrence, and from the town of Malpeque to Tracadie. This beautiful farming region is relatively flat along the southern coast, while towards the northern coast it offers pretty landscapes of valleys and rolling farmland leading to splendid steep cliffs and some of the most beautiful fine sandy beaches of the island. A unique ecosystem makes up an important part of this coastline and is protected in Prince Edward Island National Park.

The northern coast is called "Anne's Land" because it was here, in New London, that Lucy Maud Montgomery was born and it was this idyllic corner of the island that inspired the author to write *Anne of Green Gables*. Montgomery worshippers from around the world can make a virtual pilgrimage to the spots that marked the childhood of the island's biggest star. The southern region, called "Charlotte's Shore" because of its biggest attraction, is dotted with little coastal villages, including the adorable town of Victoria.

Take the TransCanada when leaving Charlottetown to Cornwall, then Route 19 (follow the sign for the Blue Heron Tour) south to Rocky Point.

Rocky Point ★

Rocky Point is located at the end of a point of land, at the mouth of the West River and in front of the Hillsborough River, which was always a strategic point in the defense of Charlottetown and the back-country against an eventual attack from the sea. This site was of particular interest early on to the colonial empires who would fight battles to win control of the island. The French were the first to establish themselves here in the 1720s, by founding Port la Joye, captured in 1758 by the British who then founded Fort Amherst. The fine-tuning of the fort came that same year when the war between France and England began in earnest. The British garrison had the important role of protecting the island from French invasion and controlling maritime traffic in the Northumberland Strait throughout the whole war. However, as of 1763, with the end of the war, the fort's importance decreased significantly and was abandoned by the British in 1768. The **Port La Joye - Fort Amherst National Historic Site ★** *(free admission; end of Jun to early Sep 10 AM to 6 PM; Route 19; ☎ 675-2220)* houses a small interpretive centre presenting an exhibit on the various documents related to the French colony (Port La Joye) and the British presence at the site (Fort Amherst). There is also a short documentary film on the history of the Acadians of Prince Edward Island. Very

little remains today of Fort Amherst. There is however a lovely view of the surrounding fields and of the city of Charlottetown from the site. The **Micmac Village** *(adults $3.25; Jun, 10 AM to 5 PM, Jul, 9:30 AM to 7 PM, Aug, 9:30 AM to 6 PM; Route 19, ☎ 675-3800)* is also worth a stop, when visiting Rocky Point. There is a small museum, a gift shop and a reconstruction of a Micmac village, the natives that inhabited the island before the arrival of European colonists.

The road from Rocky Point to Victoria is calm and there are several great views of the strait along the way. This tranquil country region consists essentially of farms, small peaceful hamlets and provincial parks. Here and there along the road, are the small fruit and vegetable stands of farmers selling offerings from their harvest.

Victoria ★

The beautiful residences lining the streets of this charming and peaceful coastal town are evidence of the opulence of another era. Founded in 1767, this seaport played a significant role in the local economy up until the end of the 19th century, when bit by bit the development of the railway on Prince Edward Island outmoded it. Fishing trawlers can still be seen, however bobbing about just beyond the once busy harbour. Today the interest in Victoria lies mostly in its old-fashioned character and in the friendliness of its residents. Country life on the island is best represented here. There are two inns, a few restaurants, and a famous chocolatier...

When arriving from the east you'll first come to **Victoria Provincial Park** (see p 175), extending to the water and including a small beach and a picnic area. The **Victoria Seaport Museum** *(free admission; Jul to early Sep, Tue to Sun 10 AM to 5 PM; Route 116; ☎ 658-2602)* is located close by in a lighthouse. Besides the several photographs of Victoria on display, you can also climb to the top of the lighthouse for a view of the village, the coast and surroundings.

Just a few streets make up the centre of Victoria. Here and there are several shops, restaurants as well as **The Victorian Playhouse** which presents, good quality concerts and theatre all summer long, adding to the charm of town.

Borden

This town has little to offer visitors. It is however one of the most visited spots on the island, since this is where the ferry between Prince Edward Island and New Brunswick arrives and departs from (see p 160). There are several businesses and restaurants, which come in handy while waiting for the ferry, as well as a good tourist information centre.

If you are not be continuing west to Summerside (see Tour D: Western P.E.I.) from Victoria or Borden, we suggest taking the secondary road Route 231, which joins with Route 2 to reach Burlington.

Burlington

One of the most popular attractions where children are concerned, **Woodleigh** *($7.35; end of May to Jun, 9 AM to 5 PM, Jul to early Sep, 9 AM to 8 PM, Sep to Oct, 9 AM to 5 PM; Route 234; ☎ 836-3401)*, is the brainchild of Col. Ernest Johnstone, who constructed replicas of famous buildings and monuments on his property

---

A Bridge to the Island?

Talk has abounded for years, but following an election promise of the current federal government, that old dream of a bridge linking Prince Edward Island to the mainland may yet materialize before 1997. A bridge between Cape Tourmentine (N.B.) and Borden (P.E.I.) would span no less than 12.7 km across the Strait of Northumberland. This is a bold project demanding the latest technology and the hiring of 1,000 local workers. At a cost of about 840 million (1992 estimation), Canadian financing may be hard to come by which means foreign investors may be needed. After so many broken promises Islanders are putting off the celebrations, they'll believe it when they see it!

---

after his return from the first World War up until his death 50 years later. The site was opened to the public in 1958 and now has more than 15 wooden and stone buildings, several of which can be visited, and a variety of other monuments dispersed across the pretty wooded property. The most impressive building is probably the replica of the Tower of London. Celtic music shows are organized, usually on Sundays.

Park Corner

Anne of Green Gables Museum at Silver Bush ★ *(adults $2.50; Jun, 9 AM to 6 PM; Jul and Aug, 9 AM to 8 PM; Sep and Oct, 9 AM to 6 PM; ☎ 886-2807)* was actually a favourite house of Lucy Maud Montgomery, it belonged to her aunt and uncle, Annie and John Campbell. She adored it and was married here in July, 1911. Today it is a historic house, decorated with period furniture and many of the author's and her family's personal effects.

New London

The small community of New London has the distinguished honour of being the birthplace of the writer who has done the most for Prince Edward Island abroad. The main attraction is the house where she was born, the **Lucy Maud Montgomery Birthplace** *(adults $1; Jun, 9 AM to 7 PM; Jul and Aug, 9 AM to 7 PM; Sep to mid-Sep, 9 AM to 6 PM; mid-Sep to early Oct, 10 AM to 5 PM; at the intersection of Routes 6 and 8, ☎ 885-2099 or 436-7329)*. Personal objects, inluding L.M. Montgomery's wedding dress, can be viewed in this simple house.

Cavendish ★

Cavendish is a sacred spot for tourists to P.E.I.. Located next to some of the most beautiful beaches on the island, and several big tourist attractions, Cavendish has many lodging possibilities, restaurants and shops. It is for many a gateway to the national park, and therefore has an excellent tourist information centre.

Green Gables House ★ *(free admission; mid-May to end of Jun, 9 AM to 5 PM; end of Jun to early Sep, 9 AM to 8 PM; early Sep to end of Oct, 9 AM to 8 PM; Route 6, west of Cavendish, ☎ 672-6350)* is the house that inspired Lucy Maud Montgomery, and it is also where she situates the action of her famous novel *Anne of Green Gables*. Built towards the middle of the last century, the house belonged to David and

It was November 30th, 1874 that Lucy Maud Montgomery was born, in New London, P.E.I. But early in her childhood she had to leave New London to live with her grandparents, Alexander and Lucy MacNeill, in Cavendish, who raised her after the death of her mother. Her first novel Anne of Green Gables, inspired by her own orphan life, was a huge success as soon as it appeared in 1908, it has since been translated into 16 languages. L.M. Mont-gomery, later published 23 novels up until her death in 1942. Her most famous work remained however the story of Anne, that enchanting little orphan with the red hair and freckled face.

Margaret MacNeil, older cousins of the author's. L.M. Montgomery used to love strolling down "lover's lane", located in the woods on her cousins' property. She was so inspired by the surroundings that it became the backdrop for her novel. By 1936 the novel was so popular that the federal government made a classified site of the house, and thus today it can be visited.

Prince Edward Island National Park ★★★ (see p 174)

South Rustico ★

The quaint town of South Rustico, like the neighbouring towns has a large Acadian population. Two significant institutions in the history of the Acadian community on the north of the island, are actually located right next to each other. The **Banque des Fermiers** ★ or Farmer's Bank, a museum today *(adults $1; end of Jun to early Sep, Mon to Sat 9:30 AM to 5 PM, Sun 11:30 AM to 4 PM; Route 243, ☎ 963-2505)*, was founded in 1864 by Father George-Antoine Belcourt, with the aim of providing Acadians with the opportunity to take their place in the economic development. It was the first people's bank in the country, and for a certain time, the smallest chartered bank in Canada. The exhibit tells of Father Belcourt's work, the building is located on a historic site. Right next door, the modest **Saint Augustine Church** *(Church Street)* is the oldest Acadian church on the island.

Brackley Beach ★

This small hamlet on the shores of Rustico Bay is worth a visit to see the **Brackley Beach Lighthouse** *(adults $2, end of May to end of Jun, 9 AM to 6 PM; Jul and Aug, 9 AM to 9 PM; at intersection of Routes 15 and 16, ☎ 672-3478)* and its exhibit of photographs of lighthouses on the island. The view from the top is superb. Another recommended stop, close by is **The Dunes Art Gallery** *(free admission; May, 10 AM to 6 PM; Jun to Sep, 9 AM to 10 PM; Oct, 10 AM to 6 PM; Route 15, ☎ 672-2586)* where the works of the biggest artists of the island are on display. There is also a charming little restaurant.

■ Tour C: Eastern P.E.I. ★

Extending to the east of Charlottetown is a lovely rural region that will delight visitors seeking the tranquillity of deserted beaches, the busy atmosphere of small fishing villages and enchanting bays that appear around every bend in the road. Somewhat hilly to the north, this region presents a varied landscape,

that may not always be spectacular, but is often pretty and harmonious. None of the communities in this part of the island have more than a few hundred inhabitants, and life here revolves mainly around fishing and agriculture. A tour of eastern Prince Edward Island thus offers visitors an opportunity to discover a lovely part of the province while experiencing a way of life that remains directly dependent on nature.

Orwell

A visit to the **Orwell Corner Historic Village** ★ *(TransCanada Highway, 30 km east of Charlottetown; ☎ 651-2013)* is a must for anyone interested in discovering what life was like in rural Prince Edward Island back in the 19th century. This delightful village is made up of restored buildings, including a pretty little school that looks as if it came straight out of an L.M. Montgomery novel, a church, a shingle factory, several barns, a forge and a farmhouse that doubles as a general store and a post office. The atmosphere is enlivened by characters in period dress, who are available to answer visitors' questions. Orwell Corner may be smaller than other similar historic villages, such as Kings Landing in New Brunswick, but its size gives it a charming authenticity.

A few hundred metres from Orwell Corner, tucked away in an enchanting setting, lies the **Sir Andrew Macphail Homestead** *(30 km east of Charlottetown; ☎ 651-2589)*. A native of Prince Edward Island, Andrew Macphail (1864-1938) had an extraordinary career in the fields of research and medicine, and also as an author and journalist. His house, furnished as it was at the beginning of the century, is a lovely part of the local heritage. There is a small dining room, where light meals are served. Visitors can also explore the vast grounds by taking a pleasant walk along a 2 km trail.

Point Prim

Not far from the village of Eldon, Route 1 intersects with Route 209, a small road leading to the **Point Prim Lighthouse** *(free admission; Jul and Aug, Mon to Wed 10 AM to 5 PM, Thu and Fri 10 AM to 6 PM, Sat and Sun 10 AM to 7 PM; Route 209, ☎ 659-2692)*, designed and built by Isaac Smith, architect of Charlottetown's Province House, in 1845. The lighthouse is open to the public, and the surrounding area is perfect for a picnic. The **view ★** of the sea is worth the short detour.

Wood Islands

Wood Islands, the boarding point for the ferry to Pictou, Nova Scotia (see p 160), has a large tourist information centre. Close by, in **Wood Islands Provincial Park**, is a pretty unsupervised beach.

Murray Harbour

Antique lovers should stop at the **Log Cabin Museum** *(adults $2; Jul to early Sep, 9 AM to 6:30 PM; Route 18A; ☎ 962-2201)*, which displays a curious collection of objects of varied origins.

Murray River

Excursions out of Murray River are organized by **Captain Garry's Seal & Bird Watching Cruises** *(adults $13.50; mid-Apr to Sep; ☎ 962-2494 or 1-800-561-2494)* (see p 178).

Montague ★

Montague might not be very big, but it is nevertheless one of the largest communities in the eastern part of the province. It is home to several businesses, shops and restaurants, as well as the interesting **Garden of the Gulf Museum ★** *(adults $2.50; Jul to early Sep, 9 AM to 6:30 PM; 2 Main Street, ☎ 838-2467)*, set up inside the former post office. The exhibit deals with both local and military history. Montague is also the point of departure for excursions organized by **Cruise Manada Seal Watching Boat Tours** *(adults $13.50; mid-May to end of Aug; on Main Street, near the bridge, ☎ 838-2444)* (see p 178). Other excursions start at the Brudenell Marina.

Georgetown

The small fishing port of Georgetown witnessed the golden age of wooden ship-building. Right before Georgetown, visitors will find the superb **Brudenell River Provincial Park** (see p 176), which boasts a beach, a beautiful golf course, a good hotel and a number of camping sites.

Cardigan

A small community looking out onto the bay of the same name, Cardigan was a ship-building centre in the 19th century. It is now home to several interesting craft shops.

Souris ★

The little town of Souris, with its 1,600 or so inhabitants, is the largest community in the eastern part of Prince Edward Island. Accordingly, it offers a range of services, several restaurants and hotels and a tourist information centre. Not far away lies **Souris Beach**

Provincial Park , where visitors will find a picnic area and an unsupervised beach. The town's Main Street is graced with several pretty buildings, which bear witness to Souris' prominent role in this region. The most striking of these are the **Town Hall** and **St. Mary's Church**. The town port is the boarding point for the ferry to Québec's Îles-de-la-Madeleine.

Red Point

Make sure to stop for a picnic, a stroll or a swim at the magnificent white sand beach in **Red Point Provincial Park** *(Route 16, north of Souris)* (see p 176).

Basin Head ★

Ideally located on one of the island's loveliest sandy beaches, not far from some magnificent dunes, the **Basin Head Fisheries Museum ★★** *(adults $3; mid-June to early Sep, Tue to Sun 9 AM to 5 PM; Route 16, ☎ 357-2966)* offers visitors an opportunity to learn about all different facets of the wonderful world of fishing around Prince Edward Island. The museum exhibits an interesting collection of artifacts related to the lives and occupation of the fishermen of old. The building itself is flanked by sheds, in which vessels of various sizes and periods are displayed, as well as a workshop where local artisans make wooden boxes like those used in the past for packing salted fish. An old canning factory stands a little farther off. In all respects, this is one of the most interesting museums in the province. To make the most of a visit, however, don't miss a chance to stroll along the neighbouring beaches and dunes as well.

East Point

For a magnificent view of the ocean and the area's coastal landscape, head to the **East Point Lighthouse ★** *(free admission; Jul and Aug; Route 16; ☎ 687-2295)*, which stands on the easternmost tip of the island. During summer, visitors can climb to the top of this old lighthouse, which dates back to 1867.

Elmira

A tiny rural village near the easternmost tip of the island, Elmira is home to one of the Prince Edward Island Museum and Heritage Foundation's six museums, the **Elmira Railway Museum ★** *(adults $1.50; mid Jun to early Sep, Tue to Sun 10 AM to 6 PM; Route 16A; ☎ 357-2481)*. Located in a bucolic setting, it occupies the town's former train station, which has been closed since 1982. In addition to the main building, there is a warehouse and a railway car, which is stationed on one of the tracks. This museum's excellent exhibit is a reminder of the glorious sense of adventure that accompanied the construction of Prince Edward Island's railway.

St. Andrews

After Elmira, the TransCanada Highway passes through several tiny rural communities. A brief stop in St. Andrews is a must, in order to visit the little **chapel** *(free admission; end of Jun to Aug; ☎ 961-3323)*, which has been moved twice. Built in 1803 on its present site, it was transported down the frozen Hillsborough River to Charlottetown in the winter of 1964, where it was used as a girl's school. It was restored in 1988 and moved back to its original site two years later.

The Golden Era of the Railway

The history of the railway is closely linked to that of Prince Edward Island and its accession to Canadian Confederation. In the 1860s and 1870s, the island's inhabitants began demanding a railway, which in those years, was the most efficient means of communication and transport throughout North America, as well as a virtual guarantee of economic growth. In August of 1871, the island's government passed the Railroad Act, and construction of the railway began two months later. By the following year, however, construction costs had led to an unprecedented crisis in the island's public finances. On the verge of bankruptcy, the government had no other option but to transfer its debt to the Canadian government and join Canadian Confederation in July 1873. Two years later, the island's railway began operating. Its main track linked Alberton, in the west, to Georgetown, in the east, and later to Elmira. Another line linked Tignish, in the west, to Souris, in the east. For nearly a century, the railway was the backbone of the island's development. Starting in the 1960s, however, the emergence of new and more efficient means of transportation forced Canadian National to cut back its services all over the country, including on Prince Edward Island. In 1989, the island's last line was closed, bringing the golden era of the railway to an end.

■ **Tour D: Western P.E.I.** ★

The western part of Prince Edward Island is home to the province's second largest town, Summerside, as well as its most isolated area, the northwest. Southwest of Summerside, visitors can explore the Acadian region of Prince Edward Island, the domain of the Arseneault, Gallant and Richard families, among others, who live in a string of tiny coastal villages with colourful names like Baie-Egmont, Saint-Chrysostome, Mont-Carmel, Maximeville, etc. Here, in the Évangéline region, inhabitants proudly preserve the French language and Acadian culture handed down to them by their ancestors. A tour of the western part of the island offers visitors an opportunity to discover this Acadian legacy, as well as to visit a peaceful, picturesque region whose inhabitants live mainly on fishing and potato-farming. The scenery is pretty and sometimes even spectacular, especially near North Cape.

Summerside ★

With a population of about 10,000, Summerside is Prince Edward Island's second largest town. It is presently experiencing an economic boom, due to the nearby construction of the bridge that will soon link the island to the province of New Brunswick. It is a pleasant town, graced with lovely Victorian residences and a pretty waterfront. As the chief urban centre on the western part of the island, Summerside also has a number of shops, restaurants and places to stay.

Eptek ★ *(adults $2; Tue to Sun 10 AM to 5 PM; on the waterfront, Water Street, ☎ 888-8373)* is a national exhibition centre, which presents travelling exhibits of Canadian art. The same building houses Prince Edward Island's Sports Hall of Fame.

Through a collection of photographs and other articles, the **International Fox Museum** *(free admission; May to Sep, Mon to Sat 9 AM to 6 PM; 286 Fitzroy Street, ☎ 436-2400)* traces the history of fox-breeding on Prince Edward Island. After a timid start at the end of the last century, this activity represented 17% of the province's economy by the 1920s. In those years, a pair of silver foxes could fetch as much as $35,000. Efforts are now being made to revive this once prosperous industry.

Miscouche

In Miscouche, barely 8 km west of Summerside, the **Acadian Museum of Prince Edward Island** ★ *(adults $2,75; Jun to early Sep, Mon to Fri 9:30 AM to 5 PM; early Sep to May, Mon to Fri 9:30 AM to 5 PM; Route 2; tel. 436-6237)* offers an excellent introduction to the world of the local Acadians. The museum's exhibit recounts the history of the island's Acadian community, from 1720 to the present day, with the help of artifacts, writings, numerous illustrations and an audiovisual presentation, shown on request, which lasts about 15 minutes. The museum also houses Prince Edward Island's *Centre de Recherches Acadiennes*, which has a library and archives that may be used for genealogical research.

The Acadian Presence

Although Acadians didn't settle in the Evangeline region until 1812, their presence on Prince Edward Island dates back to the 1720s, when the island was a French colony named Île-Saint-Jean. These first colonists, who came from the area then known as Acadia (present-day Nova Scotia), founded the settlements of Port-LaJoye, Pointe-Prime and Malpèque, among others. In the following decades, the Acadian population gradually increased, then began growing rapidly in 1755, due to the arrival of refugees fleeing deportation from Nova Scotia (the former Acadia). In 1758, however, Ile-Saint-Jean also fell into the hands of the British, who deported about 3,000 of the 5,000 Acadians living on the island. After the war, the remaining Acadians, along with those who returned to the island, lived mainly in the area around Malpèque Bay. It wasn't until 1812 that some families left this region to settle in the southwest, founding La Roche (Baie-Egmont) and Grand-Ruisseau (Mont-Carmel).

Mont-Carmel

Mont-Carmel, known for many years as Grand-Ruisseau, was founded in 1812 by the Arseneault and Gallant families. The splendour of the **Église Notre-Dame-du-Mont-Carmel** ★ *(Route 11)*, which lies in the heart of the parish, bears eloquent witness to the prominent role played by Catholicism in Acadian culture.

Located on the site of the very first settlement, Grand-Ruisseau (now known as Mont-Carmel), the **Acadian Pioneer Village** ★ *(adults $3; Jun to mid-Sep, 9:30 AM to 5 PM; Route 11; 1.5 km west of the church, ☎ 854-2227)* recreates the rustic lifestyle of early 19th century Acadians. The village includes a church and presbytery, two family homes, a smithy, a school and a barn. Most of the furniture in the buildings was donated by citizens of neighbouring villages. A comfortable hotel stands at the entrance of the pioneer village, along with the restaurant Étoile de Mer, which offers visitors a unique opportunity to enjoy Acadian cuisine.

Cap-Egmont

A pretty fishing village looking out on the Northumberland Strait, Cap-Egmont, often referred to locally as Grand-Cap, lies in the most peaceful setting imaginable. Visitors can stop at the **Bottle Houses** *(adults $3.25; mid-Jun to end of Jun, 10 AM to 6 PM; end of Jun to early Sep, 9 AM to 7 PM; early Sep to mid-Sep, 10 AM to 6 PM; Route 11; ☎ 854-2987)*, three buildings made out of a total of 25,000 bottles, set in the midst of a park filled with flowers.

O'Leary

A village typical of this region, which produces large quantities of potatoes, O'Leary is home to the **Prince Edward Island Potato Museum** ★ *(adults $1.50;*

Jun to Sep, Mon to Fri 10 AM to 5 PM, Sat 11 AM to 4 PM, Sun 2 PM to 4 PM; 22 Parkview Drive, ☎ 859-2039), the only museum in Canada devoted to the history of potato-growing. The well-designed exhibit clearly illustrates this tuber's role in the history of food. Visitors will also learn the various techniques used to grow potatoes. This is an excellent and interesting museum regardless of the peculiar nature of its subject matter.

West Point ★

A stop at West Point offers an opportunity to explore one of the most peaceful, picturesque spots on the island, **Cedar Dunes Provincial Park** ★ *(Route 14)*, which features endless deserted beaches and dunes. Another interesting spot nearby is the **West Point Lighthouse** *(adults $2; end of May to Sep, 8 AM to 8 PM.; Route 14; ☎ 859-3606)*, which dates back to 1875 and is one of the largest in the province. In addition to housing a museum and a restaurant, it is the only lighthouse in Canada to be used as an inn.

North Cape ★

The scenery around North Cape, the northernmost tip of the island, is not only pretty, but often spectacular, with red sandstone cliffs plunging into the blue waters of the Gulf of St. Lawrence. North Cape itself occupies a lovely site along the coast. Here, visitors will find the **Atlantic Wind Test Site** *(adults $2; Jul and Aug, 10 AM to 8 PM; at the end of Route 12; ☎ 882-2746)*, where wind technology is tested and evaluated. A small exhibit explains the advantages of using this type of energy.

Alberton

During his first trip along the coast of what would eventually be Canada in 1534, Jacques Cartier apparently stopped at the present-day site of Alberton, an attractive little village adorned with a number of pretty buildings. Set up inside the former curthouse, built in 1878 and now a historic site, the **Alberton Museum ★** *(adults $2; Jun to early Sep 10 AM to 8 PM; Church Street,* ☎ *853-4048)* offers a wonderful introduction to the history of this region. The collection on display includes such varied objects as furniture, dishes and old farming instruments.

Port Hill

The **Green Park Shipbuilding Museum ★★** *(adults $2.50; June to early Sep, Tue to Sun 9 AM to 5 PM; Route 12;* ☎ *831-2206)* reminds visitors that shipbuilding was the mainspring of Prince Edward Island's economy for the greater part of the 19th century. It presents an exhibit on the various techniques used in shipbuilding and the history of the trade. The site includes a reconstructed shipyard, complete with a ship in progress. Right nearby stands the Yeo house, the lovely former home of James Yeo, Jr., who owned a shipyard in the 19th century.

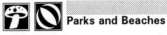

Parks and Beaches

The craggy, breathtakingly beautiful landscapes, endless beaches and unique plant and animal life are among the most spectacular attractions of this red crescent-shaped island, which lies cradled on the waves 40 km east of continental Canada. A number of parks

have been created in order to highlight the natural beauty of parts of the island. The most well known is Prince Edward Island National Park, but there are 29 provincial parks as well. More than forty lovely beaches with sands in countless shades of pink also help make this island a veritable paradise for vacationers.

■ Parks

The parks provide all sorts of services for vacationers (camping sites, picnic areas, supervised beaches) and feature a variety of activities intended to familiarize visitors with various natural settings; nature trails and welcome centres offer information on the local plant and animal life. These parks are an inexhaustible source of discovery for the entire family.

About fifteen of the provincial parks have **camping** facilities *(☎ 652-2356 for reservations in the eastern part of the island, and ☎ 859-8790 for the western part)*. Visitors can also camp in the national park, but the conditions vary (see below).

Central P.E.I.

A visit to the island wouldn't be complete without a trip of at least one day to **Prince Edward Island National Park ★★★** *(three welcome centres: in Cavendish, near the intersection of Routes 6 and 13,* ☎ *963-2391; opposite the Dalvay-by-the-Sea Hotel,* ☎ *672-6350; Brackley welcome centre, at the intersection of Routes 6 and 15,* ☎ *672-2259)*, which stretches 40 km along the northern coast of the island, from Blooming Point to New London Bay. The park was created in 1937 with the goal of preserving a unique natural environment, including sand dunes, with their fragile ecosystem, red sandstone cliffs, magnificent beaches and salt-water marshes. While exploring the park, visitors will be constantly delighted by stunning views of the sheer coastline, the sudden appearance of a red fox or one of the many activities that may be enjoyed here.

There are trails leading right into the heart of the park. On the Reeds and Rushes trail, visitors can observe the animal life in a pond from a floating footbridge. Other species of plant and animal life may be discovered on one of the four other marked trails, suitable for all ages, that crisscross the park. The beaches here are also terrific for families. Be careful around the neighbouring sand dunes, however, since the piping plover, a small, endangered species of bird, sometimes nests there. Footbridges have been laid out in order to protect this fragile environment; please respect the signs.

There are four **camping sites** in the park. On **Rustico Island**, visitors can camp by the sea in the most peaceful setting imaginable. Reservations are not accepted, however, and there is no shower. The **Cavendish** camping site, on the other hand, is fully equipped, as is the one in **Stanhope**. The **Brackley** camping site does not accept groups *(reservations required,* ☎ *672-6350)*.

The road between Charlottetown and Victoria passes through two attractive parks, **Victoria Provincial Park** and **Argyle Shore Provincial Park**, both of which are pleasant places to relax. Visitors can stop at either one to enjoy a picnic, sit and gaze at the sea or take a swim.

The Piping Plover

In all of Prince Edward Island National Park, there are just 25 pairs of these little birds, which measure about 19 cm and have sandy beige plumage, with a few black feathers on the head and neck. The piping plover feeds on insects and tiny crustaceans, and may often be seen combing the beach in search of nourishment. It also builds its nest in the sand, a little bit above the waterline at high-tide. During the 28-day incubation period of their eggs and until the baby birds set off on their own at the end of July, the parents watch over the nest, which is well-hidden in the sand, safe from predators. Unfortunately, the nests are also well-hidden from people strolling along the beach, who can inadvertently cause irreparable damage to them. The number of piping plovers has diminished greatly over the past ten years, and if the population is to grow, the nests must be protected from any disturbance. While walking along the beach, therefore, it is crucial that visitors pay careful attention to all signs.

Strathgartney Provincial Park lies alongside the West River. It is an excellent spot for camping, with sites available for both tents and trailers.

Eastern P.E.I.

Stretching along the banks of the river after which it was named, **Brudenell River Provincial Park ★** is beautifully located, offering a stunning view of the water. A large, 18-hole golf course also lies within its bounds.

Red Point Provincial Park ★ was created to protect the island's magnificent red sandstone cliffs, and some of the views here are picture-perfect. Visitors will also be charmed by the beach, a long strip of fine sand along the Northumberland Strait. The park has lovely picnic areas, too, and campers are welcome.

Western Prince Edward Island

Located at the mouth of Mill River, where it flows into Cascumpec Bay, **Mill River Provincial Park ★** stretches forth like a huge garden. It also features a superb golf course.

■ Beaches

The island is fringed with a series of exquisite white and red sand beaches, especially along the north coast, in **Prince Edward Island National Park** and along the east coast. The park boasts no fewer than seven of the island's most beautiful beaches, the most renowned being the ones in **Cavendish, North Rustico, Brackley** and **Dalvay.** The east coast has its share of magnificent beaches as well, including those in **Basin Head, Red Point Provincial Park, Campbells Cove Provincial Park** and **Panmure Island Provincial Park.** On the west coast, the beaches in **Cedar Dunes Provincial Park** and on **Nail Pond** are both worthy of note.

Outdoor Activities

Hiking

The various trails in **Prince Edward Island National Park** enable hikers to learn about the plant and animal life that have developed in this part of the island.

The **Reeds and Rushes Trail** (0.5 km) leads through the forest to a marsh spanned by a wooden footbridge, from which hikers can observe a wide variety of insects, plants and animals.

The **Farmlands Trail** (2 km) leads into the heart of the park, passing through different types of vegetation, including a spruce forest, along the way.

The **Bubbling Springs Trail** (2 km) also passes through a spruce forest, then leads to an observation post on the banks of a pond, where visitors can observe various species of water birds.

Three other trails lead into the heart of the forest: **Homestead** (5.5 to 8 km), **Haunted Wood** (1.6 km) and **Balsam Hollow** (1 km).

There are hiking trails in the provincial parks as well, particularly **Mill River, Brudenell** and **Strathgartney Parks.**

Bird-watching

Nearly 315 different species of birds may be observed along the shores of the island. From the remarkable great blue heron to the kingfisher, bluejay and rare piping plover, the island has plenty to offer amateur ornithologists. In **Prince Edward Island National Park,** there are observation points at **Brackley Marsh, Orby Head, Covehead pier** and all along the **Rustico Island floating bridge**. It isn't necessary to go to the park to observe many of these birds, which can be spotted in many different parts of the island; just keep your eyes peeled.

 Bicycling

The island is a pleasant place to go bicycling, since the traffic is never heavy and there are many quiet roads crisscrossing the fields. In **Prince Edward Island National Park**, cyclists can enjoy magnificent scenery without having to worry about cars. For information on cycling excursions, contact **Sport PEI** *(tel. 368-4110)*.

The following places also organize excursions:

MacQueen's Bike Shop
Charlottetown
☎ 357-2453

Singing Sands Sea Breeze Bicycle Expedition
Charlottetown
☎ 357-2371

Bike rentals are available all over the island. Here are a few options:

MacQueen's Bike Shop
Charlottetown
☎ 1-800-667-4583

Sunset Campground Bike Rentals (starting at $10 a day)
Cavendish
☎ 963-2440

North Shore Windsurfing and Bike Rentals ($14 a day)
Brackley Beach
☎ 672-2022

 Golf

Prince Edward Island has a lot to offer golfers, since it features several excellent greens, laid out on sites that not only make for a good game, but also offer breathtaking views of the sea and the cliffs.

The 18-hole **Green Gables Golf Course** *($24; Cavendish, ☎ 963-2488)* is located in **Prince Edward Island National Park**.

In **Mill River Provincial Park** *($25; ☎ 859-8790)*, there is an 18-hole golf course, which stretches 5,944 m along the banks of the Mill River.

The **Links at Crowbush Cove** *($35; Lakeside, ☎ 961-2800)* occupies a magnificent site, offering incomparable views of the ocean. The course is exceptionally pleasant.

The 18-hole golf course in **Brudenell River Provincial Park** *($30; Roseneath, ☎ 652-2342)* boasts a lovely site as well. Golfers also get to enjoy the vast, peaceful park surrounding the green.

For more information on the island's golf courses, write to:

GOLF PEI
P.O. Box 2653
Charlottetown
C1A 8C3
☎ 368-4130

Boating

Visitors wishing to head out to sea can take part in one of a variety of short cruises offered by local companies.

Mill River Boat Tour (adults $15)
☎ 856-3820

Cardigan River
Cardigan (sailing)
☎ 583-2020

■ **Seal-watching**

Groups of seals regularly swim near the shores of the island. Visitors interested in observing these large sea mammals can take part in an excursion organized for that express purpose.

Cruise Manada (adults $13.50, children under 12 $7)
☎ 838-3444
Departures:
From the Montague Marina
Everyday 2 PM. (mid-May to Jun)
Everyday 1 PM, 3:30 PM and 7 PM (early Jul to Aug)
From the Brudenell Marina
Everyday 2:30 PM (Jul and Aug)

Garry's Seal Cruises
☎tel. 962-2494 or 1-800-561-2494
Departures:
Murray River pier
Everyday 1 PM, 3:30 PM and 6:30 PM (Jun)
Everyday 8:30 AM, 10:30 AM, 1 PM, 3:30 PM and 6:30 PM (Jul to mid-Sep)

 Fishing

Several companies offer deep-sea fishing excursions, giving visitors a chance to test their fishing skills while enjoying an exciting outing on the water.

Excursions of this type set out from **Covehead Harbour:**

Richard's Deep-Sea Fishing ($15)
☎ 672-2376
Salty Seas Deep-Sea Fishing ($15)
☎ 672-3246

A company in Alberton arranges similar outings:

Andrew's Mist ($25)
Alberton
☎ 853-2307

 Accommodation

■ **Tour A: Charlottetown**

The **Youth Hostel** *($12.50 members $15 non-members; 153 Mount Edward Road,* ☎ *894-9696)* provides the least expensive lodging in the provincial capital region. It's a friendly spot set up in a barn-like building about 3 km west of downtown, near the university. During summer, rooms are also available at the **University of Prince Edward Island** *($23;* ☎ *566-0442)*.

The **Duchess of Kent Inn** *($48; 7 rooms, tv; 218 Kent Street, C1A 3W6,* ☎ *566-5826 or 1-800-665-5826)* occupies a lovely old house built in 1875. The place exudes charm.

The **Islander Motor Lodge** *($58; 49 rooms, tv, ℜ; 146-148 Pownal Street, C1A 3W6,* ☎ *892-1217 or 1-800-268-6261,* ⇄ *566-1623)* offers motel-style accommodation, but in pleasantly-furnished, quality rooms. This is a convenient place for families since it's just a few steps from the main sites and has a small inexpensive restaurant. If you are travelling on a small budget, reserve in advance to get the less expensive rooms.

The **Heritage Harbour House Inn** *($60; 5 rooms; 9 Grafton Street, C1A 1K3, ☎ 892-6633)* is an excellent bed and breakfast located on a residential street, just a stone's throw from the Arts Centre. The rooms are impeccably clean, as are the shared bathrooms. The house itself is warm and inviting, and guests have use of a day room where they can relax, read or watch television. Each morning, Bonnie, the owner and a charming hostess, serves a continental breakfast.

The **Dundee Arms Inn** *($95; 18 rooms, tv, ℜ; 200 Pownal Street, ☎ 892-2496)* is an elegant inn set up inside a large Queen-Anne style residence built at the beginning of the century. The beautifully-decorated bedrooms and common rooms will take you back in time. The inn also features a highly-reputed dining room. Finally, there are comfortable, slightly less expensive motel rooms available in an adjoining building.

The **Charlottetown Rodd Classic** *($99; 109 rooms, tv, ℜ, ≈; corner of Kent and Pownal Streets, C1A 1L5, ☎ 894-7371 or 1-800-565-7633)* is an excellent downtown hotel with a rather stately appearance, built to meet the needs of both businesspeople and vacationers. The inviting rooms are modern and tastefully furnished. The hotel also houses a good restaurant.

Part of the Canadian Pacific hotel chain, The **Prince Edward Hotel** *($150; 211 rooms, tv, ℜ, ≈; 18 Queen Street, C1A 8B9, ☎ 566-2222, ⇄ 566-2282)* is without a doubt the ritziest and most comfortable hotel on the island. It is also perfectly situated, looking out over the port of Charlottetown. The interior is modern and well designed, with four restaurants and all the facilities one would expect to find in a hotel of this calibre. Business meetings and conferences are often held at the Prince Edward. Its conference rooms can accommodate up to 650 people.

■ **Central P.E.I.**

Strathgartney

Right near Strathgartney Provincial Park, the **Strathgartney Country Inn** *($69; 10 rooms, ℜ; R.R. 3, C0A 1C0, ☎ 675-4711)* is set up inside a superb upper-class residence built in 1863 on a property covering about ten hectares. The fine food served in the dining room adds to the charm of this magnificent house, which is adorned with period furniture. A good choice for anyone wishing to relive the charm of the Victorian era in a rural setting.

Victoria

The clean and charming **Victoria Village Inn** *($42.50; 4 rooms; in the centre of the village, C0A 2G0, ☎ 658-2483)* is actually a bed & breakfast set up inside a well-preserved old house dating back to the 1870s. The lovely rooms have a somewhat old-fashioned look about them.

The **Orient Hotel** *($69; 6 rooms; ℜ, tv; Main Street, C0A 2G0, ☎ 658-2503)* fits in perfectly with Victoria's old-fashioned atmosphere. Built at the beginning of the century, it is a delightful place with decorations and furniture from days gone by. It is comfortable without being overly luxurious, and guests receive a warm welcome. The Orient also has a dining room and a pretty tea room, which looks out onto the street. Breakfast is included in the price of the room.

Sea View

During summer, scores of cottages are available for rent all along the north shore of the island. There are over a dozen of these at **Adams Sea View Cottages** *($69; 13 rooms, tv, ℜ, C, R.R. 2, COB 1M0, ☎ 836-5259)*, all lined up along a pretty beach. Each cottage has two bedrooms, a kitchenette and a refrigerator, making this an economical option for families or groups wishing to stay in the area. The rooms are sparsely furnished.

Cavendish

In the heart of Cavendish, about 500 m from the beach, the **Shining Water Country Inn** *($60; 10 rooms, Route 13, COA 1N0, ☎ 963-2251)* combines comfort with charm. A lovely old house with spacious porches all around, this inn features comfortable rooms and friendly service. Guests can relax in a pleasant, airy living room. There are cottages behind the house, which are available for about $15 extra.

In the heart of what could be considered the village of Cavendish, but not right on the beach, the **Cavendish Motel** *($72; 35 rooms, tv, ℜ; at the intersection of Routes 6 and 13, COA 1M0, ☎ 963-2244 or 1-800-565-2243)* offers clean, pleasant, modern rooms.

Furnished with antiques and exquisitely decorated, the **Kindred Spirits Country Inn** *($110; 14 rooms, tv, Route 6, COA 1N0, ☎ 963-2434)* offers quality accommodation less than a kilometre from the Cavendish beach. Guests can relax in one of several common rooms, including a superb living room.

South Rustico

The **Barachois Inn** *($95; 7 rooms, Church Road, C1A 7M4, ☎ 963-2194)*, a magnificent house built in the 1870s, has superb rooms furnished with antiques and adorned with works of art. It offers guests an excellent opportunity to savour the atmosphere of a sumptuous 19th century home.

Little Rock

Dalvay-by-the-Sea *($150 including breakfast and dinner; 27 rooms, tv, ℜ; Route 2, COA 1P0, ☎ 672-2048)* is probably the most highly renowned establishment in northern Prince Edward Island. A big, beautiful Victorian house built around 1885, it lies less than 200 m from a magnificent beach. The interior is exquisite, the decor, tasteful and the food, excellent.

■ Eastern P.E.I.

Little Sands

One of the most charming establishments of its type on the island, the **Bayberry Cliff Inn Bed & Breakfast** *($35; 8 rooms, tv; Route 4, 8 km from Wood Islands, COA 1W0, ☎ 962-3395)* offers quality accommodation at rates ranging from $35 to $75 per night. The warm interior, with its rich woodwork, was designed with taste and care, and the rooms, each different from the next, are very inviting. Large windows have been added to the back of the house, to let the sun in and provide an excellent view of the sea. The property is bordered by a red sandstone bluff.

Roseneath

Visitors who like to spend all day playing golf should choose the **Rodd Brudenell River Resort** *($85; 88 rooms, ℜ, ≈, tv; Roseneath, COA 1G0, ☎ 652-2332 or 1-800-565-7633)*, erected on a pretty, verdant site along a river in Brudenell River Provincial Park, right near the fantastic golf course. There are about fifty hotel rooms and almost forty cottages, set on the banks of the river. The rooms are modern, comfortable, well-furnished and equipped with balconies. The Rodd also offers family activities.

Little Pond

A haven of peace, the **Ark Inn** *($65; 8 rooms, ℜ, tv; Route 310, COA 2B0, ☎ 583-2400, ⇄ 583-2176 or 1-800-665-2400)* stands on a large property with access to a private beach. The comfortable rooms feature futons, modern furniture and large windows. One thing that sets the Ark Inn apart is that most of its rooms are split-level, with the upper portion affording a lovely view. Some rooms are also equipped with a whirlpool. There is a pleasant restaurant on the ground floor.

Bay Fortune

One of the most sumptuous and charming inns on the island, the **Inn at Bay Fortune** *($110; 11 rooms, ℜ, tv; Route 310, COA 2B0, ☎ 687-3745)* offers high-quality food and accommodation. The building has a unique architectural design, it stands on a lovely, verdant site, offering a superb view of the bay after which it is named. The rooms are furnished in an elegant and original fashion, each one different from the last. Some even have a fireplace. An excellent choice!

Souris

The **Hilltop Motel** *($60; 14 rooms, tv, ℜ; Main Street, COA 2B0, ☎ 687-3315)* has clean, comfortable rooms and the advantage of being located within a few minutes from the boarding point for the ferry to the Îles de la Madeleine, Québec. Breakfast is included in the price of the room.

■ Western P.E.I.

Summerside

The **Arbor Inn** *($35; 6 rooms, tv; 380 MacEwen, C1N 4X8, ☎ 436-6847)*, located in a new residential neighbourhood, offers a variety of rooms, some of which are the least expensive in Summerside. The rooms, are furnished rather plainly, but are nevertheless comfortable. Breakfast included.

At the entrance to town, is a series of inexpensive motels. One of these is the **Mulberry Motel** *($38; 37 rooms, tv; 6 Water Street, C1N 1A1, ☎ 436-2520 or 888-2912)*, whose rooms are decent (but no more), offering a fairly standard level of comfort for this type of accommodation.

The beautiful **Silver Fox Inn** *($60; 6 rooms, ℜ; 61 Granville Street, C1N 2Z3, ☎ 436-4033)* lies a short distance from the port in an old residential neighbourhood, and is surrounded by a pretty little garden. All of the rooms are well-furnished, inviting and equipped with a private bath. Overall, the inn is elegantly decorated. The atmosphere is reminiscent of turn-of-the-century high-society.

The **Quality Inn - Garden of the Gulf** *($69; 84 rooms, tv, ℜ, =; 618 Water Street East, C1N 2V5, ☎ 436-2295)* features several sports facilities, including a 9-hole golf-course and an indoor swimming pool. This modern hotel is pleasant and well-designed, making wise use of natural lighting.

The most comfortable hotel in Summerside, the **Loyalist Country Inn** *($69; 50 rooms, tv, ℜ; 195 Harbour Drive, C1N 5B2, ☎ 436-3333, ⇄ 436-4304)* boasts an excellent location in the heart of town, with a view of the nearby port. Although they are modern, the rooms still have character, and are tastefully furnished. This hotel is a real favourite with businesspeople. Its restaurant, furthermore, is highly recommended (see p 185).

Mont-Carmel

There is no more luxurious hotel in the Evangeline region than the **Complexe Le Village** *($72; 60 rooms, tv, ℜ; Route 11, COB 2E0, ☎ 854-2227)*, located beside the Acadian Pioneer Village (see p 173) and the famous restaurant Étoile de Mer (see p 186). The complex is actually too big for the number of tourists who visit this region, so its clean, comfortable rooms are often empty.

West Point

The only inn in Canada set up inside a lighthouse (only one room is actually inside the lighthouse; the others are in the adjoining building), the **West Point Lighthouse** *($70; 10 rooms, tv, ℜ; Route 14, COB 1V0, ☎ 859-3605)* is a good spot to stop for a day or two, long enough to explore the magnificent dunes and beaches along the nearby shore. This is a friendly place, and the rooms are decent.

Alberton

The **Traveller's Inn Motel** *($40; 15 rooms; tv, ℜ; Route 12, COB 1B0, ☎ 853-2215 or 1-800-361-7829)*, on the edge of Alberton, is not exactly charming, but nevertheless offers acceptable accommodation for the price.

Woodstock

The **Rodd Mill River Resort** *($90; 90 rooms, tv, ℜ, Route 2, COB 1V0, ☎ 859-3555 or 1-800-565-7663)* is ideal for sports buffs. Not only is there an excellent golf-course nearby, but the resort itself has an indoor pool, tennis courts, a gym and squash courts. The rooms, furthermore, are very comfortable.

Tyne Valley

The **Doctor's Inn Bed & Breakfast** *($40; 2 rooms, ℜ; Route 167, COB 2C0, ☎ 831-2164)* is a country home typical of the 1860s with a pleasant garden. Its two decent, but not very luxurious rooms are available year-round. The place is very calm, and excellent evening meals are available.

 Restaurants

■ **Tour A: Charlottetown**

A fun, friendly and truly inexpensive place, the **Island Rock Café** *($; 132 Richmond Street)* is conveniently situated on the street that runs along the back of the Confederation Arts Centre. It looks and feels like a pub, while the menu includes pasta, burgers, natchos, fish & chips, etc. The dishes are simple, but well prepared. In the evenings, people come as much for drinks and socializing as for a meal.

Just outside the Prince Edward Hotel, on the same side as Peake's Wharf, the **Anchor and Oar House Grub & Grog** *($; Prince Edward Hotel, Water Street, ☎ 566-2222)* has a simple menu ideal for lunch. Most dishes are less than $6. There is a selection of salads and sandwiches, and several fish and seafood dishes round out the offerings.

Centrally located, **Cedar's Eatery** *($; 81 University Street, ☎ 892-7377)* offers an inexpensive, change of pace. *Kebab, falafel, shawarma* and *shish taouk*, Lebanese cuisine's most famous exports, are the headliners. The atmosphere is young, friendly and unpretentious, and the portions are generous.

Peake's Quay *($-$$; 36 Water Street, ☎ 368-1330)* should win the trophy for the best-situated restaurant in Charlottetown. The pleasant terrace looks directly out over the city's marina. An economical menu of simple dishes, including excellent seafood crepes, is offered at breakfast time. In the evening, the menu is more elaborate but still affordable. For less than $20, you can have, among other things, a delicious plate of lobster. Peake's Quay is also a pub where people linger over a drink or two.

Perhaps surprisingly for a city of this size, Charlottetown does hide a few gems in terms of restaurants, namely the **Off Broadway Café** *($$; 125 Sydney Street, ☎ 566-4620)*. Its relaxing, romantic and tasteful atmosphere and excellent, deliciously-concocted menu make it the hottest restaurant in town. A variety of dishes, many with a French touch, are served. And seafood

connoisseurs will not be disappointed by the main dishes and appetizers featured. Rounding up the menu is a choice selection of desserts including many crepes.

The Lord Selkirk *($$$; Prince Edward Hotel, 18 Queen Street, ☎ 566-2222)* is one of the province's finest tables. There is a varied menu featuring several seafood dishes. Among the appetizers, the lobster-garnished linguine is particularly succulent. As main dishes, the parboiled Atlantic salmon, Atlantic halibut filet and duck roasted with red pepper are excellent. The ambiance at the Lord Selkirk is of course very chic, but at the same time very inviting.

■ **Central P.E.I.**

Victoria

In the centre of the charming little village of Victoria, near the two inns and almost directly opposite the chocolate shop, visitors will find the **Landmark Café & Craft** *($; Main Street, ☎ 658-2286 or 658-2599)*, an extremely friendly, warm and simple place whose walls are adorned with pretty handicrafts. The menu consists of light home-made dishes—quiche, *tourtière*, pasta, salads, desserts, etc.

For afternoon tea or a more substantial meal, head to **Mrs. Profitt's Tea Room** *($$; Main Street, Orient Hotel)*, in the charming setting of Victoria's historic Orient Hotel. The menu is not very elaborate, but does include a variety of sandwiches and desserts, as well as fresh lobster, lobster salad and lobster quiche.

Cavendish

The **Shining Waters Tea Room** *($; Route 13, ☎ 963-2251)* is a charming spot for a noontime meal or afternoon snack. The menu lists salads, several different types of sandwiches, including the obligatory lobster roll, and a good selection of desserts.

St. Ann

For more than 30 years now, **St. Ann's Church Lobster Supper** *($$; Route 224,* ☎ *964-2385)*, a non-profit organization, has been serving lobster everyday from 4 PM to 9 PM. The menu, like those of other similar local restaurants, consists of a salad, fish soup, mussels, lobster and dessert— all for about $20. This is the type of tradition that visitors to Prince Edward Island should definitely not miss out on.

New Glasgow

The **Prince Edward Island Preserve Co.** *($; Route 13 at the intersection of Routes 234 and 258,* ☎ *964-2524)* is actually a shop selling delicious natural products. It also has a café, which serves good sandwiches and salads, as well as other dishes, including lobster quiche, a smoked fish platter and mussels *à la provençale*.

Looking out on the Clyde River, the **New Glasgow Lobster Suppers** *($$; Route 224,* ☎ *964-2870)* is one of the island's classic eateries. Since opening, it has served over a million customers! During summer, hundreds of people pass through its two dining rooms every evening between 4 PM and 8:30 PM. The charm of this place lies in its simplicity; in the dining rooms, there are rows of plain tables covered with red and white checked tablecloths. The menu, obviously, revolves around lobster. Each meal includes an all-you-can-eat appetizer, one lobster and a

home-made dessert. Prices vary depending on the size of the lobster you choose, but $20 per person is about average.

North Rustico

A well-known local institution, **Fisherman Wharf Lobster Suppers** *($$; Route 6,* ☎ *963-2669)* also serves traditional lobster meals, with unlimited fish and seafood soup, a vast choice of salads, bread, a lobster and a dessert for about $20. The place can seat approximately 500 people, which doesn't exactly make it intimate, but that's part of its charm.

Oyster Bed Bridge

Both elegant and inviting, the **Café St-Jean** *($$; Route 6,* ☎ *963-3133)* is a small restaurant set up inside a rustic-looking house looking out on the Wheatley River. In the evening, the food is fairly elaborate, with not only seafood on the menu, but also a fair number of other well-prepared, original dishes. The less expensive lunch menu consists of light dishes. The name of the café refers to the time before the British conquest, when the island was known as Île-St-Jean and the Acadian presence was very strong in this region.

Brackley Beach

The **Dunes Café** *($$; Route 15,* ☎ *672-2586)* is the only place of its kind on the island. Set up in a complex with original modern architecture, which also houses a remarkable art gallery, it serves local and international cuisine in an airy decor. The lunch menu is less elaborate and easier on the pocketbook. Live music is often featured in the evening.

■ **Eastern P.E.I.**

Orwell Corner

Located on the historic site of the Sir Andrew Macphail Homestead, the **Tea Room Restaurant** *($; Route 1, ☎ 651-2789)* is a pleasant place to enjoy a good, light meal at lunchtime or take a break in the afternoon. Though the menu is simple, the food is tasty. Reservations are required for dinner. The elegance and atmosphere of the Macphail Homestead make this a very appealing little restaurant.

Montague

In the purest Prince Edward Island tradition, the **Lobster Shanty North** *($$; Route 17, ☎ 838-2463)* offers first-rate lobster suppers consisting of a seafood appetizer, a lobster and dessert for about $20 altogether. Guests sit in a simply decorated dining room looking out on the Montague River. This restaurant has had the honour of serving Her Majesty Queen Elizabeth II and Prince Philip in 1973, as well as Prince Charles and Lady Diana in 1983. In addition to its seafood, the place is also known for its char-broiled steaks.

Cardigan

Set up inside the former railway station, the **Cardigan Craft Center and Tea Room** *($; Route 1, ☎ 583-2450)* has a simple, inexpensive menu made up of sandwiches, salads and other light dishes.

Set up inside a century-old general store, **Cardigan Lobster Suppers** *($$, Route 17, ☎ 583-2020)* serves traditional lobster meals at reasonable prices from 4 PM to 8:30 PM every night.

This type of supper, consisting of a seafood appetizer, a lobster and dessert, is an island tradition that is not to be missed.

Bay Fortune

Without question one of the finest restaurants in the region, the dining room of the **Inn at Bay Fortune** *($$$; Route 310, ☎ 687-3745)* has a beautiful lay-out and offers a magnificent view of the bay. Chef Michael Smith, one of the great chefs of the province, prepares dishes using ingredients fresh from the market. The cuisine is both exquisite and original, and the service, highly professional.

■ **Western P.E.I.**

Summerside

With its extremely relaxed, pub atmosphere, **Brothers Two** *($-$$; 618 Water Street East, ☎ 436-9654)* is one of the liveliest and most popular spots in Summerside. People come here to eat or simply to have a drink. As in many restaurants on the island, fish and seafood are highlighted on the menu, which nevertheless lists a variety of other specialties as well. The portions are generous here.

The **Prince William Dining Room** *($$; 195 Harbour Drive, ☎ 436-3333)* offers well-prepared food and a fairly elaborate menu, including a wide choice of appetizers and main dishes. Seafood and fish make up a good part of the offerings, but various steak and chicken dishes are also available. On some evenings, a specific dish is featured, such as the excellent surf and turf, consisting of a small steak and a lobster tail. The service is courteous, and the atmosphere, elegant but relaxed.

Mont-Carmel

A visit to the Evangeline region offers a good opportunity to enjoy a meal at the most famous Acadian restaurant on the island, **Étoile de Mer** *($-$$; Route 11, ☎ 854-2227)*, located at the entrance to the pioneer village. Dishes prepared according to the best-known Acadian recipes, such as *râpure, fricot au poulet, fricot aux palourdes* and *pâté acadien* are served in a cozy dining room. None of these traditional dishes costs more than $5.25. The menu also lists a good number of other (more expensive) dishes, mostly lobster and other types of seafood and fish. This is a good place for a first encounter with the island's Acadian community.

West Point

A good place to stop for a break during a tour of western Prince Edward Island, the **West Point Lighthouse** is an inn whose **restaurant** *($-$$; Route 14, ☎ 859-3150)* is open from daybreak to 9:30 PM. The lunch menu consists of a variety of light dishes, including the usual lobster rolls, chowders and other seafood. In the evening, the cuisine is a bit more sophisticated, with more elaborate appetizers and main courses, such as a fisherman's platter, made up of five different kinds of seafood or fish for less than $20. The menu also lists steak, chicken Kiev and pasta. The restaurant is laid out in a simple fashion in the building adjoining the lighthouse. Guests can also eat on the terrace outside.

North Cape

At the same location as the Atlantic Wind Test Site museum, the **Wind & Reef** *($$; at the end of Route 12)* is a perfect place to dine on seafood and fish. The menu includes other dishes as well, but people come here mainly for the lobster, shrimp, oysters, fisherman's platter, etc. Although the prices are not exorbitant, you do have to pay a little extra for the lovely setting. Lighter, less expensive meals are available at breakfast time.

 Entertainment

■ **Tour A: Charlottetown**

Each summer, for more than three decades now, the Confederation Arts Centre has presented the musical ***Anne of Green Gables*** *(Confederation Arts Centre, ☎ 566-1267 or 1-800-566-1207)*, inspired by the work of Prince Edward Island's foreign ambassador Lucy Maud Montgomery. Both funny and touching, the story of little "Anne with an e" is now a classic of children's literature all over the world. It is amazing to see to what point Anne has affected young Japanese, who now make up an important percentage of tourists to the island. The musical is well done and makes for a fun night out.

At the **Festival Dinner Theatre** *(Charlottetown Hotel, ☎ 892-6633)* guests enjoy a meal while watching (and sometimes even participating in!) an entertaining play. You'll laugh with, and at, everyone. The young actors and actresses wait the tables, sing and play music.

For fans of Irish music, the **Olde Dublin Pub** *(131 Sydney Street)* is the place for a Guiness and a jig. There is often live music, and simple meals are also served. Drinks can also be had at the **Island Rock Café** *(132 Richmond Street)* or on Kent Street at **Miron's**

(151 Kent Street) and **Tradewinds** *(189 Kent Street)*.

Horse-racing junkies can get their fix at the **Charlottetown Driving Park** *(Kensington Road,* ☎ *892-6823)*. Races are held two to four times a week during the summer.

Something for kids of all ages: see Charlottetown from a London-style double-decker bus. **Abegweit Sightseeing Tours** *(departure from Confederation Arts Centre,* ☎ *894-9966)* crisscross the town several times a day; tours of the northern and southern shores are also available.

■ Central P.E.I.

Victoria

Almost every night in July and August, the **Victoria Playhouse** *(about $12;* ☎ *658-2025 or 1-800-925-2025)* presents enjoyable plays and concerts in its little theatre. With its quality performances, the Victoria Playhouse is as charming as the city itself.

■ Western P.E.I.

Summerside

The **Feast Dinner Theatre** *(Water Street, Brothers Two restaurant,* ☎ *436-7674)*, which has been presented on summer evenings (starting at 6:30 PM) for the past 15 years or so, is a dinner accompanied by a non-stop blend of music, songs and theatre. The show was designed to make the audience laugh.

Mont-Carmel

The **Cuisine à Mémé** *(Route 11, the Village,* ☎ *854-2228 or 1-800-567-3228)* brings Acadian Prince Edward Island to life through songs, music and theatre. These shows, held in the evening, are combined with a meal.

 Shopping

■ Charlottetown

In Charlottetown, visitors can go to **Peake's Wharf** to stroll along the pier and enjoy the seashore while getting in some shopping in one of the pretty boutiques. There is something for everyone here—crafts, souvenirs, t-shirts, etc.

Clothing

Both children and their parents will enjoy picking out one of the funny t-shirts and sweatshirts available at **Cow's** *(opposite the Confederation Arts Centre)*. Make sure to sample the store's excellent ice cream at the same time.

La Cache *(119 Kent Street,* ☎ *368-3072)* sells comfortable cotton clothing, as well as kitchen goods and tablecloths.

Anyone who likes Liz Claiborne clothing won't want to miss the low prices at the **Liz Claiborne Factory Outlet** *(on the TransCanada, opposite the Rodd hotel)*.

Visitors looking for warm woolens should head over to the **Wool Sweater Factory Outlet** *(Prince Edward Hotel,* ☎ *566-5850)*, which offers a lovely selection of high-quality, casual sweaters.

Crafts

All sorts of beautiful crafts, books and souvenirs are available at **The Two Sisters** *(150 Richmond Street,* ☎ *894-3407).*

Anne fans can poke around in one of the two **Anne of Green Gables Souvenirs** shops *(Confederation Court Mall* and *Peake's Wharf).*

■ Central P.E.I.

Victoria

The melt-in-your-mouth home-made chocolates at **Island Chocolate** *(Main Street)* are an absolute delight.

New Glasgow

The **Old Country Store** *(Route 13;* ☎ *964-2769)* features a lovely selection of local crafts, quilts and *Anne of Green Gables* articles — souvenirs related to the story of that famous little redhead. Visitors are sure to find a worthwhile memento here.

The **Prince Edward Island Preserve Co.** *(at the intersection of Routes 224 and 258;* ☎ *964-2524)* sells a wide selection of excellent jams containing very little sugar.

Cavendish

The **Cavendish Boardwalk** *(Route 6)* has all kinds of adorable little shops, some, like **Two Sisters**, specializing in t-shirts and souvenirs. Visitors will also find a

branch of **Roots** (sportswear) and **Cow's**, with its cute clothing and terrific ice cream. At the front of the store, there is a selection of slightly flawed Cow's clothing at reduced prices.

The shop **Island Treasures** *(at the intersection or Routes 6 and 13;* ☎ *963-2350)* is another good place to purchase local crafts and many other articles for the house.

■ Eastern P.E.I.

Murray River

Those who enjoy exploring cute little souvenir and craft shops should make sure to stop at Murray River, which boasts two of the loveliest craft shops in the region, if not on the entire island. **The Old General Store** *(tel. 962-2459)* features a delightful selection of housewares and quilts. **The Primrose Path** *(Route 3)* is a worthy competitor.

■ Western P.E.I.

Summerside

In summer, there is nothing more pleasant than strolling about **Spinnaker Landing**, with its pretty string of shops along the waterside. This complex, built on piles, also has a little outdoor theatre where a variety of activities are organized.

Tyne Valley

Shoreline Sweaters is a small shop where visitors will find top-quality wool sweaters hand-knit on the premises, as well as a variety of souvenirs.

INDEX

Aboiteau Beach (Cap-Pelé) 80
Acadia University (Wolfville) 120
Acadia University Art Gallery
  (Wolfville) 121
Acadian Museum (Caraquet) . . . 77
Acadian Museum of Prince
  Edward Island
  (Miscouche) 172
Acadian Odyssey National His-
  toric Site
  (St-Joseph-de-Memra..
  .) 71
Acadian Pioneer Village
  (Mont-Carmel) 173
Acadian Presence (P.E.I.) 172
Accommodation 31
Air Travel 23
Aitken Bicentennial Exhibition
  Centre (Saint John) . . . 65
Alberton (P.E.I.)
  Accommodation 182
  Exploring 174
Alberton Museum (Alberton) . . . 174
Alexander Graham Bell National
  Historic Site (Baddeck) . 133
Algonquin Hotel
  St. Andrews By-the-Sea 60
Alma (New Brunswick)
  Accommodation 89
  Exploring 68
Amherst (Nova Scotia)
  Accommodation 143
  Exploring 115
Amherst Shore Provincial Park
  (Nova Scotia) 137
Andrew & Laura McCain Gallery
  (Florenceville) 57
Annapolis Royal (Nova Scotia)
  Accommodation 144
  Exploring 122
  Restaurants 152
Annapolis Royal Historic Gar-
  dens (Annapolis Royal) . 122
Annapolis Tidal Project
  (Port-Royal) 122
Anne Murray Centre (Springhill) . 116

Anne of Green Gables Museum
  at Silver Bush (Park
  Corner) 166
Antigonish (Nova Scotia)
  Accommodation 150
  Exploring 135
Antique Automobile Museum
  (Saint-Jaques) 54
Argyle Shore Provincial Park
  (P.E.I.) 175
Art Gallery of Nova Scotia
  (Halifax) 112
Arts and Culture 17
Atlantic Salmon Centre (St.
  Andrews By-the-Sea) . . 62
Atlantic Wind Test Site (North
  Cape) 173
Aulac (New Brunswick)
  Exploring 71
Baddeck (Nova Scotia)
  Accommodation 148
  Exploring 133
  Restaurants 154
  Shopping 157
Banks 28
Banque des Fermiers (South
  Rustico) 168
Barachois (New Brunswick) 72
Barbour's General Store (Saint
  John) 65
Barrington (Nova Scotia)
  Exploring 124
Bartibog Bridge (New Bruns-
  wick)
  Exploring 75
Basin Head (P.E.I.) 176
  Exploring 170
Basin Head Fisheries Museum
  (Basin Head) 170
Bath (New Brunswick)
  Exploring 57
Bathurst (New Brunswick)
  Accommodation 92
  Exploring 77
Bay Fortune (P.E.I.)
  Accommodation 181

Restaurants 185
Bay St. Lawrence (Nova Scotia) . 134
Beaches 39
Beaches (New Brunswick) 80
Beaches (Nova Scotia) 136
Beaches (P.E.I.) 176
Beaconsfield Historic House
        (Charlottetown) 164
Beaverbrook Art Gallery
        (Fredericton) 50
Bed and Breakfasts 31
Beechwood (New Brunswick)
        Exploring 56
Bicycling 27, 39
Bicycling (New Brunswick) 81
Bicycling (Nova Scotia) 137
Bicycling (P.E.I.) 177
Bird-watching 40
Bird-watching (New Brunswick) . 82
Bird-watching (Nova Scotia) 138
Bird-watching (P.E.I.) 176
Blowers Street (Halifax) 114
Blue Rock (Lunenberg) 127
Blue Rock (Nova Scotia) 127
Bluenose II (Halifax) 112
Boating (P.E.I.) 178
Bonar Law Historic Site (Rexton)   74
Borden (P.E.I.)
        Exploring 166
Bore Park (Moncton) 70
Bottle Houses (Cap Egmont) 173
Boucanières (Cap Pelé) 72
Bouctouche (New Brunswick)
        Accommodation 91
        Exploring 72
        Restaurants 97
Boyce Market (Fredericton) 52
Brackley Beach (P.E.I.) 176
        Camping 175
        Exploring 168
        Restaurants 184
Brackley Beach Lighthouse
        (Brackley Beach) 168
Bras d'Or Lake (Nova Scotia)
        Exploring 130
Bras d'Or Scenic Drive (Bras
        d'Or Lake) 130
Brayons (New Brunswick) 55
Bridgewater (Nova Scotia)

Accommodation 146
Exploring 125
Brier Island (Nova Scotia)
        Exploring 123
Brudenell River Provincial Park
        (Georgetown) 169
Brudenell River Provincial Park
        (P.E.I.) 176, 177
Burlington (P.E.I.)
        Exploring 166
Business Hours 28
Business Hours and Public Holi-
        days 28
By-the-Sea Festival (Saint John) . 65
Cabot Trail (Nova Scotia)
        Exploring 133
        Shopping 157
Campbells Cove Provincial Park
        (P.E.I.) 176
Campbellton (New Brunswick)
        Accommodation 92
        Exploring 78
        Practical Information 47
Campobello Island (New Bruns-
        wick)
        Accommodation 87
        Exploring 62
Canoeing 39
Canoeing (Nova Scotia) 139
Canoeing and Kayaking (New
        Brunswick) 82
Canso (Nova Scotia)
        Exploring 128
Cap-Egmont (P.E.I.)
        Exploring 173
Cap-Pelé (New Brunswick)
        Exploring 72
Cape Breton Highlands National
        Park (Nova Scotia) 134, 136
Cape Breton Island
        Finding Your Way Around . . 106
Cape Enrage (New Brunswick) . . 68
Cape Fourchu (Yarmouth) 124
Cape North (Nova Scotia)
        Restaurants 155
Cape Split (Nova Scotia) 121
Cape Tourmentine (New Bruns-
        wick)
        Exploring 72

Finding Your Way Around . . .   47
Captain Garry's Seal & Bird
    Watching Cruises
    (Murray River) 169
Car Rentals   25
Caraquet (New Brunswick)
    Accommodation   92
    Entertainment   99
    Exploring   76
    Restaurants   98
Caraquet Park Beach (Caraquet) .   80
Cardigan (P.E.I.)
    Exploring 169
    Restaurants 185
Caribou Provincial Park (Nova
    Scotia) 135, 137
Carleton Martello Tower (Saint
    John)   67
Carrefour de la Mer (Caraquet) . .   77
Cathedral Church of All Saints
    (Halifax) 111
Cathedral of the Immaculate
    Conception
    (Edmundston)   55
Cavendish (P.E.I.)
    Accommodation 180
    Beaches 176
    Camping 175
    Exploring 167
    Restaurants 183
    Shopping 188
Cedar Dunes Provincial Park
    (P.E.I.) 173, 176
Ceildish Trail (Nova Scotia)
    Exploring 134
Centennial Park (Moncton)   70
Centennial Park (St. Andrews
    By-the-Sea)   60
Central New Brunswick
    Woodmen's Museum
    (Newcastle)   75
Centre d'Art de l'Université de
    Moncton (Moncton) . . .   70
Centre La Rochelle (Grand Falls) .   56
Chapel (St. Andrews) 170
Chapel Museum (Saint-Basile) . .   55
Charlotte County Museum (St.
    Stephen)   59
Charlottetown (P.E.I.)

Accommodation 178
    Entertainment 186
    Exploring 162
    Restaurants 182
    Shopping 187
Chatham (New Brunswick)
    Exploring   75
Cherry Brook Zoo (Saint John) . .   67
Chester (Nova Scotia)
    Accommodation 147
    Entertainment 156
    Exploring 127
    Restaurants 154
Chester Playhouse (Chester) . . 127
Chéticamp (Nova Scotia)
    Accommodation 149
    Restaurants 155
Children   34
Christ Church Cathedral
    (Fredericton)   52
City Hall (Fredericton)   48
City Hall (Halifax) 111
Clam Harbour Beach Provincial
    Park (Nova Scotia) . . . 137
Clifton House (Windsor) 120
Climate   29
Confederation Arts Centre
    (Charlottetown) 162
Connell House (Hartland)   57
Convent Museum (Saint-Basile) .   55
Cossit House (Sydney) 131
Courthouse (Fredericton)   48
Covered bridge (Hartland)   57
Crocker Hill Garden & Studio
    (St. Stephen)   59
Cross-Country Skiing   41
Cross-Country Skiing (New
    Brunswick)   82
Cross-Country Skiing (Nova
    Scotia) 141
Cruise Manada Seal Watching
    Boat Tours (Montague) 169
Crystal Palace (Moncton)   70
Cumberland County Museum
    (Amherst) 115
Currency   28
Currency Exchange and Banks . .   29
Customs   23
Dalhousie (New Brunswick)

Exploring 78
Dalvay (Prince Edward Island)
    Beaches 176
Dartmouth (Nova Scotia)
    Exploring 114
Deep-Sea Fishing (Nova Scotia) . 140
Deer Island (New Brunswick)
    Exploring 62
DesBrisay Museum
    (Bridgewater) 125
Dieppe (New Brunswick) 68
Digby (Nova Scotia)
    Accommodation 144
    Exploring 122
    Restaurants 153
Dingwall (Nova Scotia)
    Accommodation 149
    Restaurants 155
Dock Street (Shelburne) 124
Dory Shop (Shelburne) 125
Downhill Skiing 41
Downhill Skiing (New Bruns-
    wick) 82
Downhill Skiing (Nova Scotia) . . . 141
Downtown Beach (Caraquet) . . . 80
East Point (P.E.I.)
    Exploring 170
East Point Lighthouse (East
    Point) 170
East Quoddy Head (Campobello
    Island) 62
Echo caves (St. Martins) 67
Edmundston (New Brunswick)
    Accommodation 84
    Exploring 54
    Finding Your Way Around . . . 46
Église Notre-Dame-du-Mont-Car
    mel (Mont-Carmel) 173
Église Saint-Bernard
    (Saint-Bernard) 123
Église Sainte-Cécile (Ile
    Lamèque) 76
Église Sainte-Marie
    (Pointe-de-l'Église) 123
Electricity 34
Elmira (P.E.I.)
    Exploring 170
Elmira Railway Museum (Elmira) . 170
Embassies and Consulates 20

Emergencies 30
Entrance Formalities 19
Eptek (Summerside) 172
Escuminac (New Brunswick)
    Exploring 75
Escuminac Provincial Park (New
    Brunswick) 75, 80
Extended Visits 19
Ferguson Beach (Grande-Anse) . . 77,
    80
Ferries 27
Festival Acadien (Caraquet) 77
Festival International de la
    Francophonie
    (Tracadie-Sheila) 75
Firefighters Museum (Yarmouth) 124
Fisheries Festival (Shippagan) . . . 76
Fisheries Museum of the Atlan-
    tic (Lunenberg) 126
Fishing 39
    New Brunswick 82
Fishing (Nova Scotia) 140
Fishing (P.E.I.) 178
Florenceville (New Brunswick)
    Exploring 57
Flower pots (Hopewell Cape) . . . 68
Foire Breyonne (Edmundston) . . . 54
Fort Anne National Historic Site
    (Annapolis Royal) 122
Fort Beauséjour National His-
    toric Site (Aulac) 71
Fort Edward National Historic
    Site (Windsor) 118
Fort Howe (Saint John) 67
Fort McNab Historic Site
    (Halifax) 114
Fort Sainte-Marie-de-Grâce
    Museum (La Have) . . . 125
Fortress of Louisbourg
    (Louisbourgh) 131
Franco-Frolic (Saint John) 65
Fredericton (New Brunswick)
    Accommodation 83
    Entertainment 98
    Exploring 47
    Finding Your Way Around . . . 44
    Practical Information 47
    Restaurants 93
    Shopping 99

Fundy Geological Museum
(Parrsboro) 116
Fundy National Park (New
Brunswick) 68, 79
Accommodation 89
Gaelic College (South Gut St.
Ann's) 134
Gagetown (New Brunswick)
Accommodation 86
Exploring 58
Restaurants 94
Shopping 100
Ganong Chocolatier (St.
Stephen) 59
Garden of the Gulf Museum
(Montague) 169
Geography 10
Georgetown (P.E.I.)
Exploring 169
Giant axe (Nackawic) 58
Giant salmon (Campbellton) 78
Glace Bay (Nova Scotia)
Exploring 132
Glenora Distillery (Mabou) 134
Golden Era of Railway (P.E.I.) . . . 171
Golf 40
Golf (Nova Scotia) 140
Golf (P.E.I.) 177
Grand Falls (New Brunswick)
Accommodation 84
Entertainment 98
Exploring 56
Restaurants 93
Grand Falls Museum (Grand
Falls) 56
Grand Manan Island (New
Brunswick)
Accommodation 87
Exploring 63
Grand Parade (Halifax) 111
Grand-Pré (Nova Scotia)
Exploring 120
Grand-Pré National Historic Site
(Grand-Pré) 120
Grande-Anse (New Brunswick)
Exploring 77
Restaurants 98
Grassy Island National Historic
Site (Canso) 128

Green (Fredericton) 50
Green Gables House
(Cavendish) 167
Green Park Shipbuilding
Museum (Port Hill) . . . 174
Greenock Church (St. Andrews
By-the-Sea) 60
Gulf Shore Provincial Park (Nova
Scotia) 136,
137
Haliburton House (Windsor) . . . 120
Halifax (Nova Scotia)
Accommodation 141
Entertainment 156
Exploring 108
Finding Your Way Around . . 104
Practical Information 107
Restaurants 150
Shopping 156
Halifax Citadel National Historic
Site (Halifax) 110
Hartland (New Brunswick)
Accommodation 85
Exploring 57
Health 30
Heather Provincial Park (Nova
Scotia) 137
Hector Heritage Quay (Pictou) . 135
Hiking 39
Hiking (New Brunswick) 81
Hiking (Nova Scotia) 137
Hiking (P.E.I.) 176
Historic church of
Saint-Henri-de-Barachoi
s (Barachois) 72
Historic Properties (Halifax) . . . 112
Historic Quaker House
(Dartmouth) 115
History 10
Acadia 12
The 20th Century 16
The Arrival of the Loyalists . . 14
The Deportation 13
The Golden Age and Cana-
dian Confederation 15
Hitchhiking 27
HMCS Sackville (Halifax) 114
Holidays and Public Holidays . . . 28

Hopewell Cape (New Brunswick)
Exploring 68
Hubbard House (Campobello
Island) 63
Hubbards (Nova Scotia)
Accommodation 147
Huntsman Marine Science
Centre and Aquarium
(St. Andrews) 60
Hydroelectric dam (Mactaquac) . 58
Hydroelectric power station
(Beechwood) 56
Île Lamèque (New Brunswick)
Exploring 76
Île Miscou (New Brunswick)
Exploring 76
Île Miscou Beach (New Bruns-
wick) 80
Île Miscou Lighthouse (Ile
Miscou) 76
Imperial Theatre (Saint John) . . . 65
Ingonish Beach (Nova Scotia)
Accommodation 149
Restaurants 155
Ingonish Ferry (Nova Scotia) . . . 134
International Baroque Music
Festival (Ile Lamèque) . . 76
International Festival (St.
Stephen) 59
International Fox Museum
(Summerside) 172
Irving Nature Park (Saint John) 67, 79
Isle Madame (Nova Scotia)
Exploring 130
James Roosevelt House
(Campobello Island) . . . 63
Joggins Fossil Centre (Amherst) . 115
Jost House (Sydney) 131
Jost Vineyards (Malagash) 136
Kejimkujik National Park (Nova
Scotia) 125, 136
Kejimkujik Seaside Adjunct
National Park (Nova
Scotia) 125,
136
Kent County Museum
(Bouctouche) 74
Kings Landing (New Brunswick)
Shopping 100

Kings Landing (Prince-William) . . 58
Kingsclear (New Brunswick)
Accommodation 85
King's Square (Saint John) 65
Kirk Presbyterian (St. George) . . 62
Kouchibouguac National Park
(New Brunswick) . . 79, 80
La Have (Nova Scotia)
Exploring 125
Lawrence House (Maitland) . . . 118
Leper cemetery (Tracadie-Sheila) . 76
Les Jardins de la République
(Saint-Jacques) 54
Les Jardins de la République
Provincial Park (Saint-
Jacques) 78
Lieutenant-Governor's residence
(Charlottetown) 164
Lighthouse Museum
(Fredericton) 52
Lions Park (St. Martins) 68
Little Pond (P.E.I.)
Accommodation 181
Little Rock (P.E.I.)
Accommodation 180
Little Sands (P.E.I.)
Accommodation 180
Liverpool (Nova Scotia)
Accommodation 146
Exploring 125
Lobster festival (Shediac) 72
Log Cabin Museum (Murray
Harbour) 169
Long Island (Nova Scotia)
Exploring 123
Lookoff (Cape Split) 121
Loomcrofter Studio (Gagetown) . 59
Louisbourg (Nova Scotia)
Accommodation 148
Exploring 131
Restaurants 154
Loyalist Days (Saint John) 65
Loyalist House National Historic
Site (Saint John) 65
Lucy Maud Montgomery Birth-
place (New London) . . 167
Lunenburg (Nova Scotia)
Accommodation 146
Exploring 126

Restaurants 153
Shopping 157
MacDonald Farm Historic Site
    (Bartibog Bridge) 75
Machias Seal Island (New Bruns-
    wick) 63
Mactaquac (New Brunswick)
    Exploring 58
Mactaquac Provincial Park
    (Mactaquac) 79
Mactaquac Provincial Park (New
    Brunswick) 58
Madawaska Museum
    (Edmundston) 55
Madawaska Weavers
    (Saint-Léonard) 55
Magnetic Hill (Moncton) 70
Mahone Bay (Nova Scotia)
    Accommodation 147
    Exploring 127
Maisonnette (New Brunswick)
    Exploring 77
Maisonnette Provincial Park
    (Maisonnette) 77, 80
Maitland (Nova Scotia)
    Exploring 118
Malagash (Nova Scotia)
    Exploring 136
Malobiannah Centre (Grand
    Falls) 56
Marconi National Historic Site
    (Glace Bay) 132
Margaree Salmon Museum
    (Northeast Margaree) . . 134
Margaree Valley (Nova Scotia)
    Accommodation 150
Marine Centre and Aquarium
    (Shippagan) 76
Maritime Museum of the Atlan-
    tic (Halifax) 112
Market Square (Saint John) 65
Martinique Beach
    (Musquodoboit Har-
    bour) 128
Martinique Beach Provincial Park
    (Nova Scotia) 137
Mary's Point (New Brunswick) . . 68
Mavilette Beach Park (Nova
    Scotia)

Accommodation 145
McCulloch House (Pictou) 135
McNabs Island (Halifax) 114
Meat Cove (Nova Scotia) 134
Meetinghouse (Barrington) 124
Melmerby Beach (Nova Scotia)
    Exploring 135
Melmerby Beach Provincial Park
    (Nova Scotia) 135
Micmac Village (Rocky Point) . . 165
Military Compound and Guard
    House (Fredericton) . . . 48
Military museum (Halifax) 110
Military museum (Oromocto) . . . 58
Mill River Provincial Park (P.E.I.)176, 177
Miner's Museum (Glace Bay) . . 133
Ministers Island Historic Site
    (St. Andrews
    By-the-Sea) 60
Mirabel Airport 23
Miramichi Salmon Museum
    (Newcastle) 75
Miscouche (P.E.I.)
    Exploring 172
Moncton (New Brunswick)
    Accommodation 89
    Entertainment 99
    Exploring 68
    Finding Your Way Around . . . 46
    Practical Information 47
    Restaurants 95
Moncton Jazz Festival
    (Moncton) 68
Moncton Museum (Moncton) . . . 70
Mont-Carmel (P.E.I.)
    Accommodation 182
    Entretainmene 187
    Exploring 172
    Restaurants 186
Montague (P.E.I.)
    Exploring 169
    Restaurants 185
Monument (Escuminac) 75
Mount Allison University
    (Sackville) 71
Mount Carleton Provincial Park
    (Saint-Quentin) 79
Murray Beach Provincial Park
    (New Brunswick) 80

Murray Harbour (P.E.I.)
  Exploring 169
Murray River (P.E.I.)
  Exploring 169
  Shopping 188
Musée Acadien (Moncton) 70
Museum (Grand Manan Island) . . 63
N. S. Fisheries Exhibition and
      Fisherman Reunion
      (Lunenberg) 126
Nackawic (New Brunswick)
  Exploring 58
Nail Pond (P.E.I.) 176
National Exhibition Centre
      (Fredericton) 48
Néguac (New Brunswick) 75
New Brunswick 43
  Accommodation 83
  Beaches 80
  Entertainment 98
  Exploring 47
  Finding Your Way Around . . . 44
  Outdoor Activities 81
  Parks 78
  Practical Information 47
  Restaurants 93
  Shopping 99
New Brunswick Botanical Gar-
      den (Saint-Jacques) . . . 54
New Brunswick College of Craft
      and Design
      (Fredericton) 48
New Brunswick Museum (Saint
      John) 65
New Brunswick Power and
      Electricity Museum
      (Fredericton) 48
New Brunswick Sports Hall of
      Fame (Fredericton) 50
New Denmark (New Brunswick)
  Exploring 56
New Glasgow (P.E.I.)
  Restaurants 184
  Shopping 188
New London (P.E.I.)
  Exploring 167
Newcastle (New Brunswick)
  Exploring 75
Newspapers 35

Nicolas Denys Museum (St.
      Peters) 130
North Cape (P.E.I.)
  Exploring 173
  Restaurants 186
North Rustico (P.E.I.)
  Beaches 176
  Restaurants 184
Northumberland Fisheries
      Museum (Pictou) . . . 135
Nova Scotia 103
  Accommodation 141
  Entertainment 156
  Finding Your Way Around . . 104
  Outdoor Activities 137
  Parks and Beaches 136
  Practical Information 107
  Shopping 156
Nova Scotia Museum of Natural
      History (Halifax) 110
Odell Park (Fredericton) 52
Officer's Square (Fredericton) . . . 50
Old Burying Ground (Halifax) . . 114
Old Carleton County Courthouse
      (Hartland) 57
Old City Market (Saint John) . . . 65
Old Home Week (Hartland) 57
Old Loyalist Cemetery
      (Fredericton) 52
Old Sow (Deer Island) 62
Old Town Clock (Halifax) 110
Oromocto (New Brunswick)
  Exploring 58
Orwell (P.E.I.)
  Exploring 168
Orwell Corner (P.E.I.)
  Restaurants 185
Orwell Corner Historic Village
      (Orwell) 168
Outdoor Activities 37
  Beaches 39
  Bicycling 39
  Bird-watching 40
  Canoeing 39
  Cross-Country Skiing 41
  Downhill Skiing 41
  Fishing 39
  Golf 40
  Hiking 39

Parks 37
Seal Watching 40
Snowmobiling 41
Summer Activities 38
Whale-watching 40
Winter Activities 41
Ovens Natural Park (Rose Bay) . . 126
Owens Art Gallery (Sackville) . . . 71
Oyster Bed Bridge (P.E.I.)
    Restaurants 184
O'Leary (P.E.I.)
    Exploring 173
Panmure Island Provincial Park
        (P.E.I.) 176
Papineau Falls (Bathurst) 78
Paquetville (New Brunswick)
    Restaurants 98
Park Corner (P.E.I.)
    Exploring 166
Parks 37
    (P.E.I.) 174
Parks (New Brunswick) 78
Parks (Nova Scotia) 136
Parks (P.E.I.) 174
Parlee Beach Provincial Park
        (New Brunswick) . . . 72, 80
Parrsboro (Nova Scotia)
    Exploring 116
Partridge Island (Saint John) . . . 67
Passport 19
Pays de la Sagouine
        (Bouctouche) 74
Peake's Wharf (Charlottetown) . . 164
Peggy's Cove (Nova Scotia)
    Exploring 127
Perkins House (Liverpool) 125
Pictou (Nova Scotia)
    Accommodation 150
    Exploring 135
    Restaurants 155
    Shopping 157
Piping Plover (P.E.I.) 175
Plaster Rock (New Brunswick)
    Accommodation 85
Playhouse (Fredericton) 50
Point Pleasant Park (Halifax) 114
Point Prim (P.E.I.)
    Exploring 169

Point Prim Lighthouse (Point
        Prim) 169
Pointe Daly Reserve (Bathurst) . . 77
Pointe Wolfe (New Brunswick) . . 79
Pointe-De-l'Église (Nova Scotia)
    Exploring 123
Politics and the Economy 16
    New Brunswick 16
    Nova Scotia 17
    Prince Edward Island 17
Pomquit Beach Provincial Park
        (Nova Scotia) 137
Pope Museum (Grande-Anse) . . . 77
Port Hastings (Nova Scotia)
    Exploring 130
Port Hill (P.E.I.)
    Exploring 174
Port La Joye - Fort Amherst
        National Historic Site
        (PEI) 165
Port of Charlottetown
        (Charlottetown) 164
Port-Royal (Nova Scotia)
    Exploring 121
Port-Royal National Historic Site
        (Port Royal) 122
Post Office (St. George) 62
Post Offices 28
Practical Information 19
    Accommodation 31
    Advice for Smokers 33
    Business Hours and Public
        Holidays 28
    Children 34
    Climate and Clothing 29
    Currency 28
    Currency Exchange and
        Banks 29
    Customs 23
    Embassies and Consulates . . 20
    Entrance Formalities 19
    Finding Your Way Around . . . 23
    General Information 34
    Health 30
    Restaurants and Bars 33
    Safety 34
    Shopping 30
    Taxes and Tipping 32
    Time Difference 28

Tourist Information 22
Transportation 25
Weights and Measures 34
Wine, Beer and Alcohol 33
Prescott House Museum (Starrs
    Point) 121
Prince Edward Hotel
    (Charlottetown) 164
Prince Edward Island 159
    Accommodation 178
    Airport 160
    Entertainment 186
    Exploring 162
    Ferries 160
    Finding Your Way Around . . . 160
    Outdoor Activities 176
    Parks and Beaches 174
    Practical Information 160
    Restaurants 182
    Shopping 187
    Tourist Information 160
Prince Edward Island National
    Park (P.E.I.) 174,
                        176, 177
Prince Edward Island Potato
    Museum (O'Leary) 173
Prince House (Campobello
    Island) 63
Prince of Wales Tower National
    Historic Site (Halifax) . . 114
Prince-William (New Brunswick)
    Exploring 58
Province House (Halifax) 112
Province House National Historic
    Site (Charlottetown) . . . 162
Provincial Legislature
    (Fredericton) 50
Public Gardens (Halifax) 111
Pugwash (Nova Scotia)
    Exploring 136
Quaco Head lighthouse (St.
    Martins) 68
Randall House Historical
    Museum (Wolfville) . . . 121
Red Point (P.E.I.)
    Beaches 176
    Exploring 170
Red Point Provincial Park (P.E.I.) . 176

Red Point Provincial Park (Red
    Point) 170
République de Madawaska (New
    Brunswick) 54
Restaurants and Bars 33
Restigouche Gallery
    (Campbellton) 78
Restigouche Regional Museum
    (Dalhousie) 78
Reversing Falls (Saint John) 65
Rexton (New Brunswick)
    Exploring 74
Richibucto (New Brunswick)
    Accommodation 91
Riverview (New Brunswick) 68
Robichaud (New Brunswick) 72
Rockwood Park (Saint John) . . . 67
Rocky Point (P.E.I.)
    Exploring 165
Roosevelt House (Campobello
    Island) 63
Roosevelt-Campobello Interna-
    tional Park
    (Campobello Island) . . . 63
Rose Bay (Nova Scotia)
    Exploring 126
Roseneath (P.E.I.)
    Accommodation 181
Ross Farm Museum (Chester) . 127
Ross Memorial Museum (St.
    Andrews By-the-Sea) . . 60
Ross Thomson House
    (Shelburne) 125
Rustico Island (P.E.I.)
    Camping 175
Sackville (New Brunswick)
    Accommodation 90
    Exploring 71
    Restaurants 96
Safety 34
Saint Augustine Church (South
    Rustico) 168
Saint John (New Brunswick)
    Accommodation 88
    Entertainment 99
    Exploring 63
    Finding Your Way Around . . . 46
    Practical Information 47
    Restaurants 95

Shopping 101
Saint-Basile (New Brunwick)
    Exploring 55
Saint-Bernard (Nova Scotia)
    Exploring 123
Saint-Jacques (New Brunswick)
    Exploring 52
    Practical Information 47
Saint-Joseph-de-Memramcook
        (New Brunswick)
    Exploring 71
Saint-Léonard (New Brunswick)
    Exploring 55
Salmon Festival (Campbellton) . . 78
Sanctuaire
        Sainte-Anne-du-Bocage
        (Caraquet) 77
Sea View (P.E.I.)
    Accommodation 180
Seal-watching 40
Seal-watching (P.E.I.) 178
Settlers Museum (Mahone Bay) . 127
Shand House (Windsor) 120
Shediac (New Brunswick)
    Accommodation 90
    Exploring 72
    Restaurants 96
Shelburne (Nova Scotia)
    Accommodation 145
    Exploring 124
    Restaurants 153
Shelburne County Museum
        (Shelburne) 125
Sherbrooke (Nova Scotia)
    Exploring 128
Sherbrooke Village (Sherbrooke) . 128
Sheriff Andrews' House (St.
        Andrews By-the-Sea) . . 60
Shippagan (New Brunswick)
    Accommodation 91
    Exploring 76
    Restaurants 97
Shopping 30
Sir Andrew Macphail Homestead
        (Orwell) 168
Smoking 33
Snowmobiling 41
Snowmobiling (New Brunswick) . 82
Snowmobiling (Nova Scotia) . . . 141

Souris (P.E.I.)
    Accommodation 181
    Exploring 169
Souris Beach Provincial Park
        (Souris) 169
South Gut St. Ann's (Nova
        Scotia) 134
South Rustico (P.E.I.)
    Accommodation 180
    Exploring 167
Spring Garden Road (Halifax) . 114
Springhill (Nova Scotia)
    Accommodation 143
    Exploring 115
Springhill Miners' Museum
        (Springhill) 116
St. Andrews (P.E.I.)
    Exploring 170
St. Andrews Blockhouse (St.
        Andrews By-the-Sea) . . 60
St. Andrews By-the-Sea (New
        Brunswick)
    Accommodation 86
    Entertainment 99
    Exploring 59
    Restaurants 94
    Shopping 100
St. Ann (P.E.I.)
    Restaurants 184
St. Dunstan's Basilica
        (Charlottetown) 164
St. Francis Xavier University
        (Antigonish) 135
St. George (New Brunswick)
    Accommodation 87
    Exploring 62
St. Martins (New Brunswick)
    Accommodation 89
    Exploring 67
    Restaurants 95
St. Mary's Church (Souris) 170
St. Patrick's Church (Sydney) . . 131
St. Paul Church (Halifax) 111
St. Paul's Anglican Church
        (Charlottetown) 164
St. Peters (Nova Scotia)
    Exploring 130
St. Stephen (New Brunswick)
    Accommodation 86

Exploring 59
Practical Information 47
Shopping 100
St. Thomas University
    (Fredericton) 52
Stanhope (P.E.I.)
    Camping 175
Starrs Point (Nova Scotia)
    Exploring 121
Strathgartney (P.E.I.)
    Accommodation 179
Strathgartney Provincial Park
    (P.E.I.) 175
Strathgartney Provincial Park
    (P.E.I) 176
Summer Activities 38
Summerside (P.E.I.)
    Accommodation 181
    Entertainment 187
    Exploring 171
    Restaurants 185
    Shopping 188
Summerville Beach (Nova
    Scotia)
    Accommodation 146
    Restaurants 153
Sunbury Shores Arts & Nature
    Centre (St. Andrews
    By-the-Sea) 60
Swallowtail Light (Grand Manan
    Island) 63
Sydney (Nova Scotia)
    Accommodation 148
    Exploring 131
    Restaurants 154
Tatamagouche (Nova Scotia)
    Accommodation 150
    Exploring 135
Tatamagouche Provincial Park
    (Nova Scotia) 135
Taxes 32
Taylor Head Provincial Park
    (Nova Scotia) 137
Tetagouche Falls (Bathurst) 78
The Dunes Art Gallery (Brackley
    Beach) 168
The Victorian Playhouse (Vic-
    toria) 166

Théâtre Populaire d'Acadie
    (Caraquet) 77
Thomas Williams House
    (Moncton) 70
Tidal bore (Moncton) 70
Tidal bore (Truro) 116
Tidnish Dock (Nova Scotia)
    Exploring 136
Tidnish Dock Provincial Park
    (Nova Scotia) 136
Tilley House (Gagetown) 58
Time Difference 28
Tipping 33
Tourist Information 22
Town Hall (Souris) 170
Tracadie Historical Museum
    (Tracadie-Sheila) 76
Tracadie-Sheila (New Bruns-
    wick)
    Accommodation 91
    Exploring 75
    Restaurants 97
Transportation 25
    Bicycling 27
    By Bus 26
    By Car 25
    By Plane 27
    By Train 26
    Ferries 27
    Hitchhiking 27
Truro (Nova Scotia)
    Accommodation 143
    Exploring 116
Tyne Valley (P.E.I.)
    Accommodation 182
    Shopping 188
Université Sainte-Anne
    (Pointe-de-l'Église) . . . 123
University of New Brunswick
    (Fredericton) 52
Val-Comeau (New Brunswick) . . 75
Victoria (P.E.I.)
    Accommodation 179
    Entertainment 187
    Exploring 165
    Restaurants 183
    Shopping 188
Victoria Park (Charlottetown) . . 164
Victoria Park (Truro) 116

Victoria Provincial Park (P.E.I.) . 165, 175

Victoria Seaport Museum (Victoria) 166

Village Historique Acadien (Caraquet) 77

Visitor Reception Centre (Canso) 128

Water Street (St. Andrews By-the-Sea) 60

Waterfall (Grand Falls) 56

Waterfall (St. George) 62

Waterfowl Park (Sackville) 71

Weights and Measures 34

West Point (P.E.I.)
  Accommodation 182
  Exploring 173
  Restaurants 186

West Point Lighthouse (West Point) 173

Westport (Nova Scotia)
  Accommodation 145

Whale-watching 40

Whale-watching (New Brunswick) 81

Whale-watching (Nova Scotia) . . 138

White Point (Nova Scotia)
  Accommodation 146

Wile Carding Mill (Bridgewater) . . 126

William F. deGarthe Memorial Provincial Park (Peggy's Cove) 127

Wilnot United Church (Fredericton) 48

Windsor (Nova Scotia)
  Accommodation 144
  Exploring 118

Winter Activities 41

Wolfville (Nova Scotia)
  Accommodation 144
  Exploring 120
  Restaurants 152

Wood Islands (P.E.I.)
  Exploring 169

Wood Islands Provincial Park (P.E.I.) 169

Wood Islands Provincial Park (Wood Islands) 169

Wooden Mill (Barrington) 124

Woodleigh (Burlington) 166

Woodstock (New Brunswick)
  Accommodation 85
  Exploring 57
  Restaurants 94
  Shopping 100

Woodstock (P.E.I.)
  Accommodation 182

Woolastook Provincial Park (Longs Creek) 79

Yarmouth (Nova Scotia)
  Accommodation 145
  Exploring 123

Yarmouth Country Museum (Yarmouth) 123

York County Courthouse (Fredericton) 50

York-Sunbury Museum (Fredericton) 50

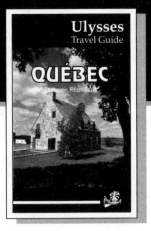

MONTRÉAL

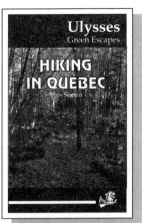

HIKING IN QUÉBEC

ONTARIO

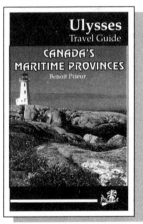

CANADA'S MARITIME PROVINCES

Restaurants, hotels, inns, bars and nightclubs...
adresses for every budget and every taste.

Complete practical and cultural information.

The largest selection of walking, bicycling and driving tours.

The widest range of regional and city maps.

Travel better... enjoy more

DISTRIBUTORS
United States: Seven Hills Book Distributors, ☎ 1-800-545-2005 - Fax (513) 381-0753
Canada: Ulysses Travel Publications, ☎ (514) 843-9882 - Fax (514) 843-9448

■ ULYSSES TRAVEL GUIDES

☐ Affordable Bed & Breakfasts
   in Québec . . . . $9.95 CAN
                              $7.95 US
☐ Canada's Maritime
   Provinces . . . . $24.95 CAN
                              $14.95 US
☐ Dominican Republic
   2nd Edition . . . . $22.95 CAN
                              $14.95 US
☐ Guadeloupe . . . . $22.95 CAN
                              $14.95 US
☐ Honduras . . . . $24.95 CAN
                              $16.95 US
☐ Martinique . . . . $22.95 CAN
                              $14.95 US
☐ Montréal . . . . $19.95 CAN
                              $12.95 US
☐ Ontario . . . . $14.95 CAN
                              $12.95 US
☐ Panamá . . . . $22.95 CAN
                              $14.95 US
☐ Provence -
   Côte d'Azur . . . . . . $24.95 CAN
                              $14.95 US
☐ Québec . . . . $24.95 CAN
                              $14.95 US
☐ El Salvador . . . . $22.95 CAN
                              $14.95 US

■ ULYSSES GREEN ESCAPES

☐ Hiking in the Northeastern
   United States . . . . $19.95 CAN
                            $12.95 US
☐ Hiking in Québec . . . . $19.95 CAN
                            $12.95 US

■ ULYSSES DUE SOUTH

☐ Cartagena (Colombia) . . $9.95 CAN
                            $5.95 US
☐ Montelimar (Nicaragua) $9.95 CAN
                            $5.95 US
☐ Puerto Plata - Sosua - Cabarete
   (Dominican Republic) . . $9.95 CAN
                            $5.95 US
☐ St. Barts . . . . $9.95 CAN
                            $7.95 US
☐ St. Martin . . . . $9.95 CAN
                            $7.95 US

■ ULYSSES TRAVEL JOURNAL

☐ Ulysses Travel Journal . $9.95 CAN
                            $7.95 US

QUANTITY	TITLES	PRICE	TOTAL

Name : _____

Address : _____

City : _____

Postal Code : _____

Sub-total	
Postage & Handling	3.00 $
Sub-total	
G.S.T. in Canada 7 %	
TOTAL	

Payment : ☐ Money Order ☐ Visa ☐ MC ☐ Cheque

Card Number : _____

Expiry Date : _____

Signature : _____

ULYSSES TRAVEL PUBLICATIONS

4176, Saint-Denis
Montréal, Québec
H2W 2M5
Tel : (514) 843-9882
Fax: (514) 843-9448

Figure 2